WHAT THIS COUNTRY NEEDS

WHAT THIS COUNTRY NEEDS

Paul A. Kienel

Foreword by
Tim F. LaHaye

BETA BOOKS • SAN DIEGO

WHAT THIS COUNTRY NEEDS
Copyright © 1976, 1977 by Paul A. Kienel.
Beta Books, 10857 Valiente Court
San Diego, California 92124

All Rights Reserved

No portion of this book may be reproduced in any way without the written permission of the publisher, except for brief excerpts in magazine reviews, etc. Printed in the United States of America.

Scripture quotations in this book credited NASB are from the *NEW AMERICAN STANDARD BIBLE,* © 1971, the Lockman Foundation, La Habra, Calif. Other Bible quotations are from the King James Version.

Library of Congress Cataloging in Publication Data

Kienel, Paul A
  What this country needs.

  First published in 1976 under title: America needs Bible centered families and schools.
  1. Religious education--United States.
I. Title.
LC368.K53 1977   370.11'4   77-340
ISBN 0-89293-015-2

Dedicated to

My mother
Who has reminded me often
that
"What we are
shows in everything we do"

Contents

1. Back to Basics...for Families and Schools — **15**
2. Children are Parent Watchers — **21**
3. Grades in School...are Not the Only Measure of Your Child's Worth to the World — **29**
4. The Importance of Parental Love — **35**
5. Is There a Proper Masculine-Feminine Balance in Your Home? — **41**
6. Your Home — The Number One Influence...in the Life of Your Child — **47**
7. Discipline at Home and at School — **55**
8. Should Your Child Have a Good Self-Image? — **63**
9. Why Christian School Education is Right for Your Child — **71**
10. The Academic Quality of Christian School Education — **79**
11. What Method of Classroom Instruction is Best...for Your Child? — **87**
12. "Our Public Schools are Not Working" — **95**
13. Evolution and the Christian School — **103**
14. Why Many Former Public School Teachers...Now Teach in a Christian School — **109**
15. Answers to Common Questions About Christian Schools — **117**

Foreword

God founded two institutions: the home and the church. They should never compete with one another, but they are both entrusted by God with the training of children. Years ago the Church wisely started Christian schools to specialize in the area of educating these children and young people in academics as well as spiritual subjects so they would be properly prepared to take their place in society.

Two sad things gradually happened. Many parents began abdicating their responsibility for training their children by assuming the school would do it; and then, very subtly, atheistic humanists took over the school system and secularized it. Consequently, the teaching of Christianity, morals, and character building are no longer a part of education.

During the last one hundred years or more the Church began to emphasize "Sunday School" classes and youth meetings to give children the Bible training they no longer received in schools. Since World War II many churches have awakened to their educational responsibilities and have begun starting Christian day schools. As the public school system degenerated the Christian school movement increased until it has become the fastest growing school movement in America.

Unfortunately, the trend still continues with too many parents who think the Christian school and the Church should train their children. God has entrusted that responsibility to the parents, particularly the fathers (see Deut. 6:7, Eph. 6:4, and others). The home has always been the greatest educational institution in the world; it has the child during the most pliable stage of his life—birth to fifteen years of age. The parent who gives himself fully to the task of training, loving, and disciplining his child during those years rarely has the heartache of a "teenage time bomb" ten years later.

The Church, Christian school, and parents must work together in this very serious business of raising our children to love God and to help equip them to serve Him and their fellow man. It is refreshing to see Paul Kienel, one of the nation's most foresighted Christian educators and a devoted father, speak out on this issue. He is an active church leader who has rightly recognized the need to put into the hands of parents valuable information that will help them, their church, and Christian schools as together they bring up their children "in the nuture and admonition of the Lord" (Eph. 6:4). All concerned parents will find this book exceedingly helpful.

Dr. Tim F. LaHaye, president
Christian Heritage College

Preface

It is appropriate that the subject of home and school be discussed within the same context. Each is vital to the survival of the other. I honestly believe if there is any hope for our beloved country, it lies in a revitalization of strong Bible-centered families, Bible-centered schools and an equally revitalized Bible-centered church community.

I mention in the opening chapter of this book that the Christian world, since World War II, has concentrated on reviving the church. As long as the church is peopled by mortals it will never be fully revived but comparing the present Bible-believing church world to churches in the early forties, we have come a long way. In my view, we have concentrated on reviving the church to the point that we have neglected an equal concern for families and schools. In the process of succeeding with the church, we have created a spiritual imbalance for our children. Bible-believers in growing numbers are beginning to realize that to have a revived church with weak Christian homes and a sterile secular educational system is to have a triad of confusion for our youngsters. The next generation desperately needs not only the support of revived churches but revived families and revived schools.

This book will reflect my strong personal conviction, and perhaps yours, that fathers must take a stronger position of leadership in our children's home training environment. Do you realize that 83% of our children's time is spent in our home environment? We should also realize that our children spend 16% of vital prime time in the process of school education. Martin Luther wrote the following important prophetic words: *"I am much afraid that the universities and schools will prove to be the gates of hell, unless they diligently labor in explaining the Holy Scriptures and engraving them in the hearts of youth. I advise no one to place his child where the Scriptures do not reign paramount."*

As you well know, the "Scriptures do not reign paramount" in our tax-supported public schools and colleges. I stated in my previous book, *"The Christian School: Why It Is Right For Your Child"* (Victor Books), *"It is time for the Christian community to declare an educational program that will not kick the spiritual stuffings out of the next generation!"* It is also time for parents to investigate, evaluate and upgrade the quality of life for their children in the sacred sanctuary of their homes. Someone has said, *"Church, home and school, Christ in all three - the divine ideal."* To my knowledge, there is no verse of Scripture that permits any of us to hold a view contrary to that "divine ideal."

The General Electric Company says *"Progress is our most important product."* That may be right for General Electric but for parents, the lives of our children is our ultimate concern and they are much more than just a product. This book is written to help parents and Christian school educators bring honor to Christ in the lives of children and young people at home and at school.

For the past ten years, I have been writing about Bible-centered homes and schools. This particular work is the product of those years of thought, writing and observation. I am aware that I have included some strongly worded statements. I am sure some will not agree with them. I apologize in advance if my statements or quotations are offensive to anyone. As always, I have tried to chart a course of viewpoint as close to Biblical authority as possible.

I am particularly indebted to Lee Kay and Laurie McGuyre, loyal members of my staff who have carefully edited and typed my manuscript. I am also indebted to Joe Smith, James Braley and Eunice Dirks, talented Christian leaders who serve God with me on the WACS Executive Staff, to the nineteen members of the WACS Executive Board who have been my professional sounding board and to my wife, Annie, and my daughters, Sandi, Colleen and Cheryl, for putting up with my "mess in the dining room" while I hammered out the manuscript.

Paul Kienel
1641 Sheffield Dr.
La Habra, California 90631

**Bible-centered families
+ Bible-centered schools**

= . . . a better America

1

Back To Basics For Families and Schools

Mr. Gable, tapping a small bell on his desk, said, "Class, please come to order. We will now salute the American flag." With hands over hearts, my four classmates and I stood proudly for the pledge of allegiance to the American flag. We said solemnly, "I pledge allegiance to the flag of the United States of America..." The words were a bit awkward because it was my first day of school in September, 1939. I was the only student in the first grade. In fact, there were only five students in the school. There were twin girls in grade three, a girl in grade four and a boy in the eighth grade who had remained in that particular grade for several years. Lest you feel sorry for us in our little red school house nestled in the wheat fields of north central Oregon, please don't. It was an academic heaven on earth! In the nineteen years of my formal education that followed, the quality of instruction never surpassed the learning intensity of that little public school in Oregon. In a very real sense I had five teachers, Mr. Gable and the four other students. They all helped me, especially the twin girls in the third grade. Our aging eighth grader was not particularly helpful to me academically but he was great at recess time. He and I played softball and teamed up against Mr. Gable and the girls. Most often we won, especially when it was our turn at bat and we had left green grasshoppers in the fingers of the catcher's mitt.

Our school's heating system consisted of a potbellied stove fueled by wood that we students carried from the woodpile located at the back of the school. The restroom facilities were small one-room structures located on either side of the main school house.

Our school was deprived of an asphalt parking lot, landscaping, air-conditioning, a multi-media learning center and even electricity. We had no busing problems because we had no buses.

The rural area surrounding our school was peopled by farmers who knew each other by name. They helped one another during harvest season and through difficult times of sickness. Our teacher, Mr. Gable, and other professional people such as doctors and ministers were highly revered in our community.

I consider myself fortunate to have begun my educational career at the end of a unique era. It was the trauma and heartbreak of the second

Back to Basics . . . / 17

world war in the forties that shattered the tranquility of my early educational years. As our country mobilized for global war, Americans by the multiplied thousands moved from farming areas to the cities to work for the "war effort." Sons and young fathers were drafted for military service. Family groups were separated and marriage bonds were weakened and often severed. Life for children during these uncertain years was unsettling. It was a period of dramatic transition from peace time to war time. Even in rural Oregon we observed curfews and blackouts. We heard and saw the ominous aerial parade of twin-tailed B-24 bombers and P-38 fighters conduct day and night practice missions over our community and along the cliffs and valleys of the beautiful Columbia River Gorge. Long caravans of U.S. Army jeeps and trucks rumbled along our highways, especially at night. Tanks and bomb casings were ever present on railroad flat cars headed for shipping ports on the Oregon coast for transport.

The life style of Americans changed rapidly during these years. Writing of the war years in his book, *The Family First,* Dr. Kenneth Gangel says:

> World War II defense plants reached their long, noisy arms into the kitchens of American families to create "Rosie the riveter." While G.I. Joe was off shooting the bullets, his wife, girl friend or sister was back home making them. What apparently was not foreseen in those early forties was that the new working status of women was destined not to be a temporary stopgap measure to assist America in the war, but a whole new pattern of life which has now come to

18 / America Needs: . . .

ugly fruition in what is loosely called the *"Women's Liberation Movement."* A cigarette commercial reminds American women, *"You've come a long way baby,"* but it stops short of suggesting which direction.

From the forties on, the climate of the classroom and the environment of the home would never be the same. The Bible-believing church community was a minor influence in the early forties. The tragedy of the second world war came to a close in 1945 and Americans who had drifted spiritually saw their need for a basic Bible message and responded to Bible-centered churches. Old line liberal churches waned but Bible-preaching churches soared into prominence and popularity.

In the meantime, a counterforce was at work in the nation's public school system. Because the government's secular public schools were based on a sterile secular philosophy, they had no way of responding in times of spiritual renewal. In the forties and fifties, for example, instead of responding to spiritual revival, they were responding with great vigor to the philosophy of a man who believed *"that traditional belief in God is an unproven and outmoded faith."* He was the first president of the American Humanist Association. His name was John Dewey, Professor of Philosophy and Pedagogy at the University of Chicago and later at Columbia University. His views on pragmatic progressive education became the philosophic touchstone for all teacher training institutions across America. His humanistic progressive educational theories reached full force in the nation's

Back to Basics . . . / 19

public school system in the forties and fifties and continued into the sixties. Only now, in the seventies his views are beginning to wane. Even though the public school system through the years has been peopled by more Christians per capita than any other profession in America, the ability of Christians to use the system as a means of presenting Christ as Savior and Lord was and still is severely limited. While the church was being revived in the fifties, sixties and seventies, the American home and our children's educational system was lagging far behind.

Therefore the purpose of this book is to nurture the new wave of interest in the revitalization of Bible-centered families and the development of Bible-centered schools. America needs Bible-centered families and schools as never before. As we move from chapter to chapter discussing the Christian home and the Christian school, I urge you to contemplate the full ramifications of a verse of Scripture that has become a foundational principle for me. The verse is Colossians 1:18, "...that in all things He might have preeminence." □

"You can count on it! Your children are watching you. Whether you realize it or not, they are observing your every move. They are learning more from you than from all their teachers, preachers and peers combined."

2

Children Are Parent Watchers

Do you have fun with your children? I do with mine. My children, along with their friends, are wall-to-wall entertainment for me. We make up crazy games of all kinds. I usually end up the loser in most of them. We tell jokes. We have fights with bean bags (I win most of these because I am bigger). As often as possible, we go camping in the Southern California desert. My wife and I purchased a camper and two small *Christian* motorcycles. I have declared them *Christian* because they are small and relatively safe. Because I am handy with tools, I have made three carts out of bicycle wheels and bucket seats and attached one behind the other. With my three daughters in the carts pulled by one of our *Christian* cycles, we zip around our desert camping area terrifying jack rabbits,

22 / America Needs: . . .

lizards and all other desert creatures who race across our path. We are a strange sight as we go weaving our way through the sage brush, over knolls and valleys but in the process we have genuine family fun together.

My children know I definitely enjoy being with them no matter where we are or whatever the activity. My wife and I center our leisure *fun-time* around our children. Because we enjoy life, they enjoy life. And in the midst of all our pleasant family activity we as parents are, by example and by instruction, guiding our children through some of the hard lessons of life that every child must learn. Our practice of parent to child instruction is a valid scriptural pattern. Moses in Deuteronomy 6:6-7 said, "And these words, which I am commanding today, shall be on your heart; and you shall teach them diligently to your sons and shall talk of them when you sit in your house and and when you walk by the way and when you lie down and when you rise up." (N.A.S.B.).

In God's book the Bible, the family is clearly established as the basic unit of society. Dr. Gangel said, *"There is no question about the Biblical position on the primacy of the family. Long before God called into existence schools and churches, He designed the basic unit of society in the Garden of Eden. There is no evidence in scripture that this emphasis has ever changed. Parental right is a natural right which is neither bestowed nor legalized by the state."* The family has precedence over the church, the school, government and every other institution known to man. Such institutions

Children are Parent Watchers ... / 23

are vitally important but they survive only when our family units are strong and Christ is preeminent in our homes. As parents we have a responsibility to live our lives in a manner pleasing to God and inspiring to our children. The writer of Ephesians says, ". . . do not provoke your children to anger" (Ephesians 6:4 N.A.S.B.), implying our homes should be happy places where parents have learned to lead happy lives as living examples for the children God has given us.

Remember the American Cancer Society's television ad about the boy who imitated his father in a sequence of typical father and son outdoor activities? Then the two sat under a tree to rest. The father lit a cigarette and put the pack of cigarettes beside him. The boy picked up the cigarettes and looked inside the pack. At that point, the scene ended, leaving the viewer with the clear impression that the boy was about to follow his father's example and smoke a cigarette. The ad effectively accomplished its purpose. We shuddered at the thought of that child following in his father's footsteps.

The best legacy you as a parent can leave your children is the memory of a father and mother who genuinely loved God, who loved each other, who loved their children and had a positive outlook on life. If you are a happy, positive Christian parent, it is very likely your children will be happy, positive Christian children.

You can count on it! Your children are watching you. Whether you realize it or not, they are observing your every move. They are learning more from

24 / America Needs: . . .

you than from all their teachers, preachers and peers combined. For example, your youngsters learn about God and the Bible at church and Christian school but they are looking to you for the down-home example of what a Christian is like as translated into a day-to-day pattern of living. The attitude you have toward spiritual matters and spiritual leaders will be mirrored in the attitudes of your children. If you *roast principal, roast teacher or roast preacher* at your dinner table each evening, your children will develop a disregard for their spiritual academic/leaders.

One evening as my wife and I prayed with our three daughters, each had woven into her prayer, *"Thank you, Father, for all the good things you have given to us."* In our prayers my wife and I have inspired our daughters to be thankful to the Lord for His day-to-day blessings to our family.

Your children and my children are also watching us in times of crisis and stress in our families. The Scripture reminds us, "in everything give thanks," (I Thess. 5:18 N.A.S.B.). Are you equally thankful to the Lord in times of distress as in times of blessing? How you react in a crisis is carefully observed by your children.

As you know, life is made up of positives and negatives. There is a positive and a negative side to everything. The cup is either half full or half empty depending on your point of view. If you, as the attitude pace-setter for your children, are living on the positive side of life and you thoroughly enjoy living every day to its fullest, your children will sense your positive attitude and have a simi-

Children are Parent Watchers ... / 25

lar outlook on life.

I personally enjoy being positive. Who wants to be negative when he can be positive! I could become totally depressed with the national debt, the ever-present possibility of a nuclear war or any one of a dozen fatal diseases which could afflict me or members of my family. If my thoughts majored on these possibilities I would be a negative, dismal, neurotic wreck and my wife and children would suffer because of it. I choose rather to concentrate on the amazing grace of our Heavenly Father, to enjoy the beauty of another day, the friendship and fellowship of my colleagues and the warmth and love of my own family. I thoroughly enjoy living for Jesus Christ. I do not live a positive life just because of my children. It's the way I want to live. I am fully aware that my children are *reading me* and because I enjoy living, they are learning to live a positive, joyful Christian life. It is beautiful to see.

You may not consider yourself in the teaching profession; but if you are a parent, like it or not, you are a teacher. And the intensity of instruction and learning between you and your children for better or worse is greater than all the years of formal classroom education your children will receive. As a parent, you are the prime teacher of your children.

There isn't a parent in the world who is adequately qualified on his own to be the model teacher for his children. That is why I pray every day that God in Heaven will give me the moment by moment wisdom I need to be the parent-teacher

God would have me be.

As a leader in the burgeoning Christian school movement, I believe whole-heartedly in Christian school education. I will go to any sacrifice necessary to make it available for my youngsters. But it is not a substitute for my role as a parent. Your children and my children are parent watchers. It is our responsibility before God to live lives that will be an unforgettable source of inspiration to the next generation. ☐

"If your youngster is struggling in school, don't lose faith in him. There is hope!"

3

Grades In School Are Not The Only Measure Of Your Child's Worth To The World

When our Lord selected His twelve disciples, He did not choose candidates whose academic records showed them to be in the top ten percent of their class. He called common men, mostly who were uneducated, to perpetuate His Gospel to all future generations.

Even at less lofty levels than the Lord's disciples, there have been men and women who were honored in their adult years as great individuals but as children in school they were perpetual candidates for *the least likely to succeed* group.

Perhaps a classic example is the well known story of a boy named Albert. Albert was so slow learning to talk that his parents thought he was abnormal. His teachers called him a misfit and classmates avoided him. He failed his first college

30 / America Needs: . . .

entrance examination. To the amazement of everyone, he turned out to be one of the greatest scientists in the world. His name—Albert Einstein.

Winston Churchill was less than a bright boy in school. As a matter of fact, he was the lowest achiever in his class through his early years of education. He stuttered so badly that his parents and teachers could barely understand him. In later years as Prime Minister of Great Britain, he became known as one of the most eloquent statesmen in history. In 1953 he won the Nobel Prize for Literature.

If your youngster is struggling in school, don't lose faith in him. There is hope! Of course, success in later life is not guaranteed to the youngster who struggles in school even as success is not assured the student who is a *straight 'A' genius*. It is interesting to observe how many times children who trudge a continual uphill road in school develop a quality of determination in their character that makes them valuable citizens in their later years. If your youngster is less than an *academic whiz*, perhaps you will take comfort in the following survey of 342 graduates of Columbia University. According to the findings, *"Those who had graduated from Columbia University with honors, who had won scholastic medals, who had been elected to Phi Beta Kappa, were more likely to be in the lower professional levels than in the top levels!"*

I suppose the best interpretation of such findings is that students who always succeed in school never learn the valuable lessons reserved only for

Grades in School . . . / 31

strugglers and uphill climbers. Those who whiz through school very often have some basic qualities of determination missing from their fibers and are afraid to attempt anything where the risk of failure is a possibility. The individual who struggles in school will attempt most anything in life because he has coped with failure so often one more failure is not all that traumatic to him. And because he keeps trying in the face of setback and disappointment, he eventually finds his niche and becomes a roaring success. This is not to say that you have to be mentally dull and have a difficult time in school to succeed in life. Brilliance is not a liability. But in the Lord's economy of people, He has graciously balanced the scales and our worth to the kingdom is not determined totally on our academic prowess. God can use dim bulbs as well as bright bulbs! He can take our liabilities and turn them into assets and our lives will bring honor to His name as long as we are willing to submit ourselves to His direction.

I believe in quality academic instruction in our schools. In a later chapter, I will discuss achievement test scores which demonstrate that Christian school education is significantly superior to the national norms established by public schools. Unfortunately, however, many parents take the academic grades of their children too seriously and judge their youngster's worth to the world on their current academic achievement. As parents, we should admonish our children to always do their best in school to bring honor to Christ but never should we attempt to force them into a specific

32 / America Needs: . . .

academic plateau in an effort to bolster our own parental ego.

If your child is honestly doing his best in school and if his best is less than impressive to you, don't fall apart over it. Your child may be developing qualities that cannot be measured in academic grades. Permit me to list a few qualities that are of immeasurable value to the impact your child will have in later life:

1) *A Total Commitment to Jesus Christ as Savior and Lord*

Your child will be better adjusted emotionally and consquently better prepared to meet the stresses of life if he has trusted Christ as his Savior. Proverbs 3:5-6 says, "Trust in the Lord with all thine heart; and lean not to thine own understanding. In all thy ways acknowledge Him, and He shall direct thy paths." I can testify personally that this verse has been true in my life.

2) *A Total commitment to a Project of His Interest*

Perhaps your youngster is less than enchanted with history at school but has a project at home that requires commitment, hard work, skill and a series of trial and error sequences that are of great value to his learning processes.

3) *A Sense of Love and Compassion for Others*

This is seldom a natural characteristic. We come into this world as self-preservationists. Your child is far ahead of his peers if he has a genuine sense of compassion for others. Perhaps more than any other, this is a characteristic learned from parents. At the Kienel household during our family prayers we often ask the Lord to *"make us a blessing to other people."* This important concept is now bearing fruit in the lives of my children.

4) *A Sense of Responsibility*

If your youngster has developed a basic sense of responsibility and trustworthiness, he is already developing qualities of greatness that will be of significant value in later years. In Matthew, Christ reminds us, "... you were faithful with a few things, I will put you in charge of many things..." (Matt. 25:21 N.A.S.B.).

5) *A Spark of Creativity*

A problem Albert Einstein had in school was the fact that his mind was often on a creative mental adventure far removed from the subject being taught in the classroom. True creativity and imagination may not always be reflected on your child's report card.

Never lose faith in your child. There is hope for him. There is hope especially if the love of Christ is preeminent in your child's home and if you as his number one earthly example truly love him and assure him of your love often. The importance of parental love for children will be the topic of our next chapter.

"It is imperative to the mental and emotional well-being of your child that love be expressed to him by his parents on a regular basis and in a variety of ways."

4

THE IMPORTANCE OF PARENTAL LOVE

Whatever the natural liabilities or assets your child may reflect in school, his potential worth to the world is greatly enhanced if he loves God and has strong love ties at home. Your child can weather every storm if he knows Christ loves him and his parents love him. It is imperative to the mental and emotional well-being of your child that love be expressed to him by his parents on a regular basis and in a variety of ways.

I am sure observers of the Kienel household would characterize our family as an affectionate family. For example, when I arrive home from the office, I kiss my wife and daughters and I tell each one that I love them. This is important. Life for children and adults can be complicated. The simple day-to-day contact with people at any age level is enough to do us in emotionally. We all need a home base where no matter what happens to us we know without question that we are loved. To those of us who are members of the family of God, we know that our Heavenly Father loves us "...with an everlasting love" (Jeremiah 31:3 N.A.S.B.). This principle must be translated into the day-to-day relationship between parents and children. Not only is it important for children to know that their parents love them but it is vital to their emotional stability to know that everything is all right between mom and dad. Each evening at our house after the family has finished eating, we usually talk for a little while. I go around the table and kiss my wife in full view of my children. I tell her I love her and then I tell her, "Thanks for the tremendous dinner." I don't do that just for show in front of my girls. I thoroughly enjoy family affection.

If your relationship with your family has cooled and crusted over, I strongly recommend that you start rekindling the family fires of affection again and let your spouse and children know that you love them. Love is a flame that one way or another must be refueled everyday.

When your children leave for school each morning, it is vital to their emotional state of mind to know that mom and dad love them and love each other. As a former teacher and principal, I have watched the *before* and *after* drama of a child whose parents have separated and divorced. If more couples could see what happens emotionally to their children at school when they divorce if

The Importance of Parental Love . . . / 37

they have a normal range of compassion for children, they would never go through with it. When a child's home is falling apart, it is not uncommon to see him vomit his lunch, cry uncontrollably or stare into the distance for long periods of time. His grades almost always take a nose-dive and he often becomes a discipline problem. Children can bounce back from many abuses but I am convinced the divorce of parents is a shattering trauma from which they never fully recover. God's institution of family for them as children is never quite the same again.

In my view, next to our love for God and His Word should be our constant love for our families. The key to family security is a Bible-centered family where the love of Christ controls every family member. In our complicated world, we as parents need wisdom beyond our own to properly raise our boys and girls.

God never intended that any of us should win the world and lose our own families. The average father spends less than fifteen minutes a day with his children. Fathers in this category have obviously lost sight of their priorities. Children desperately need a masculine father and a feminine mother and know, without a doubt, they are loved by both.

Your child's ability to surmount the every day pressures of school, church and neighborhood are enhanced many times over if he has the security of God's love in his heart and the security of knowing he has a home where he is understood and loved. As valuable as Christian school education is and as

38 / America Needs: . . .

valuable as the church is, they are secondary to a Christian home where Christ-honoring parents truly love their children.

> "An important part of our parental responsibility is to establish a proper masculine-femine balance in our homes."

5

IS THERE A PROPER MASCULINE-FEMININE BALANCE IN YOUR HOME?

This past summer I was flying from Chicago to Los Angeles. As I boarded the plane in Chicago, I noticed two men ahead of me on the boarding ramp to our DC-8 jet. Along with numerous other passengers, I noticed them because they wore ponytails and held hands. They were as engrossed with each other as newlyweds of the ordinary masculine-feminine variety. The two times I observed them during the flight, they were in their seats locked arm in arm, enraptured by each other's presence. After touchdown in Los Angeles, I saw them again at the baggage carousel. Somewhere between the plane's unloading ramp and the baggage area, they were met by two ponytailed fellows just like themselves. The reunion ceremony included an exchange of roses and a round of

42 / America Needs: . . .

affection. By this time, the level of shock and disgust at the sight of them had risen noticeably among the passengers as they waited at the carousel. I, too, was shocked but I prayed for them as they left the airport. Only the amazing grace of God can reach out to confused mortals like these.

I am sure we need to have Christian compassion and pity for these gay persons but lest we be caught up in the world's growing tolerance for homosexuality, we would do well to read Romans 1:26-28:

> *For this reason God gave them over to degrading passions; for their women exchanged the natural function for that which is unnatural, and in the same way also the men abandoned the natural function of the woman and burned in their desire towards one another, men with men committing indecent acts and receiving in their own persons the due penalty of the error. And just as they did not see fit to acknowledge God any longer, God gave them over to a depraved mind, to do those things which are not proper. (N.A.S.B.).*

As a general rule, homosexual tendencies are created when there is a masculine-feminine imbalance in a child's home experience. Because we have an exploding trend in our country of mothers playing a dominant role over fathers, we are producing a generation of effeminate boys. They are patterning themselves after their mothers instead of their fathers. When these effeminate boys become young men, most young ladies are not attracted to them, consequently their affections are diverted from ladies to other lonely effeminate men who have the same basic problem.

On the other side of the masculine-feminine

Masculine-Feminine Balance . . . / 43

ledger, the effect of a dominant mother on girls is not as immediate and dramatic as it is on boys. Girls who pattern themselves after a dominant mother tend to marry weak, non-aggressive men over whom they can easily maintain control. As a result, the *imbalanced home* is perpetuated and boys and girls born to such a union are affected by this continuing cycle of imbalance.

The concept that marriage is a *fifty-fifty proposition* is not a Biblical idea. The Apostle Paul said,
> *For the husband is the head of the wife, as Christ also is the head of the church. He Himself being the Savior of the body. But as the church is subject to Christ, so also the wives ought to be to their husbands in everything. Husbands, love your wives, just as Christ also loved the church and gave Himself up for her; (Ephesians 5:23-25 N.A.S.B.).*

The fact that mothers all too often become the head of the household is not always the fault of mothers. Dads are often guilty of simply not accepting their responsibility as the spiritual head, husband and father of their household. Mother emerges as head because the family is leaderless. Perhaps we need a stronger dose of pulpit preaching that deals candidly with this problem.

Mother may also emerge as family leader because the father is deceased or perhaps the father is absent as a result of divorce. Today, the latter is more often the case.

Single-parent families function with a predictable disadvantage. All of the problems resulting from lack of proper masculine-feminine balance in the home are potentially present in the single-parent household. But with God's help and some

44 / America Needs: . . .

basic understanding of the potential problem, the dilemma can be overcome.

Permit me to speak from experience on this point. My father, Paul Kienel III, a minister of the gospel, died when I was seven years old. Mother was left as the leader of our family; two younger sisters and me. Needless to say, those were difficult times for us. I was the only boy in our newly created single-parent family. As you can quickly see, I was surrounded by a totally feminine environment. I am grateful to this day to an evangelist friend of ours. He suggested to my mother that I needed the masculine influence of some wholesome families complete with fathers and sons.

I needed, as every boy needs, a masculine model as a guide toward normal manhood. My mother went to great effort to follow the counsel of our evangelist friend. She initiated a crusade of friendship with wholesome Christian families in and around our community in northeastern Oregon. Our families were knit together in a wide range of fellowship activities. I was accepted as brother and son in wholesome disciplined family environments that provided me and my sisters with the masculine-feminine balance we needed. I patterned my interests after the boys and fathers of these families. As time off from work, school and church permitted, we went camping, hunting, fishing, flying, skiing and generally had a good time. Many of the attitudes, convictions and personal standards I have today about family, church, integrity, work and friendships, I trace back to those marvelous families with whom we affiliated when

I was a boy.

To seek wholesome family friends whose children are good models for your children is wise counsel for single-parent families and equally wise counsel for families who are blessed with both parents.

The basic unit of society is the family. As parents of the children God has given to us, we have the joyful responsibility of living our lives so that our children will look forward to the day they can live their adult years as we have lived ours. An important part of our parental responsibility is to establish a proper masculine-feminine balance in our homes or compensate by close family friendships with those who can provide the appropriate models your family needs. □

"Whether or not your child grows up to be a tight wad, miser or a money-slinging spender depends on you as parent-instructor."

6

YOUR HOME - THE NUMBER ONE INFLUENCE IN THE LIFE OF YOUR CHILD

"But if any provide not for his own, and specially for those of his own house, he hath denied the faith, and is worse than an infidel." (I Timothy 5:8). The Bible does not mince words regarding parental responsibility toward children. Jesus said, "But whoso shall offend one of these little ones, which believe in me, it is better for him that a millstone were hanged about his neck, and that he were drowned in the depth of the sea." (Matthew 18:6).

If you believe in the Bible as I do, then the above Scriptures should cause you and me to carefully analyze what we are doing with the lives of our children. Because the family is the basic unit of society, your home and my home are sacred institutions vital to the needs of man.

Your home is the number one influence in the

life of your child. Dr. Howard Hendricks, in his book *Heaven Help the Home* (Victor Books), says, *"The average church has a child 1% of his time: the home has him 83% of his time; and the school for the remainder,"* which is 16%. This does not minimize the need for churches and schools, but it establishes the fact that your home is 83% of your child's world and you have only one time around to make it of maximum benefit to your child or children.

Unfortunately, because of the materialistic climate of our times, many parents interpret *maximum benefit to your child or children* as giving them a host of material *things* when all of the time the children are reaching out for their parental love, control and spiritual leadership.

Recently, Craig Johnston, an outstanding senior at Whittier Christian High School, was our guest at one of our family outings in the desert. Not only is he a credit to Christian school education and his church but his life reflects a strong family influence. While we were having lunch in our camper, Craig said, *"I feel sorry for any youngster who has not had the privilege of growing up in our family."* Perhaps you should know there are twelve children in the Johnston family and all of them attend Christian schools and colleges. This past football season, Craig, as the Whittier Christian High School running back, set a new CIF record of carrying the ball 448 yards in one game. After the record was broken and as he was coming off the field to the plaudits of a roaring crowd of enthusiastic supporters, he pointed to the sky indicating the praise belonged to the Lord. Then he embraced his father who had been cheering him on from the sidelines.

I am sure Mr. and Mrs. Johnston could provide their children with a finer home or even drive luxury cars if they were not responsible for Christian school tuition payments for their large family. But they know that children do not need material things nearly so much as they need parental love and guidance and an educational program that is not at odds with Christian philosophy in their home.

Craig is not the only outstanding member of the Johnston family. Judy, the eldest daughter, is a graduate of Biola College and is a music teacher at Brethren Elementary School in Whittier. Bruce, the eldest boy, was recently named the season's most valuable football player at Christian Heritage College in San Diego. Rick is the senior class president at Whittier Christian High School and is also an outstanding athlete. The entire family of twelve children are musically talented and recently performed as a musical team before 2,755 teachers and principals attending the 25th Annual Convention of the California Association of Christian Schools. Literally thousands of Southern Californians come to the front yard of the family home each Christmas season to see the family portray the Christmas story in music and drama.

I am sure we could name other families who are revered in their communities and considered exceptional in a variety of ways. The prevailing characteristic of all of them is the fact that mom and dad have concentrated on the character needs and the spiritual needs of their children rather than just material needs. Providing your children with material things is not a corrupting factor, in fact, children need to cope with wealth as well as with poverty. My point is that you and I as parents cannot buy our way or delegate our way out of our responsibility to be the loving, guiding lights to our children we ought to be.

Personally, I like to delegate authority. It is the only way to keep a large organization such as WACS functioning efficiently. Recently, for example, I sat down with my executive staff of three outstanding Christian leaders to plan our workload for the next several months. Each of them ended up with a work list longer than mine. I have been told this is good leadership. Careful delegation of large segments of the work under my administration may be good organization but as a parent of three lovely daughters I am responsible for 100% of their environment. The most I can delegate to the church and the school to help me do my job as a parent is 17%. My wife and I are personally responsible for the remaining 83% of our children's time.

If it is true, as Dr. Ron Chadwick of Grand Rapids Baptist Seminary says, that the curriculum in school *"in terms of courses of study is only 10% of the impact in the life of the student, while the teacher is 90%,"* then it follows that the kind of models we are before our children is of major significance.

The first order of business on the road to successful parenthood is to become a complete individual

Your Home—The Number One Influence . . . / 51

through a personal faith in Jesus Christ. Apart from Jesus Christ, the total concept of what God intends for families will never come into focus for you.

The second step on the road to successful parenthood is to set up a home training program for you children. There is a direct command to parents in Scripture that says, "Train up a child in the way he should go. . ." (Proverbs 22:6). Your training program at home need not be as formal as classroom instruction, but as a parent you have a definite teaching responsibility to your children. You say, "But I'm not a teacher. "My answer is, "You taught your children to speak the English language, didn't you?" That is of course a significant teaching accomplishment. If you have taught your children to speak the English language then it follows that you as a parent—instructor can teach your children to be courteous, to be honest to be responsible, to be on time, to be hard working and a host of other "to be's."

Many of life's important lessons are not included in the curriculum in the 17% church and school part of your child's life. For example, there is the area of thrift and spending. Whether or not your child grows up to be a tight wad, miser or a money-slinging spender depends on you as parent-instructor. This brings up the subject of tithing. Will your children tithe a tenth of their income to Christian ministries when they grow up? They will if you as parents have "trained them up in the way they should go" in your home.

How about love, marriage and sex education?

Many parents tend to turn several shades of color and run from this responsibility. The timing and manner of instruction for each child is so varied and critical on this subject that it is best taught by parents who know their children well. The fact that some parents fail at this task does not change the truth of the fact that this is a parental responsibility.

And the list goes on and on — the important lessons of life that are strictly for home education. Those of us who serve you in the 17% school and church category are valuable aids in helping you get your job done but our 17% in no way compares with your 83% responsibility. Our job is next to impossible if you are not effectively fulfilling your role as the number one influence in the life of your child.

Training your children *in the way they should go* should be the major pursuit of every parent. Beware lest you be caught up in activities less important than the preservation of your children. Paraphrasing Matthew 16:26 we might say, "What shall it profit a parent who gains a world of material and professional acclaim and loses his own family?" Raising your family for Christ must always be number one on your list of life's priorities. □

"Does America have a discipline problem? Yes, the lack of basic discipline has become the number one problem of our nation's public school system."

7

DISCIPLINE AT HOME AND AT SCHOOL

In 1954, a national woman's magazine gave the following advice to parents:

When your child has a tantrum, lies down on the floor, bangs his head and screams, or may kick and bite, scratch and cry, it is a perfectly natural thing for him to do. In most cases the reason for the tantrum lies not with the child but with the adult. He makes an issue over some insignificant situation and the child objects.

Solution: Divert the child by saying, let us go out and play or by starting a favorite game. If it does not work, My advice is to do nothing at all. No tantrum will go on indefinitely, and when it's all over, don't scold or punish your child. Try to make him happy, do what he is interested in. Punishment will only harm his development.

This trend of parental permissiveness was

56 / America Needs: . . .

spawned in the twenties and thirties by a new breed of atheistic philosophers whose teachings for several decades later diverted American families and schools away from Biblical principles of child training. These liberal philosophies began to flower and bloom in the succeeding decades of the 40's, 50's and 60's. Dr. Bruce Narramore, a well-known Christian psychologist, described the sequence of events in the March 1975 issue of "Psychology for Living" as follows:

During the 1940's a new wave swept the child-rearing educational practices of American culture. Under the names of progressive education, democracy, and child-centered homes, well-known educators and psychologists expounded the virtues of a permissive attitude toward children.

At the core of this new attitude was the belief that children could make their own choices and direct their own lives with very little outside interference. Underlying this notion was the philosophical belief that human beings are basically good and possess the capabilities to direct their own existence. This belief obviously led to a negative view toward authority. If children could make effective decisions on their own, there was little need for parental authority. As author A.S. Neil put it, "I believe that to impose anything by authority is wrong. The child shouldn't do anything until he comes to the opinion – his own opinion – that it should be done."

The influence of this new movement spread quickly. Innovative educators soon began implementing educational procedures based on this new philsophy.

Many parents were taught that physical discipline could warp their children's personalities. Soon parents developed a kind of national guilt. Every time they raised a rod or razor strop they wondered if they were somehow inflicting lasting damage to the psyches of their precious children. Because of this influence many parents refrained from setting needed limits and consistently disciplining their children.

Not until a generation later did the inadequacies of the approach become evident to many of its followers. The blatant campus rebellion of the sixties was partially the result of the permissive parenting of the forties. Children who did not learn to control their impulses and respect authority at home had little reason to respect their college leaders and administrators. Permissive parents had unknowingly undermined their children's concept of authority.

If American parents and educators had listened to Dr. Proverbs instead of Dr. Spock in the preceding few decades the embarrassing spectacle of the sick sixties would never have occurred. The writer of Proverbs is very clear regarding permissiveness: "The rod and reproof give wisdom: but a child left to himself brings his mother shame." Proverbs 29:15. Some parents and educators are tempted to say, *Small infractions when children are young can be over-looked. It is better to wait until children are older and then reason with them when they are more mature.* That may sound good to some but Dr. Proverbs says, "Chasten your son while there is hope, and let not your soul spare for his crying." Proverbs 19:18.

The emphasis during the earlier permissive decades was to be careful not to break a child's will. There was a fear if children were disciplined for their rebellion they would rebel all-the-more. Such was not the philosophy of the mother who produced

58 / America Needs: . . .

John and Charles Wesley. You will recall her sons were the great evangelists of the eighteenth century whose powerful ministry transformed morally depraved Europe and later spread revival throughout America.

Mrs. Wesley said, The first thing to be done is to conquer the children's will and bring them to an obedient temper. The subjection of their will is a thing which must be done at once. For by neglecting timely correction, they will contract a stubbornness and obstinacy which is hardly ever conquered; and never without using such severity as would be as painful to me as to the child. Whenever a child is corrected, it must be conquered; and this will be no hard matter to do, if he be not grown headstrong by too much indulgence. Self will is the root of sin and misery. No indulgence of it can be trivial, no denial of it unprofitable.

Someone may say, "Obeying God's Word turns parents into 'child beaters' and if they follow Biblical principles parents will be guilty of 'cruel and unusual punishment.' " The Bible does not advocate angry violence toward children. The writer to the Hebrews says, "For those whom the Lord loves He disciplines, and He scourges every son whom He receives. It is for discipline that you endure; God deals with you as with sons; for what son is there whom his father does not discipline?" (Hebrews 12:6-7, N.A.S.B.). Physical discipline or any other form of discipline that is based on Biblical principles is administered from genuine parental love — the kind of love that says to children, "I love you too much to allow you to do something that I know will hurt you." It's the kind of love that sets

Discipline at Home and at School . . . / 59

reasonable boundaries and limits and, if need be, uses reasonable discipline to enforce them. The Psalmist David said, "It is good for me that I have been afflicted; that I might learn thy statues." Psalm 119:71. "Before I was afflicted I went astray: but now have I kept thy word." Psalm 119:67.

Does America have a discipline problem? Yes, the lack of basic discipline has become the number one problem of our nation's public school system. *The Sixth Annual Gallup Poll of Public Attitudes Toward Education* summarized the situation as follows:

> *Lack of discipline in the public schools again heads the list of problems cited most often by survey respondents. Discipline has, in fact, been named the number one problem of the schools in five of the last six years. New evidence of its importance comes from the special survey of high school juniors and seniors. An even higher percentage of this group names discipline as the leading problem faced by the local public school.*

New Christian schools are being established at the rate of two per day across America. Christian school education has become the fastest growing educational movement in the United States. We could wish that the motivating force behind the parent interest in Christian schools for their children was a positive motivation such as the desire to follow the Biblical directive to "Train up a child in the way he should go . . ." However, many parents are reaching out to the Christian school because of a lack of discipline in the public school and a host of other negative factors. The October 8, 1973 issue of *U.S. News and World Report* reporting on the "Boom in Protestant Schools" said,

60 / America Needs: . . .

"There is rising alarm of parents over what they see as academic laxity in the public schools, along with rampant misbehavior – robbery, drug abuse, and classroom disruption. What these parents are seeking, it is said, is a learning environment for their youngsters that is more disciplined and more religious than can be found in any public school."

How important is discipline in our homes and our schools? I know as a former classroom teacher in a Christian school that discipline is vital to the process of education. Without it very little learning occurs. I also know as a parent of three children that I cannot fulfill my Biblical responsibilities of training my children without the accompanying process of discipline. Christian training and discipline go hand in hand.

It is interesting to look at the statistics of two families which illustrate the value of Christian training and discipline:

Max Jukes lived in the state of New York. He did not believe in Christian training. He married a girl of similar character. From this union 1,026 descendants have been studied. Three hundred of them died prematurely. One hundred were sent to the penitentiary for an average of thirteen years each. One hundred and ninety were public prostitutes. There were one hundred drunkards, and the family cost the state $1,200,000. They made little contribution to society.

Jonathan Edwards lived in the same state. He believed in Christian training. He married a girl of similar beliefs and character. From this union 729 descendants have been studied. Out of this family have come 300 preachers, sixty-five college professors, thirteen university presidents, sixty authors of good books, three United States congressmen and one vice-

Discipline at Home and at School ... / 61

president of the United States; and outside of Aaron Burr, a grandson of Edwards, the family has not caused the state a bit of trouble or cost the state a single dollar. The difference in the two families: Christian training in youth and heart conversions.

This article was published in *Sylmar Side Lights,* a publication of the Light and Life Christian School in Sylmar, California. The principal, Coral Ide, is one of the finest Christian school educators in the Western states.

There is no question about it, young Americans need discipline at home and at school. Now is the time to be the mothers and fathers God intended us to be. Our children are the most precious possessions we have in this life and they are all of this earth we can potentially take with us to heaven.

"John the Baptist said, 'He must increase but I must decrease" (John 3:30).

8

SHOULD YOUR CHILD HAVE A GOOD SELF-IMAGE?

There is a popular phrase making the rounds in the psychological community these days. The phrase is *Self-image*. Psychologists claim that students, and all of us for that matter, need to have a good *self-image*. They also talk about *self-love, self-esteem* and *self-concept*. If you are a fledgling Christian philosopher as I am (nothing more complicated than trying to see things as God sees them) then you are reaching for your Bible and asking, "What does God's Word have to say about this?"

Paul reminds us in Romans 7:18, ". . .in my flesh (or self) dwelleth no good thing." To those of us who have received Christ, our *love* and *esteem* have been redirected from self-centeredness to Christ-centeredness. John 1:12 joyfully announces that if we have believed on the name of Christ, we have *become the sons of God*. As sons of God we are *joint heirs with Christ* and a part of the royal family of God. That should be cause for rejoicing! However, this high position in God's family is not a reason for us to generate a great reservoir of *self-love* or *self-esteem*. The very act of receiving Christ involves turning to God *from* self. Self is dethroned and Christ becomes preeminent in our lives. Our *love* and our *esteem* is not for ourselves but for the person of Jesus Christ.

You ask, "What is the Biblical counsel for Johnny with a bad image of himself? He sees himself as a failure. He has failed so often that he expects to fail so he doesn't really try anymore."

First of all, if the child is a born-again Christian, he should not have a bad image of himself. He is a son of God, a unique creation of God and God has a unique purpose for his life. One can have a good image of himself if the image he sees is Christ and if he realizes that whatever worth he is to the world resides in his completeness in Christ. This is decidedly different from *self-love* and *self-esteem* where one draws strength from himself instead of Christ. Colossians 1:18 reminds us, "That in all things He might have the preeminence" — which includes how we look at ourselves. This counsel is equally important for youngsters who are moderately successful or extremely successful in school.

Secondly, perhaps it is God's will for Johnny to struggle in school. Sometimes the very process of academic struggle builds strength of character and determination that is a major factor to Johnny's

Should Your Child Have . . . / 65

future success. As I mentioned in chapter three, Winston Churchill and Albert Einstein were both very slow boys academically all through their early years of education to the dismay of their teachers. They became significant figures in the world. We must not slide into the world's mold of evaluating the future of a youngster on the basis of his present grades in school. Nor should we go to the other extreme and remove the ABCD grading system so Johnny will not know how poorly he is doing in school. Sheltering Johnny from the truth of his dilemma will not help him adjust to life as it comes.

Thirdly, though Johnny may have a long record of academic failure and though we may have adjusted to the idea that part of his bright future is inherent in his present struggle with reading, writing and arithmetic, there is no Biblical excuse for him to be lazy. Overcoming laziness is a major lesson of life taught by parents and teachers to every new generation of man since God created Adam. We must require our youngsters to do their very best in their academic studies and work with all their mental and physical might to bring honor to Christ. The Word of God is prolific with passages of warning to those who choose to drag through life as lazy dullards. The Apostle Paul said, "This we commanded you, That if any would not work, neither should he eat." (II Thess. 3:10).

Fourthly, if Johnny now sees Christ preeminent in himself and he is working to his full potential (although compared to others his potential is not very impressive) our attitude toward him should be one of acceptance and encouragement. He will take comfort in the counsel of the Apostle Paul who said to the Philippians, "I know both how to be abased, and I know how to abound; everywhere and in all things I am instructed both to abound and to suffer need. I can do all things through Christ which strengtheneth me." (4:12-13). If Johnny has received Christ as Savior and he is operating at his full potential, then we as parents and teachers have a responsibility to accept him as he is and give him the same degree of attention and love we give to "Straight 'A' Sam" or "Academic Alice." It is imperative to the mental and emotional well-being of every child that love be expressed to him on a continual basis and in a variety of ways.

Sometimes in the Christian world we readily adopt non-Christian words and phrases without determining whether or not they have a Biblical basis. In the bright light of Scripture, the idea of *self-love* or *self-esteem* does not ring true. Paul reminds us in Philippians 2:3, "Let nothing be done through strife or vain glory; but in lowliness of mind let each esteem others better than themselves." We are born with a natural sense of self-preservation. When Jesus admonished us to "Love thy neighbor as thyself," His emphasis was not on loving ourselves but on loving our neighbor. Our natural carnal tendency is to love ourselves a great deal more than we love our neighbor. The ultimate mark of Christian maturity is complete selflessness, *esteeming others* more than ourselves. We must realize that a non-Christian individual con-

Should Your Child Have . . . / 67

tinues to operate on a *self frequency*. Consequently he tends to build up his *self-concept* and develops a *self-esteem* and *self-love* because his strength is in himself. The idea of doing "all things through Christ which strengtheneth me" is foreign to him. John the Baptist said, "He must increase but I must decrease" (John 3:30).

As mentioned in the preface on page 11, many chapters of this book were published in a national publication *Christian School Comment*. When this particular article was published in November 1975 I received the following letter from a mother in San Jose, California:

Dear Dr. Kienel,

This letter is being written in appreciation of, and to support, your Christian School Comment, Vol. 6, No. 2.

*Since we're surrounded all the time by well-meaning friends, Sunday School teachers, (and authors) etc; who say, "You have to learn to love yourself," it's really encouraging to hear from someone who realizes that we are **born** in love with ourselves. We are told to help our child have a good "self-image," love themselves, and learn to be independent. However, it's obvious in these last days that the spirit of independence in children is very difficult to squelch! They **really** need to learn to be **dependent** on God.*

*We are the parents of four children, ages 11-24. Our two oldest were brought up, as well as we could, with God's help, in the manner you suggest. We had complete opposition from friends, neighbors, relatives, and other Christians. We were told that our "narrowness" would ruin them, since we wanted them to be **dependent**, and be concerned about their Christ-*

68 / America Needs: . . .

image rather than their self-image.

Now, both of these two have elected to attend Multnomah School of the Bible – the oldest is married to a pastoral student and is graduating this year. The letters of thanks and gratitude we receive are a fulfillment of God's promise that "our children will rise up and call us blessed."

We are rearing our younger two in the same manner, and get the same static from other Christians who are trying to push various books on us, etc.

However, the fellowship and prayer times, confessions, intercessory prayer, fun times, etc; that we enjoy with these two boys are priceless. They can't really **relax** *and have real* **unfettered** *fun until they are free of loving themselves so much! When they give up the struggle to have a good self-image, it's like a weight is lifted.*

Thanks so much for your article.

In Christ – A Christ-centered mother in San Jose.

Should your child have a good self-image? If he is not a Christian, he should be made aware that he needs Jesus Christ as his Savior. If he is a born-again Christian, his *self-image* should be completely absorbed by the indwelling presence of Jesus Christ in his life. If Christ is not Lord of every area of our life, including *self,* he is not Lord at all.

"Unless there is a nationwide-wide revival of education which is academically sound and founded on Biblical principles, there is little hope for our country."

9

WHY CHRISTIAN SCHOOL EDUCATION IS RIGHT FOR YOUR CHILD

Abraham Lincoln said, *"The philosophy of the classroom is the philosophy of the government in the next generation."* The true purpose of CHRISTIAN SCHOOL EDUCATION is to hand the torch of a Bible-centered, Christ-honoring education to your children and mine and the next generation.

George Washington said, *"True religion affords government its surest support. The future of this nation depends on the Christian training of the youth. It is impossible to govern without the Bible."*

Both of these great leaders affirm that we need to be vitally concerned with the education of youth and that the Bible must have a central place in education. This is the very heart of Christian school education and quite frankly, unless there is a nation-wide revival of education which is academically sound and founded on Biblical principles, there is little hope for our country. There are few pursuits of life more important to the future of our country than the wide-spread expansion of the Christian school ministry.

The purpose of Christian school education is to show children and young people how to face God and then with the vision of God in their hearts to face the present world and the world to come. The purpose of Christian school education is to present as clearly as possible to our children the truth about God, about life and living, about our world and everything in it and to present the Word of God as the authoritative source upon which to build a life that has purpose and meaning.

Of course a major controversy in the world of education is the age old question, "What is truth?" The late Dr. Mark Fakkema said, *"Truth is not necessarily truth because it is regarded as such by contemporary scholarship. By way of verifying His statements, our Lord did not appeal to the recognized leadership of His day. Our Lord constantly quoted Scripture as His authority. God's Word is the test of all truth. All teaching that is expressive of God's Word is true. Teaching that is not expository of the Word is falsehood."* Christian school education is right for your child because its central purpose is to develop an educational process that puts the Bible at the center and asks the student and the teacher to evaluate all they see in the world through the eyes of God — because God is Truth. All must conform to Him or it is not truth. Jesus said, "I am the Way, *the Truth,* and the Life" (John

Why Christian School Education . . . / 73

14:6). In true Christian education, students learn to use the Bible to evaluate all of life. The Bible is Life — it is the living Word — it is above every other book. In Christian school education the Word of God is not on trial. Needless to say, Christian education is the exact opposite of secular education. *Webster's New Collegiate Dictionary* defines *secularism* as *"rejection or exclusion of religion and religious considerations"* or simply stated, *"without God."* It is important to note that the definition of "atheism" is *"no God."* Secular education ignores or denies God and there is every indication the system is producing a generation that ignores and denies God. On October 14, 1973, during a speech in Phoenix, Arizona, Dr. W. P. Shofstall, Arizona State Superintendent of Schools, said: *The atheists have, for all practical purposes, taken over public education in this country.*

TOOLS OF LEARNING

Christian school education is right for your child because its purpose includes the responsibility to prepare Johnny with the basic tools of learning. Houses are built by men who have an array of tools at their disposal and have the skills to use them. Words are the tools of thought. The ability to read, the mastery of math, the ability to express thoughts orally and in writing make up the basic tools with which a student can make his way through the disciplines of learning and become a productive Christ-honoring citizen. Educators who lose sight of their basic academic responsibility of equipping Johnny's educational tool box have lost sight of what an educator is supposed to be. The next chapter will substantiate the over-all academic quality of Christian school education.

SYSTEM OF VALUES

Another purpose of Christian school education is to inspire in students a system of values consistent with the Word of God. Since spiritual values are spiritually discerned, it is incumbent upon Christian school educators to lead their students into a new life in Christ so that old things will pass away and all things will become new. Today, more than ever, we need a generation of students whose ethics and moral sense of right and wrong is clearly grounded in God's Holy Word. Though it does not necessarily follow that students will acquire Biblical ethics from teachers who are rightly related to their Creator through personal faith in Jesus Christ, it must be understood that apart from this it can never take place.

LOVE FOR COUNTRY

Not the least among the objectives of Christian school education is to instill in the hearts of your children and mine a strong love for our country. An emphasis on patriotism has always been a hallmark of Christian school education. America needs a new wave of patriotism, not a fanatical patriotism but a genuine love for the U.S.A. and

Why Christian School Education . . . / 75

our Christian heritage. There is no other group of schools in America that can speak so freely about our country's Christian beginnings as our country's Christian schools.

RESPECT FOR PARENTS

The Christian school is right because one of the high purposes of Christian school education is to uphold the sanctity of our homes and the sacredness of our churches. A mother told me recently that her child in public school was asked the question "If you had to push your mother or father over a precipice, which one would it be?" What a choice! And what a question to ask a child! Christian school educators respect the fact that they are working in behalf of parents in their educational ministry to students. All that is said and done in the classroom is done in behalf of parents because ultimately the responsibility for the education of children resides with their parents. Christian school educators are not on a crusade to drive a wedge between a child and his parents. As a matter of fact, Christian school educators know when they reinforce student respect for parents they are simultaneously supporting student respect for teachers.

REGARD FOR CHURCH

Most every Christian school is closely related to a church or works in cooperation with several churches. Virtually every Christian school

76 / America Needs: . . .

educator has a high regard for the church. This regard and respect for the church and those who serve God in the church is carried into the classroom and woven into the fabric of the school's curriculum. Regard for God's house and ministers of the Gospel is held forth in the classrooms, in student chapels and is undergirded in Bible lessons. Although some churches are still unaware of it, the Christian school is among the best friends the church has ever had.

The Christian school is right for your child because the full purpose of Christian school education is to help parents fulfill the counsel of that wise and powerful proverb we quoted in the first chapter which says, "Train up a child in the way he should go and when he is old he will not depart from it." (Proverbs 22:6)

"Reading levels range from six months to sixteen months above the national average."

10

THE ACADEMIC QUALITY OF CHRISTIAN SCHOOL EDUCATION

A recent issue of a leading Christian college magazine states that, *"many freshmen students coming from Christian schools bring high verbal comprehension, excellent study habits and a keen knowledge of God's Word. As a result, this college has risen to the challenge of providing courses of greater challenge than the tradional Bible survey and English courses structured to meet the needs of the average public school graduate."*

There has been the gnawing concern in the mind of some about the quality of Christian school education. Many have assumed because Christian schools are not funded by government tax dollars that Christian schools are academically inferior to their public counterparts. They equate expensive facilities and high salaries with quality instruction.

An old adage says, *"The proof of the pudding is in the tasting."* It has also been stated that, *"The proof of the school is in the testing."* This is not entirely true, especially in Christian schools because there is much more to evaluate than cold academics.

Academic achievement tests are not designed, nor could they be, to measure spiritual progress, love of country, parents or the church, all of which are basic to the purpose of Christian school education. But Christian school supporters need not hang their heads regarding the academic quality of instruction in our Christ-centered schools. Evidence is mounting to indicate that Christian school students are not only doing as well as their public school counterparts, but are, in fact, significantly ahead of them. Perhaps the largest sampling of the quality of academic instruction is available through a testing program administered among Christian schools who are members of the California Association of Christian Schools. The program has been administered for the past eight years by the test department of Harcourt, Brace, Jovanovich, publishers of the well known Stanford Achievement Tests. John P. Yates, a test consultant for the firm reported to CACS, *"Year after year testing shows that CACS students score higher than the national average at every grade taught."* The interesting graph which follows was prepared by Mr. Yates. The graph tells us that the reading levels range from six months to sixteen months above the national average. The actual grade by grade results are as follows:

1st graders are 6 months *above* the National Average

2nd graders are 7 months *above* the National Average

3rd graders are 9 months *above* the National Average

4th graders are 9 months *above* the National Average

5th graders are 14 months *above* the National Average

6th graders are 13 months *above* the National Average

7th graders are 12 months *above* the National Average

8th graders are 16 months *above* the National Average

The average scores of Christian school students in the upper fourth of the test sampling were as much as two years ahead of national norms at some grade levels. In a tenth grade sampling at the high school level, Mr. Yates reports that with the national average percentile score at 50, the Christian school student's average in reading was the 70th percentile; in English, the 74th; and in mathematics, the 66th. Average scores in the top 25% of the students were in the 80th and 90th percentiles. I have reports from other areas of the United States which indicate similar academic progress in Christian schools.

There are several basic reasons why Christian schools offer a better level of instruction:

1) The Christian school education environment is a positive environment where Christ is honored

and teachers and students are respected and loved. The family feeling in a Christian school is conducive to learning.

2) School discipline is positive and has as its ultimate aim self-discipline. Students are encouraged to be in control of themselves. At times corrective measures may be used to establish these boundaries. A child feels free, accepted, and content in an environment of loving discipline. Many Christian teachers, administrators and parents would evaluate these first two reasons as being most important.

3) Most Christian schools attempt to stress the *basics* of learning. They emphasize the phonetic approach to reading along with other equally effective approaches. Drill is an integral part of the learning process. Memorization is considered a positive force in learning. Many math concepts

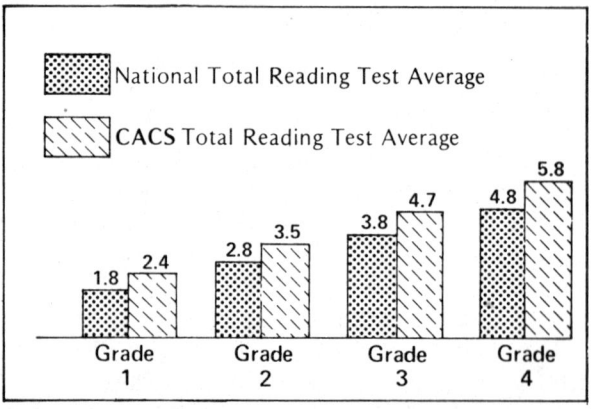

	National Total Reading Test Average	CACS Total Reading Test Average
Grade 1	1.8	2.4
Grade 2	2.8	3.5
Grade 3	3.8	4.7
Grade 4	4.8	5.8

CACS students were compared to some 225,000 students that were carefully selected to represent average students across the United States (1973). The figures represent the average (median) of all tests at

The Academic Quality ... / 83

such as the basic combinations for addition, subtraction, multiplication and division are best also learned by memorizing. Limiting class size is also a positive factor in many cases.

4) The positive attitude of students is a very dynamic factor in this process of learning. Most students in Christian schools have a real pride in their school and usually work cooperatively with the teachers, staff and other students.

5) Dedicated teachers are another positive influence on academic success. Students learn more from teachers than they learn from books or teaching machines. Teachers in Christian schools feel God has called them to this place of service and seek to serve youngsters with total dependence on Christ for strength and wisdom.

Combine all these positive factors and there is every reason to believe there should be success in

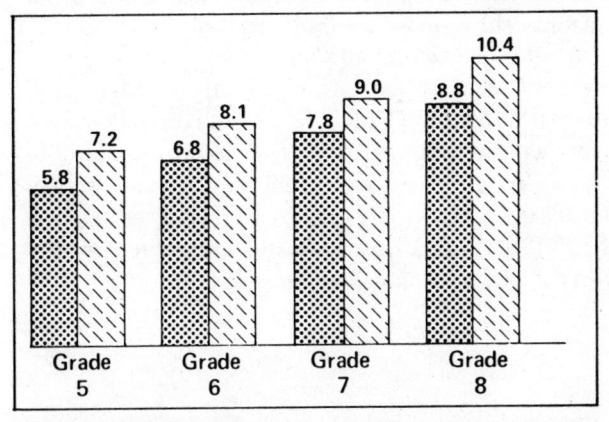

Grade 5	Grade 6	Grade 7	Grade 8
5.8 / 7.2	6.8 / 8.1	7.8 / 9.0	8.8 / 10.4

each grade level. The test used was the 1973 Stanford Achievement Test, Form A. The school year is based on ten calendar months.
—John P. Yates

academic growth. Successful learning is a natural by-product of a positive educational environment.

There is no question that most youngsters enjoy a better learning experience in a Christian school. Broad samplings of achievement test scores consistently indicate that Christian school students, at all grade levels and in every subject area achieve significantly above the national achievement test norms. Some people explain this away by saying that Christian schools are more selective in their students, their class sizes are smaller and parents generally show a greater interest in their youngster's school work because they have tuition money invested in their child's education. This may be true but it should also be said that Christian school educators are highly motivated because they consider their work a ministry unto Christ and they want to please Him and the students and parents they serve.

Academic excellence *should* be the natural outcome of positive Christian education. Above all, the child in whom Christ has done His redemptive work is free to mature, to grow spiritually, and to *learn*. To quote an experienced Christian school educator, James Braley, Christian education MUST be *"education of excellence which is distinctly and dynamically Christian."*

"It is my observation that true education flourishes best in a structured, disciplined and loving, friendly atmosphere where an inspiring and gifted teacher systematically imparts truth and knowledge to a group of students who have come together for the express purpose of learning."

11

WHAT METHOD OF CLASSROOM INSTRUCTION IS BEST FOR YOUR CHILD?

To my knowledge, there is nothing particularly sacred about the *traditional* form of education that characterizes the vast majority of thousands of Christian school classrooms around the country. No words in the sacred Scriptures are binding us to traditional education. We are bound, however, in Scripture to "teach them diligently" which implies that we are to be concerned about quality education. Christian schools have not *arrived* academically but as stated in the previous chapter the achievement test scores indicate that in the subject of reading, Christian school students average from six months to sixteen months ahead of the national norm of public school youngsters.

Even with our established record of above average test scores, a few educational prophets from the secular system (even though its test scores are lower) will occasionally suggest that Christian school educators jump on the public bandwagon and embrace a *better* form of education. Some have suggested, for example, that we follow the open classroom concept of education where the student is given a great many educational options in his classroom and complete liberty to pursue those options at his own discretion in a free atmosphere of minimum discipline. I am sure this sounds intriguing to some of our fuzzy-headed thinkers but the practical outcome is less than desirable.

Recently, I talked with Professor Gloria Graham about her views on open classroom education. Mrs. Graham is the former head of the Education Department at Biola College and is now on the administrative staff of the Teacher Training Division at California State University in Los Angeles. She is well informed on the current trends in education. She said the following regarding open classrooms:

> If Christian schools get involved in open classroom education and I suggest they don't, discipline will go down. There will be a loss of listening ability by students and a loss of their ability to follow directions. Statistics are showing that the brilliant child will achieve acceptably in an open classroom because he is self-motivated but the normal child in an open classroom is not given the basic stimulation that is needed to reach the achievement level that is developed in a traditional classroom setting.

A writer in the October 21, 1974, edition of *U.S. News and World Report* in an article entitled, "Back to Basics in the Schools" said, " . . . *all across*

What Method of Classroom Instruction . . . / 89

the nation, parents, school boards and often the pupils themselves are demanding that the (public) schools stop experimenting and get back to basics — in reading, writing, arithmetic and standards of behavior to boot." The article gives the following interesting account of two experimental schools in Pasadena, California:

There are two special public schools in Pasadena, California, that are of intense interest to parents and educators all across the country. One is the Pasadena Alternative School, a two-year-old experiment in *open education,* where students are given a maximum of individual freedom, a minimum of teacher supervision. There are no dress rules, and very few restrictions on behavior. Barefoot and blue-jeaned, the students themselves decide what and when they want to learn. Among the available options are leatherwork, gourmet cooking, weaving and something the school calls *hip lit* — all for credit. No tests measure the students' progress, instead, the teachers gauge their students in terms of creativity. Discipline, of course, is kept to an absolute minimum. "Sometimes," giggles one eighth-grader, "I even make it to class."

About three miles away stands Pasadena's other special public school, the John Marshall Fundamental School — a bastion of tradition-oriented education. Letter grades, regular examinations, strict dress codes and detention for delinquents are integral parts of the school's conservative program. Both the faculty and the student body are expected to present *an outstanding image* in dress and deportment. The curriculum is strict and basic; it features computational arithmetic . . . , reading drill in standard phonics and rigorous homework from kindergarten on.

90 / America Needs: . . .

At the *open-education* school, the kindergarten through twelfth grade enrollment is 550, and the waiting list stands at 515. At the John Marshall Fundamental School, however, a total of 1,700 pupils are enrolled and the waiting list has passed the 1,000 mark.

An article in the October 9, 1974, *Pasadena Star News* compares the the test scores of the two experimental schools: *"The Fundamental School registered the highest average gain while the Alternative School (open classroom) registered the lowest gain."* It is interesting to note that Pasadena's *experimental* traditional school was patterned after one of our Christian schools — San Gabriel Christian School near Pasadena after several visits to that school by members of the Pasadena City School Board and the administrative staff from John Marshall School.

In the last decade there had been an endless parade of new classroom innovations. Most of them have not set very well with parents or students. The October *U.S. News and World Report* article said, *"Most of the high schools and colleges that had given up grading systems in favor of the less competitive pass-fail options have returned – largely at the request of students – to the old-fashioned marks."* The article records the words of Dr. Mario Fantini, Dean of Education at a state university in New York who said, *"If a referendum were taken today, there is no doubt in my mind that 70 percent of parents would opt for the old fashioned kind of education . . . and only 10 percent for the innovations."*

It is my observation that true education flourishes best in a structured, disciplined and loving, friendly atmosphere where an inspiring and gifted teacher systematically imparts truth and knowledge to a group of students who have come together for the express purpose of learning.

In recent conversation with Dr. Walter Fremont, Dean of the School of Education at Bob Jones University, he shared with me the results of an extensive study on various forms of education. The outcome of the study indicates that a well-educated and gifted teacher is still the key to quality education.

After personally visiting hundreds of classrooms across the United States and listening to a great variety of opinions, I am convinced that Christian school education under the leadership of godly administrators and gracious God-fearing teachers is the best investment of our educational dollars.

The United States Government has invested millions of dollars in numerous schemes for changing the process of education. Every few years the pendulum swings from one extreme form of education to another when all of the time the answer is in the first four books of the New Testament where we watch Jesus the Master Teacher teach on the shores of Galilee. A reading of the sixth chapter of Mark will show that He organized His *students* in such a manner that without the aid of electronic voice amplification, chalk board, overhead projector or even a classroom, he was able to teach for hours to a student audience so quietly disciplined that His over-sized class of thousands of students

92 / America Needs: . . .

could hear His natural voice. And even today there is no substitute for the Christian teacher who has the inner dynamic of the Holy Spirit imparting to an organized class of students the sacred Bread of Life and a Bible-centered curriculum.

"In my view, the heart of the problem is the fact that the tax-supported system must function without a fixed moral base."

12

"OUR PUBLIC SCHOOLS ARE NOT WORKING"

Even though public education has long held an equal status with motherhood, apple pie and the American flag, there is a growing number of parents who are no longer listening to the oft repeated arguments against private Christian education. They feel their children are their first obligation. They simply do not believe we have a religious obligation to use our beloved children to save the public schools. These parents, as they should be, are more concerned with the outcome of their children than they are with the outcome of the local tax-supported school.

As the true nature of public education comes into focus academically and philosophically, it is becoming easier for concerned parents to lay aside the long standing idea that it is somehow advantageous to expose children to an anti-Christian educational environment.

Across America Christian schools are coming into existence at the rate of two new schools a day. Parents, by the thousands, are now enrolling their youngsters in Christian classrooms. Concerning this phenomenon ABC News Commentator, Paul Harvey said:

> Americans, hard taxed to support public schools, are willing to pay extra to provide for their children's education in a Christian environment.
>
> Several factors contribute to this phenomenon.
>
> Overcrowded public schools have motivated those who can afford it to seek the more personal teacher-student ratio of the smaller school.
>
> Grotesque misbehavior, individual and organized, which now characterizes many public schools has alienated both students and faculty.
>
> And the harvest from the bad tree is bitter fruit. Youth crime is increasing eleven times faster than youth population is increasing.
>
> Further, each student who pays extra to attend a private school saves the taxpayers from $500 to $900 a year, depending on the school district.
>
> Christian schools predate public schools in the United States by 200 years. These are not "parochial" schools. They are supported in whole or in part by a church, but each is open to anybody who is academically qualified and willing to live and work by the rules.
>
> Christian schools are the fastest growing education movement in America.

Dr. Neil V. Sullivan, a former district and county superintendent of public schools, wrote these alarming words in the September 16, 1972, edition of *Saturday Review:*

> It's no secret anymore: Our public schools are not

Our Public Schools are Not Working ... / 97

working. In many cities a third of the kids are quitting; almost as many of those still registered simply don't attend. Regular teachers and administrators are retiring early; others are on strike. Taxpayers are rebelling at the escalating costs of running the schools; many large systems face bankruptcies.

The system itself is literally coming apart at the seams. Most school administrators and board members, meanwhile say little or nothing. They are hanging on by the skin of their teeth — waiting to retire ...

The August 18, 1975 issue of *U.S. News and World Report* shows an over-all increase in *protestant schools* of 201,000 students from 1960 to 1975. In an earlier edition *The U.S. News* reported the following reason for the increase:

The big impetus, churchmen say, is coming from rising alarm of parents over what they see as academic laxity in the public schools, along with rampant misbehavior — robbery, drug abuse and classroom disruption.

Search for discipline. What these parents are seeking, it is said, is a learning environment for their youngsters that is more disciplined and more religious than can be found in any public school.

In my view, the heart of the problem is the fact that the tax-supported system must function without a fixed moral base. Permit me to quote from a Michigan Department of Education report on *Education in Moral Values*. *"To moralize and to impose morality on youngsters – especially in pluralistic society – is not within the purview of public education."*

It appears any standard of morality or even a pretense of a religious observance in a public school can be successfully challenged by one or more individuals and the practice or standard is eliminated. Recently the Evangelical News Service carried a story of a situation of this type in Santa Rosa, California. The report was as follows:

> A kindergarten song ending with the line, "Thank you, God, for everything," has been banned as unconstitutional by a Sonoma County judge.
>
> Superior Court Judge Joseph Murphy said the school board of the Rohnert Park community was wrong in permitting students to sing the song, "Thanksgiving."
>
> He ruled that use of the song, which had been challenged by a parent, did not maintain the required separation of church and state.

It is interesting to observe the accuracy of a prediction made by Dr. A.A. Hodge of Princeton University more than 100 years ago.

> It is capable of exact demonstration that if every party in the State has the right of excluding from public schools whatever he does not believe to be true, then he that believes most must give way to him that believes least, and then he that believes nothing, no matter in how small a minority the atheists or the agnostics may be. It is self-evident that on this scheme, if it is consistently and persistently carried out in all parts of the country, the United States' system of national popular education will be the most efficient and wide spread instrument for the propagation of atheism which the world has ever seen. (These statements can be found in Hodge's book *Popular Lectures in Theological Themes,* pages 281, 283).

Dr. Hodge's prediction is all the more remarkable when you realize a century ago teaching in a public school was a very circumspect occupation. Education researcher David L. Barr has brought

Our Public Schools are Not Working ... / 99

from the archives one set of rules for public school teachers which included the following:

> Teachers will not dress in bright colors. Dresses must not be more than two inches above the ankles. At least two petticoats must be worn. Teachers will not marry or keep company with men during the term of employment. Teachers will not loiter at ice cream stores. Teachers will not smoke cigarets or play at cards. It is understood that the teacher will attend church each Sunday.

Our present-day public schools and even Christian schools, except for the latter three rules, would be hard pressed for teachers if each of those policies were enforced today — a hundred years later.

Now back to the present. As Dr. Sullivan said, *"Our public schools are not working."* In addition to their lack of a fixed moral base (Christian schools have the Bible for their fixed moral point of reference) public schools are running into serious financial problems. Says Sullivan, *" ... many large systems face bankruptcy."* In the last seven years the cost of educating a public school student has doubled. According to a nation-wide survey of school-district budgets conducted by Market Data Retrieval, an educational-research company based in Westport, Connecticut, the average cost of educating a student in the nation's public schools rose from $553.95 during the 1967-68 school year to $1,108.22 during 1974-75. Unfortunately, there has not been a corresponding increase in the mental take-home pay for public school students. Suzanne De Lesseps reporting for the *New York Times,* September 9, 1975, said:

Test scores on the College Entrance Examination Board's Scholastic Aptitude Test (SAT) — a test given to help forecast how a high-school student will perform in college — have fallen steadily for the past 13 years. The average composite scores on tests administered by the American College Testing Program (ACT) have also fallen in recent years.

In recent years, less than half of the nation's school bond issues have passed indicating a grassroots disenchantment with public education. In her *New York Times* report, Suzanne De Lesseps said:

> As the fall term opens, there is a growing feeling among many parents that the public schools have not paid enough attention to the three traditional standbys — reading, writing and arithmetic.
>
> On one level, this feeling is related to dissatisfaction with the educational innovations of the 1960's and the belief that the schools have become too permissive. On another level, it is related to the growing mistrust of American institutions in general and the desire to recapture the stable, traditional values that have somehow gotten lost in the shuffle.

For the 58.9 million young Americans who are attending America's public schools, during this bicentennial year, I wish it were possible for me to quote from an impressive array of responsible educational prophets that the future of public education is on the upswing and that Biblical values and academic basics are just over the immediate horizon. Unfortunately, to the best of my knowledge, such a forecast cannot be assembled even for the most optimistic public school supporters.

In conclusion, permit me to quote the late Dr. Mark Fakkema, the leading pioneer of the modern

Our Public Schools are Not Working ... / 101

Christian school movement. He said:

> Shortly after the first quarter of the last century there lived a man in New England who has been called the "Father of the Public School." His name was Horace Mann. He was a Unitarian. He was a leader in education. He sought to bring about a change in the existing private schools of his day. It was his ambition to introduce socialized education into this country. This was not an American idea. He imported it from Prussia in Europe. Having visited Prussia, he conceived the idea of promoting a Prussian type of education in America. Copying Prussia he sought to introduce a system of education in our country which was state-controlled, state-owned, and of course, state financed.
>
> In trying to import this foreign system of education into our country, he was confronted with one great difficulty. It was this: In Prussia there was no separation of church and state. Consequently, the state schools in Prussia were free to teach the religion common to that nation. However, in America we have separation of church and state and this has increasingly been interpreted to mean that state schools do not have the right to teach the Christian religion. They may teach a Christ-ignoring philosophy but they may not teach Christ. They make comment on the books written by men but the law forbids them to make comment on the Book of God. The Bible may be contradicted by the anti-religious teaching of evolution, but the teaching of the religion of the Bible is forbidden. It should be apparent that the interpretation of Geography, Arithmetic and History in the light of Scripture — which is the only true interpretation — must needs be lost in the crucible of secular instruction.

In these brief words Dr. Fakkema brings into focus, at least for the Christian, the very heart of the problem. The public school system in America is an educational house divided against itself.

"The cat family has always produced cats and the dog family has always produced dogs and there is not one fossilized bone anywhere in the world that gives evidence to the contrary."

13

EVOLUTION AND THE CHRISTIAN SCHOOL

Is evolution taught in Christian schools? In a sense, yes, but I prefer the word *exposed* in place of *taught*. Christian school students are *exposed* to the philosophy of evolution and they are *taught* the Biblical account of creation or the *creationist view*. The word *taught* implies teaching a particular truth in a positive way. There is no scientific evidence that evolution can be construed as truth. As a matter of fact, there is a growing number of scientists who are Christian who claim it takes considerably more faith to believe the idea of evolution than it does to believe the creationist's view. In the minds of many scientists, the evolution theory, from the scientific point of view, is *out of gas* and is incapable of accounting for life on earth.

104 / America Needs: . . .

Dr. Henry M. Morris, Director of the Institute for Creation Research and Academic Vice-President of Christian Heritage College in San Diego, California, is probably the nation's leading spokesman for scientific creationism. He said:

Although widely promoted as a scientific fact, evolution has never been proved scientifically. Some writers still call it the "theory" of evolution, but even this is too generous. A scientific hypothesis should be capable of being tested in some way, to determine whether or not it is true, but evolution cannot be tested. No laboratory experiment can either confirm or falsify a process which, by its very nature, requires millions of years to accomplish significant results.

Evolution is, therefore, neither fact, theory, nor hypothesis. It is a belief – and nothing more.

Charles Darwin's philosophy of earth's creation began with his work called *Origin of Species* in 1859. The scientific community picked up his philosophy and clothed it in scientific respectability. This occured at a time when science was fast becoming the god of the intellectual community.

I recall vividly my own public high school biology teacher presenting Darwin's evolutionary ideas. In a short span of time he thoroughly shook my faith in God and my belief in the authority of the Scriptures. Other Christian students were also affected. Although I survived the ordeal, others did not. So overwhelming were the evolutionary arguments in those years that Christian leaders had few, if any, solid counter explanations. It was difficult to argue against *science*. The cloak of *scientific validity* had performed the *snow-job* of the century. Even in a Christian college I was pre-

Evolution and the Christian School ... / 105

sented with the *"Gap Theory"* — the idea that there was an evolutionary gap of several millions of years between Genesis 1:1 and 1:2. I am not critical of my Christian college professors for this error because the *"Gap Theory"* was the prevailing explanation making the rounds in the Christian community in the 1950's. Evolution was simply referred to as God's method of creation.

Gradually, in the 1960's, the walls of scientific credibility surrounding the *theory* of evolution began to crumble. A host of scientists, Christian and non-Christian, began to chip away the veneer that surrounded Darwin's hoax of the century.

Among the so-called scientific evidences supporting evolutionary ideas to come tumbling down was the Carbon-14 dating method — the *scientific* method that has *proven* that much of the earth and its fossils are millions of years old. Unfortunately for the evolutionists this method does not withstand scientific scrutiny. For example, the August 1963 issue of *Science* magazine records the work of Dr. M. S. Keith and G. M. Anderson in an article entitled, *"Radiocarbon Dating: Fictitious Results with Mollusks Shells."* In essence the article says that the shells of *living* mollusks were calculated to have been *dead* 2,300 years! It is interesting to note that Willard Libby, the inventor of the Carbon-14 dating method, won a Nobel Prize for his *"scientific achievement."*

A second evolutionary idea to collapse was the principle that the systems of nature are continually improving and getting better and better or ever evolving upward. Physicists have universally accepted the Second Law of Thermodynamics which states that *"there exists a universal principle of change in nature which is downhill, not uphill, as evolution requires."* Dr. Isaac Asimov, writing is the May 1973 issue of *Science Digest*, said, *"As far as we know, all changes are in the direction of increasing disorder, of increasing randomness, of running down."*

Of course, such scientific information is not too popular with the people who claim their ancestors evolved from a primeval cell.

A third evolutionary principle that has fallen *flatter than a fritter* is the idea that fossils buried deep in the earth prove evolution. Just the opposite is true. Man has yet to find a fossil that is in the transitional stage from one species to another species. To put it in more simple terms, the cat family has always produced cats and the dog family has always produced dogs and there is not one fossilized bone anywhere in the world that gives evidence to the contrary. To those of us who may have been shaken by evolutionary teaching, it is interesting now to see the evolution idea fast becoming the albatross around the necks of multitudes of teachers, scientists and publishers who have perpetuated the evolutionary cause in the name of science.

In the foreword of his newest book, *Scientific Creationism*, written for Christian school educators, Dr. Henry Morris makes the following statement:

The widespread movement in recent years toward the establishment of new private Christian schools has been stimulated largely by the failure of the public schools to maintain academic and philosophic objectivity. In the name of modern science and of church-state separation, the Bible and theistic religion have been effectively banned from curricula, and a nontheistic religion of secular evolutionary humanism has become, for all practical purposes, the official state religion promoted in the public schools.

The results of two generations of this evolutionary indoctrination have been devastating. Secularized schools have begotten a secularized society. The child is the father of the man and, if the child is led to believe he is merely an evolved beast, the man he becomes will behave as a beast, either aggressively struggling for supremacy himself or blindly following aggressive leaders.

Evolutionist teaching is not only harmful sociologically, but it is false scientifically and historically. Man and his world are "not" products of an evolutionary process but, rather, are special creations of God. (See Exodus 20:11; 31:17-19.)

That being true it follows that real understanding of man and his world can only be acquired in a thoroughgoing creationist frame of reference. True education in every field should be structured around creationism, not evolution.

Most Christian schools are, therefore, committed to Biblical creationism as a basic premise in their philosophy of education. The Christian school movement is urgently needed in today's world and is already making a vital impact. Fortunate is the child whose parents and church leaders think enough of his future character and his eternal welfare to see that he has a solid and thorough Christian education.

It is true that Christian school youngsters are being *exposed* to the *errors* of evolution and that they are being taught that *true* science is not in conflict with God's Word.

"As a Christian in the public school system, on numerous occasions I was in a position of compromise."

14

WHY MANY FORMER PUBLIC SCHOOL TEACHERS NOW TEACH IN CHRISTIAN SCHOOLS

As a history major in college I learned that eyewitnesses are considered *primary sources* and provide the most reliable evidence for chronicling historical facts. On that basis I think you will agree that teachers who have taught in public schools but now teach in Christian schools are believable witnesses to the difference between secular and Christian education. Shortly after the release of my first book, *The Christian School: Why It Is Right for Your Child* (Victor Books), I conducted a nationwide survey of former public school educators who now teach in Christian schools. I asked them to explain why they have chosen to teach in Christian schools. Their interesting statements follow:

As a Christian in the public school system, on numerous occasions I was in a position of compromise. As a Christian, I knew what was right but as an employee of the State, I was ordered to not do right, but to do whatever the system dictated. Discipline was decaying rapidly and students were sent out of school into society supposedly "equipped." As I let the Lord take my life completely, the compromising became impossible. No way could I go against my convictions by sanctioning rock music, moral decay, and a Godless education. I now teach the whole story beginning with accepting God's gift of eternal life. I now can teach something that is not relative but that is absolute TRUTH – His Word. Now lives are being "equipped" to stand in this world. In Colossians 2:8, Paul says, "Beware lest any man spoil you through philosophy and vain deceit, after the tradition of men, after the rudiments of the world, and not after Christ.
A seventh grade teacher
Fairhaven Christian Academy, Chesterton, Indiana

As a former public school teacher of ten and one half years, I have now decided to teach in a Christian school. It definitely is not because of the financial reward because I could earn well over double what I now earn. It is not due to lack of preparation for I have a B.S. in Education and lack only five classes having my Masters in Education. It is not due to convenience since I drive well over thirty miles one way to our Christian school each day. My only real reason is "LOVE;" love of God, love of children, love of learning, and love of life. TO HELP TO INTRODUCE A CHILD TO CHRIST'S LOVE AND HELP THE CHILD BUILD A PERSONAL RELATIONSHIP WITH GOD HAS REWARDS NOTHING ELSE CAN MATCH.
A high school teacher
Gateway Christian School, St. Louis, Missouri

Why Many Former Public Teachers . . . / 111

With each passing year while teaching in the public school, I became aware of a growing conflict between my own personal values and standards and those being instilled by the school as a whole. By being a part of the teaching team, I was actually compromising and giving my approval (silently, perhaps) to lowering moral standards, loose discipline, planned social activities, dress of students, and the humanistic viewpoint of many in the public school. Also, as Chairman of the Language Arts Department, I was likewise displaying my acceptance of all the literature being presented on both the junior and senior high school levels, some of which I felt should be neither exposed nor taught to young people. I therefore prayed to be placed in a teaching situation with Christian standards where the Bible could be read and used as a guide, problems could be prayed about together, control would be stronger, high moral standards would be upheld, dress would be modest, social activities would be Christ-pleasing, the TRUE meaning of holidays could be openly discussed and celebrated, and all literature could be analyzed from a Christian (Biblical) viewpoint.

When I left the public school and joined a Christian faculty, I was certainly not aware of the advantages of the Christian school. For instance, a real help to me each morning is the teachers' devotional time together. This helps to establish the proper outlook for the day, and it is a real encouragement to know that the teachers are a TRUE team, with the same basic Christian goals in mind. Also, after a few months teaching, I came to more fully realize that Bible study and teaching is not just an additional segment attached to the academic program of the Christian school, but is an integral part of every facet of the school day.

An intermediate and high school English teacher Calvary Baptist Christian Academy, Meadville, Pennsylvania

When I first entered public school teaching in 1952, I was able to read from the Bible freely and pray with my students. However, this still was not enough to develop an effective set of values and morals within the students. (God can't be tacked onto something. He must totally govern.) Gradually over the years, even the Bible and prayer disappeared completely and a tidal wave of secular philosophy has swept in. As a result, in 1965, after seven years of teaching and six years of administration, I felt led to leave and enter Christian school education. It has been an exciting ten years of seeing God's Hand bless and expand our school as well as the whole ministry.

Headmaster
The Christian Academy, Brookhaven, Pennsylvania

I find that teaching in a Christian school puts me in the Biblical position of authority as the teacher. Students have asked, on occasion, "Why should I obey you?" As a Christian teacher, I have an answer. It is not because I am older, or bigger, or stronger, or smarter. It is because I have been given the responsibility and authority of God being the teacher and God commands, because of my position, I am to be obeyed by my students. So even if they are bigger, stronger, or smarter than I, they still are to obey me. When this kind of Biblical authority is understood in the classroom, power struggles between teacher and students cease (or at least are infrequent). Things are in order because they are the way God intended them to be. And it becomes easier to point out the magnificence of God through biology, math or Bible since He's the one in charge of the class in the first place. God's order just makes everything easier.

A high school teacher
Baymonte Christian School, Scotts Valley, California

Why Many Former Public Teachers . . . / 113

After teaching math four years in an inner city school of Rochester, I was convicted about being part of a system that denies the existence of God, promotes the goodness of man and indoctrinates a life style of relativism. I could neither witness freely to students nor appeal to the Bible as the absolute authority for faith and practice. Under the leading of the Holy Spirit through God's Word, I left my tenured position in the public schools to teach in a Christian school where children are taught the Truth of God's Word.

A high school teacher
God and Country School, Rochester, New York

When I taught the child in only mind and body in the public school it seemed that there was so much left unfinished. Yet at that time I didn't know what it was. Now that Jesus is my Lord, Savior and Authority, I can teach His love and authority to students for application to their lives. The monetary loss does not come near the spiritual gain found in answering the Lord's call to teach in a Christian school.

A third and fourth grade teacher
Victor Valley Christian School, Victorville, California

Our nation will become what our children are taught. What goes into a child's mind comes out in his life. This is my conviction. As a former public school teacher (eleven years) I am now teaching in a Christian day school. I have never been happier in all my life. When I first started teaching in public school, in 1957, I was given complete freedom to use flannelgraph materials, etc., for devotional time along with prayer time. When I left public school in 1968, I could read only a few verses from the Bible, with NO comment and NO prayer time. Along with this, textbooks have been systematically eliminating the basic moral and philosophical precepts of Biblical Christianity and good common sense. Anti-Americanism was rampant on every hand. Disrespect to parents, teachers, and principals was a daily occurrence. I felt as though my "hands were tied." For the past three years, teaching in a Christian school has afforded a blessed opportunity to serve the Lord daily. Each year, boys and girls have come to know Christ as their personal Savior, which of course, would have been impossible in public schools. Needless to say, I am "sold" on Christian education.

A third grade teacher
Faith Christian School, Ramseur, North Carolina

For years I rationalized that I could reach more children by teaching in a public school but as one led by God to work with children, I realized six years ago that it is both my obligation and privilege to train the child in a completely Christian atmosphere. In a Christian school, each subject can be taught on the premise that mastering skills enables the Christian child to communicate more effectively with a lost and dying world. Discipline is consistent for it becomes a useful tool in molding "disciples" for the Lord's service. Since guiding and training children is not an easy task, I shall be grateful throughout all eternity that Christ is the MASTER TEACHER in my classroom.

A primary grade teacher
Florida Christian School, Miami, Florida

After nineteen years of teaching in the public school of New York state, my first year of teaching at Auburn Christian School has brought great contentment. I have been able to praise God with my class while teaching the "three R's." We are free to read God's

Word and exalt His name together. New experiences began the first week when a kindergarten boy answered my question of "Who is God?" by saying, "God is best." In prayer time circle we have talked to God about our families, neighbors, friends and leaders. We have been able to share the joys of answered prayer.
A primary grade teacher
Auburn Christian School, Auburn, New York

I think you will agree these statements by former public school educators, who now teach in Christian schools, reflect a strong sense of priorities and a firm dedication to the Lord. These characteristics are typical of thousands of Christian school educators across the country. Such dedication has made the Christian school education the fastest growing educational movement in America.

"Unfortunately they (parents) come to realize too late that sending their children to a 'free' public school is a very expensive thing to do."
Tim LaHaye

15

Answers

To Common Questions

About Christian Schools

WHAT IS THE BASIC DIFFERENCE BE-
TWEEN CHRISTIAN EDUCATION AND SEC-
ULAR EDUCATION?

The *Holt Intermediate Dictionary of American English* defines the word *secular* as *"having to do with this world and its affairs; not religious or spiritual."* Christian School education is almost the exact opposite of secular education. It is, in fact, religious and spiritual. Its purpose is not to draw away from the message of God's Word but to inspire love and respect for it. Instead of being worldly and man-centered, Christian education is Christ-centered. It is a positive form of education that inspires learning in the basics of education. It places the supremacy of God and His Word over the supremacy of man and his man-made achievements.

ARE STUDENTS IN A CHRISTIAN SCHOOL SHELTERED FROM THE COLD REALITIES OF THE WORLD?

The Christian school has been *put down* with this particular question more than any other. The question rests on several assumptions that are not true. The first assumption is that non-Christian teachers in public schools are better prepared to train Christian youngsters to live as Christians in a non-Christian world than Christian teachers in a Christian school. Pardon the mind bender sentence but the full reality of the situation is that non-Christian teachers in non-Christian public schools usually succeed in training Christian and non-Christian students to live as non-Christians in the world. Rather than adjusting to the world, they are conforming to the world.

I recently interviewed Dr. Tim LaHaye on my radio program, CHRISTIAN SCHOOL COMMENT. This program is released daily on ten radio stations in the west. Dr. LaHaye is one of the nation's best known pastors and, in my view, one of the finest Christian writers in the world today. Scott Memorial Baptist Church in San Diego, pastored by Tim LaHaye, sponsors a large Christian school program including a pre-school, two elementary schools, a large Christian High School and the well-known Christian Heritage College. During my radio interview with Dr. LaHaye I asked, "How do you feel about parents who say, 'I send my children to the public school because I don't want to shelter them?'" Dr. LaHaye answered, "In the first place, I don't think they are being objective. They are already colored by the fact they will have to pay tuition if they send their youngsters to one of our Christian schools. Unfortunately they come to realize too late that sending their children to a *free* public school is a very expensive thing to do. The shipwrecks end up in my office. That's where I was alerted to this whole problem of the devastating effect of public education on Christian young people. And in reality it is a ridiculous concept to expect a youngster to do battle with a non-Christian teacher who may be a master-degreed individual with years of experience. He knows how to jerk the rug out from under this kid and make a fool of him in the classroom. We don't send out missionaries this way. We train them over many years with graduate school and all the rest. Then we send them out to work with people who can't read or write. But all too many Christians will expose their kids to public school educators who may be mental perverts and skilled in the art of deception. To me it is insanity!"

Christian schools are often referred to as *greenhouses* or *hothouses* that create a sheltered environment for children. This brings us to our second assumption. The assumption is that a greenhouse is good for young and tender plants but somehow the semi-protected environment of a Christian school is not good for children.

The greenhouse plant-growing analogy carries some interesting parallels. Everyone knows the purpose of a greenhouse is to give young plants a head start. The ideal environment of the greenhouse protects the plants from destructive

120 / America Needs: . . .

elements during their early delicate growing season and provides them with proper conditions for maximum maturity. At a given point the young plants reach a "graduation point" and they are ready for transplant. The end result is they are larger, stronger, more productive and better prepared to ward off plant diseases than their counterparts who had their start in the wilds.

There is more to this than just theory. I could bring forward a host of witnesses who would support the idea that a wholesome Bible-centered environment at home and at school does, in fact, produce wholesome Bible-centered children and young people. I am impressed with the words of the following pastors on this subject:

Dr. David Hocking is a dynamic young pastor of the burgeoning First Brethren Church in Long Beach, California. This church has had a large Christian school ministry for 27 years which now includes a pre-school, two elementary schools, a junior and senior high school, an under-graduate college program and a graduate school offering M.A. and Ph.D. degrees in Christian ministries — the total program involves more than 1,500 students.

Dr. Hocking states, *"time has proven that youngsters in my congregation who attend our Brethren Church Schools are significantly more loyal to the church and very often take positions of leadership as they reach their adult years than their counterparts who attend the public system."* Pastor Hocking is a product of the church and school he now pastors. He began school there in the second

Answers to Common Questions . . . / 121

grade.

Pastor J. Kenneth Adams, Sr., pastors a church in Phoenix, Arizona, which is a supporting church of Phoenix Christian High School, one of the leading Christian high schools in America. He said, *"Now after years in the ministry, I can also compare the end result of students coming through Christian education and those who did not. Their years of experience have made me a sober partisan to Christ-centered education at all levels."*

In 1971, Paul B. Smith, pastor of People's Church of Toronto, Canada, a church which gives more than a million dollars to missions each year, wrote in "Child Evangelism Magazine,"

> If I had my life as a pastor to live over again, I would warn my people constantly about the dangers of the North American public school system. Over a period of 30 years I have watched with a heavy heart the devastating effects of the public schools, both on my own children and those on many of my congregation.

Pastor Smith has established a large Christian school in his church.

WILL THE U.S. INFLATIONARY PROBLEMS AFFECT THE GROWTH OF CHRISTIAN SCHOOLS?

Christian schools have had their greatest growth period in the last fives years. Consequently, as a movement, Christian schools have weathered only a few periods of national financial recession. In the past, financial recessions have slowed Christian school growth but never has there been a decline in the over-all student enrollment figures.

The growth patterns of the California Association of Christian Schools (now known as the WESTERN ASSOCIATION OF CHRISTIAN SCHOOLS) are typical of Christian school growth throughout America. Over the past ten years our association's school membership has increased from 68 to 500 schools and colleges and student enrollment has climbed from 11,388 to the current figure of 63,131.

Even though Christian schools are forced to raise tuitions because of inflation, most parents value the Christian education of their children to the point they are willing to make whatever financial sacrifice necessary to keep their children in Christian schools. Depending on the length and the severity of the current U.S. money crisis, the numerical growth of Christian schools will not be substantially affected.

IS IT UN-AMERICAN TO TAKE CHILDREN OUT OF THE PUBLIC SCHOOLS AND SEND THEM TO PRIVATE CHRISTIAN SCHOOLS?

There are no institutions in our country that are quite so American as our private Christian schools and colleges. Christian schools preceded public education in America by more than 200 years. One of the main reasons the pilgrims came to this country from Holland in 1620 was to establish private Christian schools that would reflect their views. Not only did our pilgrim forefathers establish Christian schools but sixteen years after the pilgrims landed at Plymouth Rock, Harvard University was founded as a ministerial training institu-

Answers to Common Questions . . . / 123

tion and named for Evangelist John Harvard. All of the early educational institutions in America were private Christian schools. Sending your youngsters to America's Christian schools is as American as Plymouth Rock, Betsy Ross and the Declaration of Independence!

About The Author

For the past ten years, Paul A. Kienel has served as the Executive Director of the Western Association of Christian Schools, a service organization representing 600 schools and colleges with a combined student enrollment of over 75,000 in the nineteen western states. He holds B.A. degrees from Bethany Bible College and La Verne College. His graduate work at California University at Los Angeles is equivalent to nearly two M.A. degrees. Azusa Pacific College conferred upon him an Honorary Doctorate of Humanities in 1972. On February 14, 1975, he was honored by Bethany Bible College as their "Alumnus of the Year."

Dr. Kienel has served as associate pastor and later as a teacher and principal of Westminster Christian School, Westminster, California.

In his work for WACS, Dr. Kienel travels nation-wide speaking at conventions, Christian colleges and Christian school functions. He is a member of the board of the Western Graduate School of Theology. He writes *Christian School Comment,* a WACS publication with a monthly circulation of 70,000. For the past seven years, he has been moderator of a daily radio program, "Christian School Comment." This program is now released on ten radio stations with an estimated audience of one-half million listeners. His first book, *The Christian School: Why It Is Right for Your Child* (Victor Books) is now in its third printing.

Dr. Kienel resides in La Habra, California, is married and has three daughters. □

BENEFIT, COST, AND BEYOND

BENEFIT, COST, AND BEYOND
The Political Economy of Benefit-Cost Analysis

JAMES T. CAMPEN

COLLEGE FOR HUMAN SERVICES
LIBRARY
345 HUDSON STREET
NEW YORK, N.Y. 10014

BALLINGER PUBLISHING COMPANY
Cambridge, Massachusetts
A Subsidiary of Harper & Row, Publishers, Inc.

31765

Copyright © 1986 by Ballinger Publishing Company. All rights reserved. No part of this publication may be reproduced, stored in a retrieval system, or transmitted in any form or by any means, electronic, mechanical, photocopy, recording or otherwise, without the prior written consent of the publisher.

International Standard Book Number: 0-88730-106-1

Library of Congress Catalog Card Number: 86-10718

Printed in the United States of America

Library of Congress Cataloging-in-Publication Data

Campen, James T.
  Benefit, cost, and beyond.

  Bibliography: p.
  Includes index.
  1. Cost effectiveness.   I. Title.
HD47.4.C36 1986   658.1′554   86-10718
ISBN 0-88730-106-1

For Phyllis, Georgia, and Ben

CONTENTS

Acknowledgments — xi

PART I PRELIMINARIES

Chapter 1
Introduction — 3

Defining Terms: *Conservative, Liberal, Radical* — 6
The Political Economy of BCA: A Preview — 10
Notes — 12

Chapter 2
The Nature of the Beast:
What Is Benefit–Cost Analysis? — 15

The History of BCA — 16
The BCA Paradigm: Introduction and Overview — 21
BCA and the Decision-Making Process — 25
Welfare Criteria and the BCA Objective Function — 27
Identifying and Measuring Benefits and Costs — 31
Aggregating Benefits and Costs — 37
BCA and Criteria for Choice — 43
Notes — 45

PART II LIBERALS, CONSERVATIVES, AND COST-BENEFIT ANALYSIS: THE BCA DEBATE

Chapter 3
What's Wrong with BCA: The Liberal Indictment — 51

Justification of Predetermined Positions — 52
BCA and Distribution — 55
Neglect of Significant Social Values — 58
Inaccurate Valuation of Benefits and Costs — 65
Flawed and Costly Implementation — 72
Notes — 76

Chapter 4
In Defense of BCA: Responses to Liberal Critics — 79

The Bottom Line: Lack of a Better Alternative — 80
Understanding BCA's Limited Role — 82
Exposing Misuse and Abuse of BCA — 85
Notes — 88

Chapter 5
Evaluating the BCA Debate — 91

The Positive Potential of BCA — 92
The Pro-Liberal Impact of BCA — 95
Promoting Better BCA — 99
Two Qualifications — 102
The Limits of the BCA Debate — 105
Notes — 106

PART III A RADICAL CRITIQUE OF BCA THEORY AND PRACTICE

**Chapter 6
Radical Political Economics, the Capitalist
State, and BCA: An Overview** — 109

The State in Capitalist Society — 111
Understanding BCA: A Radical Perspective — 116
Notes — 118

**Chapter 7
Serving the Powerful: The Selection
Function of BCA** — 121

BCA and the Rise of Rationality in Government — 122
The Materialistic Bias of BCA: Reinforcing Market Logic — 136
Notes — 143

**Chapter 8
Perpetuating Capitalism: The Reinforcement
Function of BCA** — 145

The Social Relations of BCA: Experts and Alienation — 148
Preferences and Interests: False Legitimation — 153
Notes — 168

**Chapter 9
Contradictions, Social Change,
and the Future of BCA** — 171

The Contradictions of BCA — 173
Economic Crisis, Conservative Ascendance, and BCA
  in the 1980s — 177
The Progressive Potential of BCA — 184
Notes — 187

*PART IV TRANSFORMING BCA AND
           TRANSFORMING SOCIETY*

Chapter 10
Toward a Participatory Alternative — 191

Elements of a Participatory Alternative — 193
A Socialist Social Setting — 201
Benefits and Costs of Participation — 207
What Is to Be Done? A Concluding Note — 212
Notes — 214

References — 219

Index — 235

About the Author — 241

ACKNOWLEDGMENTS

This book is the culmination of a protracted process of reflection on the nature and significance of benefit-cost analysis of government programs. Over the years that it has taken shape, I have incurred many intellectual and personal debts.

My initial understanding of and enthusiasm for systematic economic analysis of government programs was formed during the middle and late 1960s, under the influence of my teachers in the Harvard Economics Department and my supervisors in summer jobs with the Pentagon's Office of Systems Analysis and the U.S. Bureau of the Budget's Program Evaluation Staff. Among these were Robert Dorfman, Martin Feldstein, Henry Jacoby, William Niskanen, Howard Raiffa, Henry Rowen, Thomas Schelling, and Richard Zeckhauser.

As the 1960s drew to an end, however, I became increasingly dissatisfied with the essentially liberal view of the government's role that I had previously accepted. During three years of intense intellectual involvement with many other members of the Harvard chapter of the Union for Radical Political Economics, I came to believe that a radical perspective on U.S. capitalism makes possible a more insightful, more relevant, and ultimately more persuasive account of the way that the world works. In the mid-1970s my initial efforts to develop a radical critique of benefit-cost analysis benefitted from the assistance of several members of this group, including Sam Bowles, Herb Gintis, Arthur MacEwan, Stephen Marglin, and Paul Ryan.

As the manuscript of the present book took shape during the last two years, several generous responses to my requests for comments and suggestions on preliminary drafts have enabled me to make numerous improvements, large and small. For this, thanks are due to Les Boden, Baruch Fischhoff, Francis Green, Norton Grubb, Steve Hanke, Robert Haveman, and Peter Junger.

I have also benefitted enormously from discussions with friends who have helped me to work through many of the personal, political, and practical issues that arose during my work on this book. Those who have helped in this way include Bob Buchele, Nancy Chodorow, Margery Davies, Tom Engelhardt, Lou Ferleger, Thomas Frank, Nancy Garrity, Bill Mass, Michael Reich, Bill Tabb, and Ann Withorn.

Dick Cluster provided a thorough editing of the entire manuscript, thereby enabling me to strengthen the book's organization and argument while substantially reducing its length. I doubt that there is a single page in what follows that has not been improved by his suggestions. My editors at Ballinger, Marjorie Richman and Barbara Roth, consistently offered strong encouragement, prompt feedback, helpful advice, and challenging deadlines. The index reflects the skillful work of Jim O'Brien.

My continuing debt to Arthur MacEwan, for the last decade my colleague in the University of Massachusetts/Boston Economics Department, is particularly great. The helpful comments that he provided at every stage of this project are only one instance of how for over fifteen years his insights have helped to shape my own thinking on a variety of topics. Moreover, his friendship has been a steadfast source of personal support.

Phyllis Ewen insisted on the importance of completing the book and helped to make that possible by taking on, at considerable sacrifice to her own work as an artist, a disproportionate share of our joint parenting responsibilities. She also offered her keen editorial judgment at crucial moments. My dedication of this book to her and our two children reflects not only my appreciation for their sharing the costs that its preparation has entailed, but also my hope that they will fully share in the benefits of its finally being completed.

Cambridge, Massachusetts
March 1986

PRELIMINARIES

1 INTRODUCTION

On February 17, 1981, Ronald Reagan signed Executive Order 12291, thereby formally making benefit-cost analysis (BCA) a central element in his administration's regulatory policy. Henceforth, the proponents of a regulation would have to demonstrate that the "benefits" from its adoption would outweigh the "costs." This measure was viewed, both by those who favored it and those who opposed it, as part of the new administration's conservative agenda. Few doubted that, to the extent it was actually implemented, the effect would be to reduce social regulation in the areas of health, safety, and consumer protection. Liberal critics were quick to denounce BCA[1] for its pro-business bias, viewing it as one more tool for reducing the size and scope of big government.

Sixteen years earlier, another presidential directive was greeted very differently. On August 25, 1965, Lyndon Johnson announced that a new set of budgetary techniques was to be used throughout the civilian sector of the federal government. BCA was an important part of the package. This time, however, it was liberals, including President Johnson and his budget director, Charles L. Schultze, who were the principal advocates of the new techniques, which were grouped under the rubric of the "planning-programming-budgeting system." BCA was at that time generally viewed as a tool for guiding the *expansion* of government spending and for aiding government planning and management of its economic activities. It was perceived as a liberal, "good government" measure that would reduce the influence of special interests so that government programs could be more effective in aiding those that they were intended to aid. (The reactions to related executive orders issued by Gerald Ford and Jimmy Carter fell between these extremes.)

So BCA didn't suddenly emerge in the 1980s. In fact, as we shall see in the following chapter, it has been a continual—and controversial—feature of federal government decision-making for fifty years. Nevertheless, the nature and significance of BCA and its expanding use have not been well understood. Although a substantial body of literature exists, books and articles about BCA have too often been uncritical, focused on secondary issues, or based on confused and misleading conceptual frameworks.

In a political climate of conservative ascendancy, with the Reagan administration employing BCA in its campaign against social regulation, the current widespread perception of BCA as an inherently conservative tool is certainly understandable. It is, however, fundamentally mistaken. In itself, conservatives' use of BCA in pursuit of their objectives no more implies that BCA is inherently conservative than does conservatives' use of typewriters demonstrate the innately conservative nature of typewriting. A serious assessment of BCA's actual political bias requires a detailed examination both of its nature and of the consequences of its use. This book provides such an examination.

In 1969, as part of a series of interviews with a large number of the world's most prominent economists, the Italian journalist Arrigo Levi talked with "a thirty-year-old associate professor at MIT, Lester Thurow, a tall, fair, cheerful young man from Montana." Levi chose Thurow as a leading representative of the emerging generation of young U.S. economists. He inquired about this new generation's interest in planning and evaluating government programs and reports the ensuing conversation (Levi 1973, 104):

> "In the field of analysis of costs and benefits a lot of work is being done by young economists [Thurow responded]. But we are working on the instruments of planning, not the theory. We are interested in evolving a technique and a methodology, and applying them to concrete questions." (The answer [Levi comments] is revelatory of the pragmatic spirit of American economics today: there is little interest in big ideological questions, and structures are accepted as a fact—the important thing is to solve concrete problems more efficiently.)

"Isn't there a generation gap, or some rivalry, between you young people and the fifty-year-olds in the new economics?" I asked him. "No," he said, "the generation gap is between us and some of the very young, who read Marx according to Galbraith and would like to blow up big business. But they don't really know what to put in its place. They don't want state bureaucracy or Russian-style planning. They talk about participatory democracy, but that's no answer. They haven't really decided who ought to be in command. But such young people are a minority; the majority have a pragmatic orientation, like us."

The principal task of the present book is to contribute to two substantial intellectual projects whose existence belies Thurow's smugness and whose growing strength contradicts his assertions. The first of these projects is the radical critique of mainstream economic theory, of the social roles fulfilled by professional economists, and of the organization and operation of the U.S. political-economic system. The second is the process of envisioning desirable and historically possible alternatives to the continued evolution of U.S. capitalism.

With respect to the first, I apply the critical insights and alternative theoretical explanations developed in recent years by radical political economists to an analysis of the prevailing theory and practice of BCA. I am concerned here, contrary to Thurow's claims, with the theory and not just with the instruments involved in the analysis of costs and benefits of proposed public expenditures and regulatory policies; I do not accept existing structures; and I have written this book in the belief that there are indeed more important tasks than solving concrete problems more efficiently. With respect to the second intellectual project, I describe a participatory alternative to the prevailing mode of BCA, thereby contributing toward filling in one important part of the emerging general outline of a vision, and a program, for the growing movement that is struggling for a genuinely democratic society. Thurow is correct that radicals don't want state bureaucracy or Soviet-type planning. But contrary to what he says, participatory democracy *is* a central part of the answer to the question of what to put in the place of big business as the locus of decision-making power in the United States.

In short, *Benefit, Cost, and Beyond* explores the theory and practice of BCA in order to gain a better understanding of the nature and significance of the rise of BCA itself; to contribute to current efforts to comprehend the process of public policy determination and, more generally, the roles and functioning of the modern capitalist state; and to illuminate the nature and illustrate the explanatory power of the conceptual framework provided by radical political economics. It also explores the possibilities for a more egalitarian and democratic alternative to continued use of the current mode of BCA for evaluating proposed public expenditures and regulations.

In undertaking these tasks, this book constitutes what is, to my knowledge, the first extended analysis of the nature and significance of BCA that has been written from the perspective of radical political economics.[2] It is intended for at least three groups of readers. To those concerned with public policy in general, or with BCA in particular, it offers insights available only from a radical perspective. To those interested in radical political economics, it offers an application to a new area. And to those familiar with neither BCA nor radical political economics but involved in areas — such as occupational health and safety, environmental regulation, or health care policy — that have been subjected to BCA in recent years, it seeks to help make better sense of sometimes bewildering experiences.

DEFINING TERMS: *CONSERVATIVE, LIBERAL, RADICAL*

Given their central role in what follows, it is important to explain at the outset how the terms *conservative, liberal,* and *radical* will be used in this book. I do not seek to resolve any debates about the "true meaning" of these terms or to offer a detailed analysis of any of them. Each has acquired a variety of often incompatible meanings and has been used to label a range of divergent views. Conservatism, liberalism, and radicalism all come in several varieties, and bitter disagreements have arisen among self-defined adherents of each outlook ("we're the true conservatives"; "you've abandoned liberal principles"; "they're not really radical"). Although I have tried to use these terms in ways that conform reasonably closely to common usage, it is nevertheless important to explain briefly what I mean by each.

Conservatism versus Liberalism: The Mainstream's Two Main Streams

The most familiar classification of contending political viewpoints in the United States is into conservative and liberal, which are in fact the only political positions with a substantial presence in U.S. national life. The recent ascendancy of conservatism can be explained at least in part by its status as the sole perceived alternative to liberalism, in a period when the latter was widely regarded as a failure.

Conservatives can be distinguished from liberals on the basis of both normative and positive beliefs—that is, both in terms of value judgments and in terms of judgments on empirical questions concerning "the way the world works." Two clusters of characteristics are most important in distinguishing conservatives' views on economic theory and policy from those of their liberal counterparts.

First, conservatives tend to look much more to markets for solutions to social problems, while liberals tend to look much more to governments. Conservatives tend to believe that the private economy, left to itself, does quite well, and that government intervention aimed at bringing about better outcomes is likely instead to make things worse. They tend to minimize the seriousness of current problems and to argue that whatever social problems do exist are best dealt with by allowing market forces to bring about responses from private businesses. Conservatives tend to believe that lower government spending and less regulation are almost always better. They see government programs as at best unnecessary or ineffective and often as actually counterproductive; they regard the tax revenues needed to pay for public programs as creating inequities, inefficiencies, and perverse incentives; and they view social regulations as reducing worker and consumer welfare.

Liberals, on the other hand, believe much more in both the need for and the possibility of effective government intervention in the private economy in order to deal with major social problems. They recognize the existence of serious failures of private markets to accomplish such important societal objectives as protecting the environment, producing reasonable levels of health and safety on the job, and reducing inequality to a tolerable level. They also tend to believe that well-designed and well-implemented governmental expenditure and regulatory programs can make substantial contributions to dealing with these problems.

Second, in terms of their values and goals, conservatives tend to favor placing higher priority on the economic objectives of growth and efficiency than on social, distributional, or environmental objectives. Liberals tend to favor measures that, within the limits imposed by the imperatives of the capitalist economy, are more directly pro-poor, pro-labor, pro-equality, pro-minority, and pro-environment.

In spite of their differences, however, conservatives and liberals share a number of basic beliefs and assumptions—most fundamentally, their belief in the desirability and inevitability of capitalism—which justify regarding them jointly as constituting a *mainstream* intellectual and political framework that is accepted by the great majority of U.S. economists.

Radical Political Economics

Radical political economics provides the major alternative to the prevailing mainstream approach. Radical political economists, whom I will often refer to simply as *radicals*, are highly critical of the capitalist system itself and not just particular aspects of its current operation. They believe that capitalism does not work, both in the sense that internal contradictions render it incapable of providing sustained prosperity and in the sense that it is fundamentally a system at odds with meeting human needs. Radicals view most major economic and social problems as deeply rooted in the structure of basic capitalist institutions, rather than as representing remediable flaws in the functioning of those institutions. They see government efforts to deal with such problems as a natural result of political forces generated by the operation of the capitalist system, and even though they often support these efforts, they believe the results will inevitably be constrained by the need to ensure the conditions for profitable business investment.

Radicals tend to be closer to liberal policy preferences and liberal judgments concerning the failings of the market system, but to be closer to conservative assessments of the negative effect of greatly expanded government activities on the potential for private profit-making. While radicals reject mainstream economic analysis and its accompanying ideological and political commitments, they do not reject central mainstream values. In particular, they embrace both the belief in economic justice that motivates many liberals and the belief in economic freedom that is emphasized by many conservatives.

Just as there are varieties of liberals and conservatives, so too are there varieties of radicals. My concern in this book will be with the strand of radicalism that emphasizes democracy and participation not only as important ends but also as essential means in bringing about and maintaining a better society. This focus on democracy is central both to radical critiques of the structure and operation of present capitalist society and to visions of a transformed society.

I use the term *radical political economics* to include *Marxist political economics* but not to be synonymous with or limited to it. Not all radical political economists consider themselves to be Marxists (in refusing this appellation, they are in the company of Karl Marx himself, who once disassociated himself from the claims made by some followers with the phrase *"Je ne suis pas Marxiste!"* ("I am not a Marxist!") (Haupt 1982, 276). While the radical analysis of BCA developed below is certainly Marxist in the sense of being greatly influenced by the work of Marx and of others who have worked self-consciously in the Marxist tradition, it has also been influenced by the work of other social scientists who are critical of much that has been done within that tradition. There are many varieties of Marxist political economics, differing both in their interpretations of Marx's writings and in their applications of Marxist categories to the contemporary world. Use here of the more general term *radical* is intended both to avoid needless disputes with self-defined Marxists who may wish to deny that the analysis here is "really Marxist" and to facilitate a more openminded evaluation of what follows by those who have already concluded that Marxism, as they understand it, has nothing constructive to offer.

Political Perspectives and Public Policy

Radicals believe that the outcomes determined by the operation of private markets are unacceptable. They also have a pessimistic assessment of the potential improvements that can be achieved, given the existing economic system, through the formulation and implementation of improved public policy. The *radical political economics perspective* that underlies the analysis of Parts III and IV below therefore differs greatly from the *public policy perspective* that dominates mainstream, especially liberal, economics. Radicals see their role as attempting to contribute to the development of a broad-based movement for social change rather than as offering information and advice that will enable governmental decision-makers to formulate better public policy. Radical political economics is differentiated from mainstream economics as much by its political perspective and its perceived constituency as it is by its theoretical and methodological substance.

However, one of the most interesting conclusions to emerge from this book's analysis is that when these very different political perspectives are brought to bear on the question of determining the best practical activity in the short run, their conclusions may be surprisingly similar. Especially in a period of conservative ascendancy like the early 1980s, there are occasions for radicals to join with liberals against a common political opponent. This book reflects an emerging recognition among radical political economists of the need for an approach to analyzing and seeking to influence government economic activities that synthesizes the insights and long-run goals of the radical political economic perspective with some of the features of the more immediately relevant public policy perspective. In other words, it seeks to contribute to the development of what might be called a *progressive public policy perspective.*

THE POLITICAL ECONOMY OF BCA: A PREVIEW

While this book's central contribution lies in the analysis that it offers from the perspective of radical political economics, this analysis can be adequately understood only in contrast to the analyses of BCA that are offered from within the conceptual framework of mainstream economics. In particular, my claim that the conservative-to-liberal political spectrum, together with mainstream economic theory, is inadequate for understanding BCA's nature and significance cannot be reasonably evaluated without a good sense of how BCA is understood and treated within this conceptual framework.

I thus begin with an exposition of the nature and content of BCA as it is understood by its mainstream proponents. Chapter 2 presents a brief account of the development, spread, and central features of BCA. Although I stop well short of providing a complete exposition of BCA, I have tried to explain it sufficiently to make the present volume comprehensible to readers previously unfamiliar with BCA, while also providing bibliographic guidance for those who wish to learn more.

Part II then examines what I call "the BCA debate," the ongoing controversy initiated by strong attacks on BCA that have been offered by mainstream critics, primarily by those with a liberal orientation. Chapter 3 surveys the critiques in some detail, Chapter 4 reviews the responses of BCA proponents, and Chapter 5 evaluates the contending positions, from a mainstream point of view. I conclude that, within the conservative-to-liberal intellectual and political spectrum that dominates practical politics and limits social science discussions in this country, there are strong reasons for concluding that BCA is more liberal than conservative in terms of the forces that supported its origin and growth, the substance of its theoretical content, and the effect of its actual applications.

Part III, the core of the book, consists of an attempt to broaden the debate about BCA by offering an analysis from the perspective of radical political economics. I give special attention to understanding BCA as one aspect of the operation of the state in capitalist society, an area of increasing concern to radical political economists in recent years. I argue that both the welfare criteria embodied in the theory of BCA and the political consequences of its implementation serve to strengthen and reproduce the mode of production and the class structure that lie at the core of U.S. capitalism. Chapter 6 introduces this analysis and outlines the approaches of radical political economists to understanding the operation of the capitalist state in general. Chapter 7 explores the ways in which BCA works to promote the selection of expenditure and regulatory proposals that are conducive to profitable capital accumulation by private corporations. Chapter 8 examines how BCA reinforces the hierarchical social relations and pro-capitalist ideological beliefs that provide the supportive social context for the perpetuation of the capital accumulation process. Chapter 9 rounds out the analysis of BCA from the perspective of radical political economics by investigating its contradictions — that is, how and why BCA's development has resulted in a mode of public policy analysis that no longer effectively promotes capitalist class interests and may actually operate to undermine them.

Part IV's single chapter complements the earlier critical analysis by considering a more democratic and egalitarian method for bringing systematic, rational, quantitative analysis to bear on public expenditure and regulatory decisions. In particular, Chapter 10 identifies the central features of a participatory alternative mode of analysis and evaluation that contrasts sharply with the theory and practice of the prevailing BCA paradigm. In addition, because any mode of BCA can function only in a larger social, political, and economic environment with which it is compatible, I briefly examine some important aspects of a democratic socialist society that could facilitate the operation of such an alternative. Finally, I consider some of the vexing issues involved in determining and then achieving an optimal level of participation in the process of evaluating and choosing among contending proposals for the allocation of social resources.

Having indicated what the book will attempt to do, it is appropriate also to make clear two significant limitations of its coverage.[3] First, I concentrate specifically on BCA, rather than attempting to deal with the whole family of related techniques and procedures. Some of what I shall say is surely relevant to cost-effectiveness analysis, cost-utility analysis, risk analysis, and the like, but my direct focus will be limited to BCA per se.[4] Second, my concern is with the theory and practice of BCA in the United States (and, to a lesser extent, in the United Kingdom). The widespread use of BCA in connection with investment projects in underdeveloped countries, particularly by the World Bank and other international agencies, involves enough differences to justify excluding these applications from the scope of the present study.[5]

NOTES

1. The terms *benefit-cost analysis* (BCA) and *cost-benefit analysis* (CBA) are equivalent, and both are frequently used. The authors of recent texts in the field appear to be evenly divided between the two possibilities. However, texts using BCA tend to be written by Americans (Gramlich 1981; Halvorsen and Ruby 1981; Stokey and Zeckhauser 1978; Thompson 1980), while those opting for CBA are more often British (Mishan 1982a; Pearce 1983; Pearce and Nash 1981; Sugden and Williams 1978). One hypothesis to account for this difference is that there has been no British counterpart to the requirement, in U.S. budgetary reviews of water resource projects, that a *benefit-cost ratio* of greater than one be demonstrated for a proposed project before it could be approved. In any event, I will use CBA only when directly quoting other authors who do so.
2. I am aware of only two relatively brief articles that examine BCA from the perspective of radical political economics (Ball 1979; Waitzman 1982–83).
3. Another area of BCA use that is beyond the scope of this book is that of what legal scholar Duncan Kennedy calls "liberal law and economics . . . the body of literature and taught tradition that proposes and elaborates cost-benefit analysis as a way for a policy maker to decide what private law

rules to recommend to judges, legislators, or administrators who have the power to set those rules" (1981, 387). Kennedy's article provides a useful exposition and powerful critique of this manifestation of BCA.
4. Levin (1983, 17-31) offers a clear description of the relationship of BCA to cost-effectiveness analysis; Fischhoff et al. (1981) survey the relatively new field of risk-benefit analysis, or risk assessment; Merewitz and Sosnick (1971, 1-13) discuss BCA as one generally separable part of the set of techniques and approaches packaged together in the planning-programming-budgeting system.
5. Pearce and Nash devote a chapter of their text on BCA to explaining how and why "the idea has become accepted that substantially different methods should be used for appraising projects in developing countries from those used in developed countries" (1981, ch. 10; the quote is from p. 165).

2 THE NATURE OF THE BEAST
What Is Benefit-Cost Analysis?

Benefit-cost analysis means different things to different people. The author of one text on BCA has written that "Ultimately, it is nothing more than a logical attempt to weigh the pros and cons of a decision. And ultimately, something like it must necessarily be employed in any rational decision" (Gramlich 1981, 3). But this injunction that one should undertake a proposed action if and only if its advantages (benefits, pros) outweigh its disadvantages (costs, cons) is without practical content. My concern is with BCA as a systematic, quantitative approach to the comparative evaluation of governmental expenditure and regulatory alternatives.

The goal of this chapter is to establish an unbiased basis for critical examination of BCA by presenting a characterization that both proponents and critics can agree on as accurate. I have sought to avoid imbedding an implicit critique within this characterization. And I have tried to stay away from the sort of hostile, caricatured description of BCA that, by attributing clearly objectionable features, makes strongly critical conclusions easy to derive but at the same time is unpersuasive to those with a more realistic, balanced sense of what BCA in fact is.

BCA is frequently characterized as an area of applied welfare economics. Jacob Viner's much-quoted dictum that "economics is what economists do" therefore suggests that BCA is what benefit-cost analysts do or that it is what economists do when they are doing that variety of applied welfare economics known as benefit-cost analysis. While my description will seek to reflect the actual practice of BCA rather than some unattainable theoretical ideal, not every instance of everything labeled "BCA" will be regarded as the real thing. That is, BCA will not be characterized on the basis of its *mis*applications and *mis*use.

The body of this chapter will make use of two approaches to developing an understanding of "what benefit-cost analysts do." The first of these approaches is historical—a brief review of the development of BCA theory and practice. The second approach is to review how advocates and practitioners of BCA themselves have recently tried to explain it to others, based primarily on a careful examination of recent textbook presentations of BCA. Both approaches are based on the premise that when economists do BCA, they are not working in a vacuum; it is important to understand BCA in its historical, institutional, theoretical, and political contexts.

THE HISTORY OF BCA

Although the history of BCA in the United States[1] goes back to the earliest years of this century—the River and Harbor Act of 1902 required the army's Corps of Engineers to evaluate federal expenditures for navigation in a way that identified both commercial benefits and their cost (Hammond 1960, 3–4)—its emergence as a significant body of practice dates from the Flood Control Act of 1936. In a period of growing public works spending designed to combat the effects of the Great Depression, and of increased concern for the entire range of impacts of government programs, this landmark legislation required that the government undertake projects "for flood control purposes if the benefits to whomsoever they may accrue are in excess of the estimated costs."

For the next twenty-five years, water projects aimed at providing flood control and other benefits (e.g., hydroelectric power, recreation, and irrigation) were subjected to studies to determine if they met this standard. The Flood Control Act itself gave no guidance on the implementation of the criterion that it had set out in such general form, and the various federal agencies involved in the development of water resources (including, in addition to the Corps of Engineers, the Interior Department's Bureau of Reclamation, the Agriculture Department's Soil Conservation Service, and the Tennessee Valley Authority) evolved mutually inconsistent sets of standards and procedures for carrying out their analyses. Practice developed on the basis of tradition and in response to political and bureaucratic interests, with scant reference to economic theory. Each agency's primary concern appeared to be maximizing the extent of its own involvement in water projects; benefit-cost studies were intended to justify projects that the agencies wanted to undertake rather than designed to provide serious, critical analyses of their merits.

Under pressure from the Bureau of the Budget, the central clearinghouse and arbiter for all agency spending proposals on their way to the President and Congress, an interagency group was established in 1946 to codify an agreed-on set of principles. The U.S. Federal Inter-Agency River Basin Committee's Subcommittee on Benefits and Costs eventually produced its *Proposed Practices for Economic Analysis of River Basin Projects* (1950; rev. 1958). Although this manual, commonly known as the *Green Book*, never received official status, it was highly influential. Many of its ideas were incorporated in the U.S. Bureau of the Budget's *Budget Circular A-47* (1952), which promulgated a set of guidelines for all benefit-cost analyses of water resource projects that remained in force for the next decade. The controversies between the Budget Bureau and the agencies during this period provide a notable example of the continual struggle over whether BCA would function as a means of promoting the broad public interest or as a tool used by special interests to promote their more narrow objectives.

Although some of the central ideas of what has become BCA were set forth in a brilliant article by the French engineer/economist Jules Dupuit more than a hundred years earlier (1968 [1844]), the *Green Book* was notable for being the first significant attempt to ground the practice of BCA in economic theory. And it was not until nearly the end of the 1950s that three seminal books by economists (Eckstein 1958; Krutilla and Eckstein 1958; McKean 1958) systematically brought modern neoclassical welfare economics to bear on BCA, thereby firmly establishing an explicit theoretical framework for BCA more than twenty years after the Flood Control Act had brought about its regular application. The framework established by this body of theoretical work greatly influenced the interagency U.S. President's Water Resources Council's *Policies, Standards, and Procedures in the Formulation, Evaluation, and Review of Plans for Use and Development of Water and Related Land Resources* (1962), which supplanted *Budget Circular A-47* and was regarded as authoritative by both agencies and the Budget Bureau throughout the 1960s.

Another important influence on the later development of BCA was also taking shape during the 1950s, as analysts at the Rand Corporation, under contract to the U.S. Air Force, grappled with the resource allocation problems facing the managers of military spending programs. Although they advocated techniques of systems analysis and cost-effectiveness analysis rather than of benefit-cost analysis per se, many of the core ideas were closely related. An unclassified exposition of the conceptual approach and analytical techniques developed at Rand was provided in Charles J. Hitch and Roland N. McKean's *The Economics of Defense in the Nuclear Age* (1960). This book became known as "the Bible of the Pentagon" after newly installed Defense Secretary Robert McNamara made its coauthor Hitch an Assistant Secretary of Defense and charged him with implementing throughout the Defense Department the planning, budgetary, and analytical techniques developed at Rand; BCA-like techniques were one important component of the planning-programming-budgeting system (PPBS) that was put into place at the Pentagon in the early 1960s.

Taking off from the substantial body of theory and practice that had thus been created by the early 1960s, BCA developed rapidly during the next decade. On the one hand, there was a great spurt in the theoretical literature, as scores of papers and monographs reflected efforts to grapple with the issues that arose in attempts to carry out the deceptively simple mandate of determining whether, and by how much, a proposed project's benefits exceeded its costs — issues such as how to determine which of a project's effects should be properly regarded as benefit and costs, how to evaluate different kinds of benefits and costs, how to compare future benefits and costs to those in the present, and how to rank projects when not all of those with positive net benefits can be undertaken. A revised version of the U.S. Water Resources Council's *Principles and Standards for Planning Water and Related Land Resources* (1973) embodied one particularly important development in the theory and practice of BCA — the explicit adoption of a multiple-objective framework for project evaluation. The *Principles and Standards* required that separate accounts be kept for the results of both a formal benefit-cost analysis of contributions to the objective of "national economic development" and a somewhat less formal analysis of impacts on the objective of "environmental quality" (where appropriate, separate accounts were also to be maintained for the additional objectives of "regional economic development" and "social well-being") (U.S. Water Resources Council 1973; for a helpful descriptive summary see also Luke 1977, 1095-1102). Although BCA was by that time being used in a broad range of other applications, the water resources area retained special significance, and the WRC's adoption of a multiple-objective framework represented and influenced broader trends.

On the other hand, after a quarter century of applications almost solely in the area of water resource development, the 1960s witnessed a great expansion in the range of spending programs to which BCA was applied. First there were applications to other kinds of physical investment projects such as transportation and urban renewal. These were soon followed by applications in such areas of social spending as health, education, and income maintenance. A major impetus to this spreading of BCA was President Lyndon Johnson's August 1965 decision to implement a planning-programming-budgeting system (PPBS), based on that of the Defense Department, throughout the civilian sector of the federal government. Although PPBS itself proved to be relatively short-lived, its introduction did play an important role in bringing about a lasting increase in the use of BCA. In addition to applications at the U.S. federal government level, the use of BCA also became increasingly common both at the state and local level in this country and in the evaluation of proposed investment projects in underdeveloped countries.[2]

By the end of this rather intense decade of theoretical debate and expanded application, one reviewer of the state of BCA concluded that "dramatic advances have been made . . . in attacking formidable measurement issues" (Steiner 1974, 320). The editors of a BCA anthology noted that "a near-consensus has developed on the core principles of benefit-cost analysis . . . [although] there is not yet any generally accepted text or manual of these principles" (Niskanen et al. 1973, vi). In short, by the mid-1970s the stage was set for BCA to enter a period of consolidation. The ensuing decade has witnessed much less theoretical literature, as most of the major questions had already been thoroughly discussed—not necessarily to the point of complete agreement but at least to the point where contending positions were quite clearly understood. The survey articles and anthologies that had begun to appear in the mid-1960s to allow practitioners and nonspecialists to keep abreast of the explosion of theoretical papers and innovative applications[3] began to be replaced with a growing number of textbooks providing expositions of the "near-consensus on core principles of benefit-cost analysis." And applications continued apace.

However, along with this process of consensus and normalization, a contradictory development was simultaneously underway. The growth of public works spending during and following the Great Depression, the emergence of a permanently high level of peacetime military spending in the 1950s, and the expansion of government domestic spending at both the federal and state and local levels in the 1960s had all produced grist for the BCA mill. Now, the dramatic wave of "social regulation" enacted in the late 1960s and early 1970s was followed by attempts to use BCA to guide the growth of federal regulatory activity.[4] BCA began to be applied to economic, environmental, and health and safety regulation in addition to public expenditure projects. In response, new criticism and controversy emerged.

The nature of Executive Order 12291, issued by Ronald Reagan within a month of his inauguration, was noted in Chapter 1. Similar in many respects to Jimmy Carter's Executive Order 12044 of March 1978, E.O. 12291 nevertheless introduced important changes. The 1978 order had required that "significant" proposed regulations be subjected to "regulatory analyses" that would identify the "economic consequences" of alternative responses and that "the least burdensome of the acceptable alternatives" be chosen, but it made no use of the term "benefit-cost analysis" (many BCAs were nevertheless done in response to its mandate). In contrast, the 1981 order explicitly called for the use of BCA: "Regulatory action shall not be undertaken unless the potential benefits to society from the regulation outweigh the potential costs to society." And it specified the single evaluative standard of "maximizing the aggregate net benefits to society," implicitly rejecting a multiple-objective framework that might include environmental or distributional objectives as well as total net social benefits.[5]

The criticism of BCA that greeted the Carter administration's use of it to evaluate regulatory policy intensified in response to the Reagan administration's actions. Some critics merely attacked what they regarded as the new administration's misuse of an acceptable technique for analyzing difficult regulatory issues; some doubted the appropriateness of applying BCA in fields so far from those it was originally developed to deal with; and some vocal critics aimed their fire at BCA itself, claiming the technique was inherently and fundamentally flawed.

Thus, at the same time that BCA was undergoing a period of consolidation and stability, it was also expanding into a major new area of applications and being subjected to some of the most intense and challenging attacks it had ever received. A critical assessment of the theory and practice of BCA is therefore particularly timely.

THE BCA PARADIGM: INTRODUCTION AND OVERVIEW

When Paul Samuelson (1967, 623) wrote that "the cash value of a doctrine is in its vulgarization," he was urging that attention be paid to the forms in which theoretical frameworks become generally understood and used. The refinements, subtle distinctions, and qualifications present in scholarly articles and monographs tend inevitably to fall away and become lost in the process by which any body of theory comes to have broad practical impact. In the case of BCA, as I have noted above, the shared conception of the doctrine that coalesced by the mid-1970s has since been "vulgarized" through numerous textbook presentations.

Written by theorists with practical experience in the area, these texts reflect the actual influence on current practitioners of "classic" journal articles and monographs, as well as of the official and quasi-official manuals noted in my brief historical survey. The texts provide the best available indicator of what the proponents and practitioners of BCA understand benefit-cost analysis to be. Furthermore, they are a primary mechanism by which innovative ideas, resolutions of academic debates, and knowledge of particularly significant applications are transmitted to practitioners.

The rest of this chapter will therefore identify what might be called a "textbook ideal"—a set of commonly accepted standards for good practice of BCA. This characterization is based primarily on a careful review of ten expositions of BCA published between 1978 and 1984.[6] Although some of these texts give minor attention to applications in the underdeveloped countries, all ten are primarily concerned with the use of BCA in the United States and/or the United Kingdom.

My approach to providing such a specification of the nature of BCA is influenced by the suggestive conceptual framework of Thomas Kuhn (1962; 1970). Kuhn's analysis directs attention in any area of scientific endeavor to the "scientific community" whose members share a set of common understandings, or a *paradigm*, acquired primarily in their graduate schooling.[7] Kuhn argues that most scientific activities consist of solving problems within the framework of the accepted body of shared understandings, or further articulating the terms and categories that are contained in the existing paradigm, activities that he calls "normal science." It is noteworthy that recent BCA literature does consist primarily of "normal science"—not debates about first principles, but discussions of procedures for improved measurement in particular situations, for employing the basic methodology in novel settings, and for dealing with a variety of practical and theoretical issues left unresolved within the paradigm.

An Overview of the BCA Paradigm

A general view of BCA emerges from reviewing these texts. BCA is a systematic, quantitative method for the comparative evaluation of proposed public expenditures or regulatory activities. Its goal is to identify the alternative that will make the most efficient use of society's scarce resources in promoting social objectives—that is, that will provide the maximum net social benefits. BCA is carried out from a social or public point of view rather than from the private, profit-oriented perspective that guides the financial analyses undertaken by firms or individuals; it attempts "to take account of all of the effects of a project on members of the public, irrespective of who is affected and of whether or not the effect is captured in a financial account" (Sugden and Williams 1978, 7-8). The relevant benefits and costs "may take many different forms, occur at different times, involve different degrees of uncertainty, and affect different individuals. The economic theory of benefit-cost analysis provides a framework for taking such diversity into account" (Halvorsen and Ruby 1981, 1).

The formal, quantitative nature of BCA deserves special emphasis; the term means something much more specific than simply weighing pros and cons before making a choice, or even than undertaking such an appraisal in an organized, systematic fashion. Henry Peskin and Eugene Seskin (1975, 1) have expressed this fundamental point very clearly:

> *Cost-benefit analysis* is a formal procedure for comparing the costs and benefits of alternative policies. It differs from more informal comparisons of costs and benefits in two principal ways. First, the terms *cost* and *benefit* are defined more narrowly than in general English usage. Second, the formal procedure and basis of comparison rely on specialized techniques and principles, most of which are derived from economic theory.

Several elements are involved in carrying out benefit-cost analysis. Most of the texts discuss most of these elements, although they call attention to different relationships among them by adopting different schemes for organizing topics and chapters.

- Determining the role of BCA in the overall processes of decision-making and outcome determination: This involves answering such questions as, For whom is the analysis being done? How will it be used on its completion? What conceptions of government and of the political process underlie the BCA paradigm?
- Determining the social goals that provide the basis for the comparative evaluation of proposed alternatives: Costs and benefits can be identified and measured only relative to specific criteria or objectives that determine what is to be maximized. In the jargon of economics, it is necessary to specify an *objective function* that will provide the basis for valuing costs and benefits.
- Identifying, correctly and comprehensively, the benefits and costs of the proposed alternatives, and then measuring each type of benefit and cost: This involves determining the value of benefits and costs at the time that they occur and for the people directly affected.
- Combining, or aggregating, all of these benefits and costs together in order to determine an overall summary measure of an alternative's net benefits: Three particular types of aggregation are given a great deal of attention by the BCA paradigm: (1) aggregating benefits and costs that occur in different time periods (that is,

dealing with the issue of discounting); (2) aggregating benefits and costs that accrue to different individuals or groups of people (that is, dealing with distributional issues); and (3) aggregating benefits and costs that would occur in different possible future circumstances (that is, dealing with risk and uncertainty).

- Reaching a conclusion: This may involve using an appropriate criterion for choosing among proposed alternatives on the basis of their total benefits and costs as determined in the preceding stages of the analysis. More generally, it involves presenting the results of the benefit-cost analysis in a way that is appropriate in light of the first two elements identified here—the role of the analysis in the overall decision-making process and the nature of the objective function adopted for the analysis.

Before turning to a description of each of these elements of the BCA paradigm, however, it will be helpful to take note of three more general points. First, the BCA paradigm does not exist independently but is really a subparadigm of welfare economics and of public finance and shares a number of fundamental assumptions and approaches with these more inclusive paradigms. While all of the features of the BCA paradigm taken together make it a distinctive entity, much of what is said about it—in this book and elsewhere—has more general applicability to issues involving economics, public policy, and social welfare.

Second, although the discussion in the remainder of this chapter does indeed reflect the "near-consensus . . . on the core principles of BCA," some attention will also be given to identifying ongoing controversies within the generally shared BCA paradigm. Third, we are concerned with the application of BCA to proposed regulations as well as to proposed expenditures, even though most of the BCA texts reviewed refer solely to public expenditure evaluation (only Gramlich 1981 and Halvorsen and Ruby 1981 give explicit attention to its application to regulatory programs). This should be understood as a typical lag of textbook content behind current practice. Gramlich argues that "benefit-cost analyses of government activities need not be limited to government expenditure programs. There is no reason why the same logic could not be extended to the social regulation activities of government" (1981, 201). And indeed it has been. The particular issues concerning the application of BCA to regulatory activities result not from the inapplicability of the "logic" of the

BCA paradigm but from the special problems of identifying and valuing the benefits and costs of many regulatory programs.

BCA AND THE DECISION-MAKING PROCESS

The conception of the role played by benefit-cost analysis (and analysts) in the process of determining what proposed expenditures and regulations are actually undertaken is a central element of the BCA paradigm. This conception may be summarized by saying that benefit-cost analysts play the role of *technicians*, providing information and analysis to politically responsible *decision-makers*. The decision-makers must then somehow combine the information and analysis received from benefit-cost analysts with other considerations in the final process of reaching a decision. As one text puts it: "Sound expenditure decisions, whether made by the legislator or the executive, require detailed information regarding the merits of alternative projects. The technician can perform an important service in providing this information" (Musgrave and Musgrave 1984, 156-57). Another makes the point this way: "A well-conducted cost-benefit study can be only a part, though an important part, of the data necessary for informed collective decisions" (Mishan 1982a, 198-99). And a third: "CBA[8] is an 'input,' an 'aid,' an 'ingredient' of decision-making. It does not supplant political judgment" (Pearce 1983, 3).

In this, BCA shares the *public policy perspective* of most of current mainstream economics, according to which the major purpose of economic analysis is to contribute to the formulation and adoption of improved public policy. The provision of reasoned arguments, relevant information, and insightful analyses can make a positive contribution to better decisions and hence to improved social welfare. The characterization of the role of BCA that was articulated in a highly influential survey article a quarter of a century ago accurately reflects the view of the BCA paradigm:

> The economist must interpret the desires of *the policy people whom he is serving* and express them in an analytical form as an objective function. He then seeks to maximize this function, given the empirical relations in the economy and the institutional constraints that may be appropriate to the analysis. In this manner, the economist can play *the role of technician*, of bringing his technical equipment to bear on policy problems, with maximum effectiveness (Eckstein 1961, 445; emphasis added).

There is a spectrum of views, often implicit, on the nature of the "decision-makers" and of the decision-making process. One end of the spectrum envisions decision-makers commissioning BCAs and then taking their results into account in making more or less unilateral decisions. The other end of the spectrum sees benefit-cost analysts as providing inputs to a wide range of individuals and groups who participate in a pluralistic political process of outcome determination. All along the spectrum, BCA is viewed as an essentially neutral technique for providing helpful input to legitimate and effective decision-makers who function to represent the interests of the entire population and thereby to promote social welfare. One text states, for example, that "government is really the collective expression of the will of taxpayers" (Gramlich 1981, 4), and another explains that BCA is "carefully designed to ensure that public decisions accurately reflect what it is that the society wants to accomplish" (Stokey and Zeckhauser 1978, 136).

Within the BCA paradigm, there is one major disagreement concerning the proper relationship of BCA analysts to decision-makers. The question at issue is whether or not the identity and outlook of the decision-maker should affect the analyst's work.

One school of thought—called the *conventional approach* by E. J. Mishan who is its most forceful and persistent advocate (1982a, pt. 4; 1974; 1982b)—maintains that BCAs, like engineering analyses, ought to be based only on objective, scientifically observable data and generally acceptable principles. In this view the objective, scientifically observable data relevant to BCA are market data, and the only generally acceptable economic principle for evaluating alternative outcomes is that of economic efficiency, or maximization of total net benefits evaluated on the basis of market data. According to the conventional approach, there should be no special relationship between decision-makers and analysts: The publicly available results of the objective analyses can provide information and analytical conclusions that are broadly acceptable to all citizens, whatever their political views or value judgments about various important but noneconomic, nonobjective matters, such as the distribution of income.

The other school of thought—called the *decision-making approach* by Robert Sugden and Alan Williams (1978, chs. 7, 13, 16), who are its most systematic and persuasive advocates in the texts under review, and labeled "revisionist" by Mishan (1982b)—maintains that there should be a much closer relationship between decision-makers and analysts. Decision-makers should actively use analysts to obtain information and analysis that will be useful to them in identifying those alternatives most productive in reaching their goals. Analysts should make it clear to decision-makers that which alternative receives the most positive evaluation often depends on the values assigned to certain important parameters—and that it is the responsibility of politically responsible decision-makers to make judgments about the values to be assigned. Examples of such parameters include the relative weights to be attached to benefits accruing to different groups (organized, for example, by income level, geographic location, or race); the social attitude to uncertainty; and the value to be placed on noneconomic factors such as cultural, historical, esthetic, or ecological considerations. In this view, the analyst serves essentially in a staff role to the decision-maker, and analysis does not stop with "objective" market-based data.

The fundamental disagreement between the two approaches is nicely indicated by a comment made by Arnold Harberger and Daniel Wisecarver in their introduction to an early BCA anthology. After noting that one of the papers in the volume "explicitly encodes the subjective values of the decision-makers themselves," they assert that there is a "basic difficulty of this approach: Any change in the identity of the policy-makers would presumably mean a change in values, which would in turn imply a resultant change in optimal strategy" (Harberger et al. 1972, xviii). To the proponents of the decision-making approach that is, of course, the whole point.

Advocates of both views recognize the importance of factors that are not reflected in the narrow economic calculations of "conventional" BCA. Adherents of the "conventional" approach maintain that these other factors should be considered as other inputs, alongside the results of independent BCA calculations made on purely "objective" grounds. Adherents of the "decision-making" approach, on the other hand, maintain that only by incorporating decision-makers' judgments about these other factors within the BCA calculation itself can BCA really facilitate making difficult trade-offs among diverse objectives.

WELFARE CRITERIA AND THE BCA OBJECTIVE FUNCTION

Before it is possible to determine whether and to what extent any proposed expenditure or regulatory activity contributes to increased social welfare—that is, before it is possible to determine if a proposal's benefits outweigh its costs—it is necessary to have a criterion that specifies what is meant by "social welfare." The terms *benefit* and *cost* are themselves meaningful only in relation to such a criterion. In the jargon of economics, BCA must have a clearly defined *objective function* that specifies just what it is that decision-makers are seeking to maximize in their comparative evaluation of alternatives. Identifying the objective function that has been adopted by the BCA paradigm involves exploring the theoretical foundations of BCA, examining the value judgments that are inherent in it, and specifying the welfare criteria that it employs. Doing this will provide an understanding of why BCA is, indeed, an area of applied welfare economics.

Two basic assumptions provide starting points for the BCA paradigm's welfare criteria. Shared with the more inclusive paradigms of welfare economics and of microeconomic theory in general, these are often regarded as so obvious as to require no explicit mention. A classic statement of what he termed "the two fundamental value judgments of welfare theory" was provided by I.M.D. Little (1957, 258): "That it is a good thing that individuals should have what they want and that they themselves know best what they want."

The first value judgment is that social welfare depends on the individual welfare of the members of society, and only on these individuals' welfares. In the words of one text (Halvorsen and Ruby 1981, 13), "The basic goal of society is assumed to be the maximization of social welfare, which is specified to be a function of the well-being of each of the individuals in society." Thus, the benefits and costs of concern to BCA include much that falls outside of the revenue and outlay accounts of any governmental body; the BCA objective function is not merely a public sector analogue to a private company's concern with net profit. Social, cultural, environmental, or other consequences of a program, however, make no contribution to social welfare beyond their contributions to the welfare of individuals. The second basic value judgment is that an individual's welfare is best judged by that individual: An individual is regarded as better off if and only if that individual believes that he or she is.

The conceptual standard for measuring changes in welfare is provided by the *willingness to pay* (WTP) criterion. (My concern here is with WTP as a "conceptual standard"; the actual measurement of WTP, which may present great difficulty, will be discussed in the next section.) The increase (or decrease) in an individual's welfare that would result from any project is indicated by the maximum amount that the individual would be willing to pay (or the minimum amount that the individual would be willing to accept as compensation) to have the project happen rather than not happen. "The underlying principle of valuation is," as one text points out, "a 'market' one: we are valuing how much people *would be willing to pay* for goods if, by some means or other, they were called upon to pay for what they consume" (Sugden and Williams 1978, 178).

WTP provides the conceptual standard for measuring costs as well as benefits because the costs of any project are properly conceived of as its *opportunity costs*—that is, the benefits forgone because undertaking the project uses resources that could otherwise be used in alternative ways (Stokey and Zeckhauser 1978, 151–52; Sugden and Williams 1978, 30, 75). The impact on an individual's welfare of these forgone benefits, like the impact of a project's direct benefits, is best measured by the individual's WTP; this provides an exact measure of the change in an individual's welfare, as valued by the individual. If an individual's net WTP for each of a set of proposed alternatives is known, then so is the ranking of these projects in terms of their contributions to that individual's welfare.

Welfare economics therefore compares the relative contributions to social welfare of two alternative projects this way: When the consequences of alternative A are compared to those of alternative B, if at least one individual believes that his or her welfare is greater, and no individual believes that his or her welfare is less (that is, if at least one person has a higher WTP for A than for B and if no person has a higher WTP for B than for A), then it is legitimate to conclude that A makes a greater contribution to social welfare than does B. This welfare criterion is known as *Pareto superiority*, and a movement from situation B to situation A is called a *Pareto improvement.*

When it can be applied, Pareto superiority is a compelling criterion for choice; it would be hard to argue that bringing about a Pareto improvement would not increase social welfare. The problem with this criterion is its limited applicability: Almost every real-world proposal leaves at least one person worse off than would some available alternative. In the real world, there are not just winners and nonwinners; there tend to be winners and losers.

Welfare economics itself tends to stop at this point, on the grounds that no more can be said without making interpersonal comparisons of welfare—that is, without making judgments about the relative contributions to social welfare of the welfare of different individuals—and that the basic assumptions of welfare economics provide no basis for making such comparisons. As a consequence, welfare economics per se has not had much to say about policy choices. It has been limited primarily to theoretical demonstrations of the proposition that, given a number of (quite strong and unrealistic) assumptions, no possible economic outcomes are Pareto superior to those brought about by the operation of a competitive market economy.

In order to offer any constructive assistance to policy-makers—in order, that is, to move from theoretical welfare economics to applied welfare economics—economists had to go beyond the two relatively noncontroversial value judgments discussed above.[9] They adopted a very simple criterion for judging one alternative to be preferable to others even though it does not represent a Pareto improvement over them: For each alternative, simply add together the willingness to pay (positive or negative) of every individual and see which alternative receives the highest net total. This assumes, in effect, that a dollar's worth of increase in any one individual's welfare (as measured by that individual's WTP) makes exactly the same contribution to social welfare as a dollar's worth of increase in any other individual's welfare (as measured by that individual's WTP); stated another way, it assumes that a dollar's loss by any one individual is exactly offset by a dollar's gain by any other individual. This criterion is referred to by a number of names, including the "potential compensation criterion" and the "Kaldor-Hicks criterion" (after the two British economists who independently proposed it, in a related context, in 1939); we shall refer to it as the *potential Pareto improvement criterion* (PPIC). Sugden and Williams provide a clear statement of this criterion and its rationale (see also Halvorsen and Ruby 1981, 20–21; Gramlich 1981, 43):

> Undertaking a project provides a *potential Pareto improvement* if it is *in principle possible* to secure an actual Pareto improvement by linking the project with an appropriate set of transfers of money between gainers and losers—even if *in fact* these transfers will not take place. In other words, a project provides a potential Pareto improvement if the total sum of money that the gainers from the project would be prepared to pay to ensure that the project were undertaken exceeds the total sum of money that the losers from it

would accept as compensation for putting up with it (1978, 89-90; emphasis in original).

One other aspect of BCA's objective function stems from BCA's theoretical underpinnings in welfare economics. The major results of welfare economics—its demonstrations that no possible economic outcomes are Pareto superior to those produced by a perfectly competitive market system—are basic to the conceptual framework of mainstream economics in general. Within this conceptual framework, governmental economic activities such as public expenditures or regulatory activities are justified only in cases of "market failure"— that is, in situations where one or more of the necessary assumptions fails to obtain, so that market outcomes will not be optimal (Gramlich 1981, ch. 2). It follows, therefore, that the task of a benefit-cost analysis is to determine which government policy will best rectify this market failure. In short, the outcomes of competitive markets are respected where they exist; where they do not exist, the role of BCA is to determine analytically what would have obtained in a well-functioning competitive market—to discover a pattern of government spending and regulation that can bring about an economic outcome different from that provided by actual markets but as similar as possible to the one that would be provided by ideal markets.

IDENTIFYING AND MEASURING BENEFITS AND COSTS

The core of any benefit-cost analysis is the actual measurement of the benefits and costs of the alternatives being analyzed. First, however, it is necessary to identify precisely what is to be measured. The systematic enumeration of a set of benefits and costs (or, to refer to them jointly, a set of *effects*) involves tracing through a project's consequences in a way that neither overlooks significant ones nor includes ones that are spurious; doing this in a way that is both correct in theory and manageable in practice is not at all a trivial task.

BCA seeks to take into account all benefits and costs "to whomsoever they accrue," whether or not they are traded or valued in the marketplace. However, economists, like ecologists, know that everything is connected to everything else and that actually tracing through all of the consequences of any particular proposed action is thoroughly impractical. Economists also know that appearances may deceive and that some consequences that appear to be benefits or costs of a project in fact are not. Thus, an important part of the BCA paradigm is to provide a set of principles and guidelines for determining what should or should not legitimately be counted as a benefit or cost in order to make BCA both accurate and practical.

Benefits and costs may take a variety of different forms, accrue to different people, occur at different times, and depend on which of various possible sets of circumstances actually comes to pass. A water resources development project, for example, may provide electricity, flood control, irrigation, and recreation; the recipients of these various benefits may be Los Angeles energy consumers, Arizona ranchers, or Navajo shepherds; construction costs may occur in the near future while operating costs and benefits occur over many subsequent years; and flood control benefits may depend on such uncertain factors as amounts of precipitation and the speed of spring thaws. The process of identifying benefits and costs should involve a systematic enumeration along all of these dimensions.

Although the discussion of BCA's welfare criteria is generally carried out as though an overall willingness to pay (WTP) for each alternative were determined for each affected individual, this is not the way that BCA is carried out in practice. Instead, the general procedure is first to calculate the total net value (WTP), for all individuals combined, of each type of benefit or cost (e.g., for a water resources project: electricity generated, flood damage averted, irrigation water provided, and recreation facilities created). These are then combined to obtain the total net benefit of each alternative. Although a total WTP for each individual is never obtained in this process, the calculation of benefits and costs in this way is consistent with the use of the potential Pareto improvement criterion (PPIC), according to which only the aggregate of individual WTPs matters, not the individual WTPs themselves.

Three major distinctions concerning the nature of benefits and costs are employed by BCA to help identify and classify those that should be taken into account. *Real* effects are those that involve either additions to the welfare of final consumers of project benefits or actual use of resources that would otherwise have been used elsewhere; *pecuniary* effects, or transfers, result from price changes that increase revenues for some people by the same amount that they increase outlays for other people. For example, the provision of journeys by a new subway line is a real benefit, and the use of steel and concrete in constructing it is a real cost, but the increased rents near subway stations are pecuniary in nature: The benefits to landlords in the form of higher rental incomes are exactly equal to the costs to tenants in the form of higher rental payments; there is no net change in total WTP.[10] Pecuniary effects can be ignored when the objective function is based solely on the PPIC; if, however, the objective function is concerned with the distribution of welfare between renters on the one hand and landlords on the other, then pecuniary effects, and the persons to whom they accrue, must be included in the analysis. A concern with distribution thus adds greatly to the difficulty and magnitude of the task of measurement.

Direct, or *primary*, effects are those directly resulting from the project being evaluated. Other effects are *indirect*, or *secondary*. To continue the subway example, the trips and construction materials are direct benefits and costs, while the impact on the automobile and bicycle industries (as more people travel by subway) would be indirect. One of the important tasks for BCA is to carefully identify secondary benefits substantial enough to justify explicit measurement. Because proper identification of indirect effects is subject to disagreement, advocates of particular projects have often sought to include more secondary benefits, and to omit more secondary costs, than is appropriate, while opponents of particular projects have often sought to do the reverse. An example of the type of alleged secondary effect often inappropriately included in BCAs would be the increased sales of stores near subway stations; because the increased sales are almost certainly offset by reduced sales of stores elsewhere, they represent no net increase in total benefits for the economy as a whole. (On secondary effects see, e.g., Gramlich 1981, 56, 83–85; Sugden and Williams 1978, ch. 10.)

A third distinction is between *tangible* and *intangible* effects. The former are goods and services for which there are markets and thus market prices; the latter are not traded in markets. Important examples of intangible benefits and costs are reductions or increases in illness and death, aesthetic impacts of physical development or pollution control, and the preservation or extinction of endangered animal species. Attempts to assign values to a number of specific intangible benefits have been discussed extensively in the BCA literature. Prominent among these are the value of lives saved by health, safety, and other programs; the value of travel time saved by transportation improvements; and the value of recreational benefits provided for hikers, campers, boaters, and beach-goers. (On valuing intangibles, see, e.g., Gramlich 1981, 68–75; Sugden and Williams 1978, ch. 11.)

Valuation of Benefits and Costs When They Occur

The actual quantitative measurement of benefits and costs is, of course, the heart of BCA. The conceptual standard for benefit and cost measurement, as discussed above, is individuals' *willingness to pay* (WTP)—the size of the monetary payment that, in combination with the effects being valued, would leave an individual just as well off, in his or her own judgment, as he or she would be in the absence of the project. If a good or service produced by the project is provided to people free of charge, then a person's total WTP for that good or service is the proper measure of the benefits to that person. But if a price is charged, then the amount actually paid must be subtracted from total WTP in order to obtain a measure of a person's net benefit from increased consumption of the commodity. This net benefit is called *consumers' surplus*.

To illustrate the nature of consumers' surplus, consider a hypothetical situation where government programs reduce the costs of strawberry growers enough to result in a drop in the retail price of strawberries from $2.00 to $1.80 per quart, and an increase in total annual retail strawberry sales from 100 million quarts to 110 million quarts, as consumers respond to the lower price by purchasing more strawberries. Although there is no reason to believe that WTP for the original 100 million quarts of strawberries should have changed, the amount that consumers actually pay for them is $20 million less than before: This $20 million is the increase in consumers' surplus on the purchase of these 100 million quarts of strawberries.[11]

A completely analogous concept of *producers' surplus* is used to measure benefits that take the form of increases in the difference between revenues and monetary costs for suppliers. If, for example, a localized government program reduced the costs of producing strawberries by $0.25 per quart for the farmers in an area that produced only 1 million quarts of strawberries (assumed to be too small a portion of total strawberry production to affect either the wholesale or the retail price), these farmers would realize a producers' surplus of $250,000.

When the market for a given commodity is working properly—that is, when "market failure" is absent—market price provides a reliable guide to marginal WTP for that commodity.[12] In other cases, however, there are good reasons to believe that existing market prices do not accurately reflect WTP. Analysts may then calculate *shadow prices* that will enable consumers' surplus to be estimated more accurately. These shadow prices represent attempts to estimate analytically the price that would have been determined in a well-functioning market—that is, a price that genuinely reflects consumer preferences and real resource use. Calculating shadow prices can be a costly and time-consuming process, and there is no guarantee that estimated shadow prices will be any more accurate than the imperfect market prices. The estimation of shadow prices offers an opportunity for the influence of subjective factors and political biases, whereas "market values do give an objective, impersonal guide to measuring benefits and costs" (Gramlich 1981, 78).

The issue of when to accept market prices and when to undertake adjusting them is a basic issue in applications of BCA (Gramlich 1981, 246–47). The predominant view among adherents of the BCA paradigm is that shadow prices should be calculated only in those relatively rare cases where the distortions in market prices are believed to be substantial, where there are clear grounds for believing that a more accurate shadow price can be calculated, and where the price in question is important in terms of the overall analysis. One shadow price that has received great attention is that for the cost of using labor that would otherwise be unemployed (Gramlich 1981, 61–67; Sugden and Williams 1978, 102–04); BCA texts also discuss adjusting market prices to remove the distorting effects of excise taxes and of monopoly power.

An additional category of benefits and costs includes those for which no market price exists at all. There are a number of approaches to the problems posed by valuation of such intangibles, most of which attempt to estimate what a market valuation would be, if only an appropriate market existed:

> Where there is no market, the analyst must try to deduce, from whatever evidence he can find, how people would behave if there were one.... there are many varied and often ingenious ways in which such deductions can be made; the resulting estimates of marginal valuations may have no obvious relationship to any conventional market prices. Nonetheless, the underlying principle of valuation is a "market" one (Sugden and Williams 1978, 149, 178).

The most frequent approach of BCA to valuation of intangibles is to identify information from actually existing markets that can be used to provide information about WTP for the particular benefit in question. For example, a significant consequence of some public expenditure projects is increased noise for residents in certain areas. Although there is no market for "quietness" as such, analysts have attempted to estimate a market-based price of quietness by sophisticated statistical analysis that seeks to isolate that portion of the total housing price differentials among diverse neighborhoods that can be attributed to varying noise levels.

Another approach to the valuation of intangibles is the use of interviews with potential program beneficiaries. The appeal of this approach is its directness: To find out what someone is willing to pay to have a particular outcome, simply ask him or her. There are, however, two major reasons for questioning the value of information obtained in this way, both stemming from the fact that the interview situation imposes no requirement that people put their dollars where their mouths are. On the one hand, answers may be top-of-the-head and poorly thought through; on the other hand, people may answer strategically, giving answers that they think will increase the likelihood of the outcome that they prefer.

An alternative approach is to stop short of attempting to estimate all benefits in terms of a common monetary unit. At a minimum, nonquantifiable effects of a program can simply be noted in a brief narrative statement accompanying the quantitative analysis. A somewhat more ambitious approach is to use a multiple-objective framework (as discussed in the historical review of BCA, above). Rather than attempting to calculate a single summary measure of net benefits, an analyst adopting this approach would produce both a formal BCA of quantifiable economic effects and a companion report on other, noncommensurable consequences. For example, an analyst might report to a decision-maker that of two mutually exclusive proposed health programs, one could be expected to save 100 lives per year in addition to providing other net benefits valued at $20 million, while the other program could be expected to save 200 lives per year in addition to providing other net benefits valued at $10 million.

From Theory to Measurement

It should be clear by now that there is a considerable gap between the nature and range of the benefits and costs included in theoretical discussions of the BCA paradigm's welfare foundations, and those that are actually measured in BCA's practical applications. The theoretical discussion is based on the notion that every individual, on the basis of a complete description of the proposed alternative, has an overall willingness to pay for that alternative, based on his or her own judgment and taking into account whatever effects he or she regards as relevant. In practice, however, estimates are made for the aggregate effect on all individuals of each of a relatively small number of specific types of effects. The most significant consequence is that many effects that are viewed as relevant by individuals are not included in benefits and costs as measured by BCA in practice.

Although it is difficult to see how such effects as those on the nature of community, cultural values, social relations, or political institutions could be measured by BCA in practice, it is relevant to note that in many cases they would be part of individual WTPs for the alternatives being analyzed—sometimes even a dominant part. One text recognizes this problem by arguing that making BCA practical requires restricting attention to "economic welfare" (defined as that part of social welfare that depends only on goods and services) and "further by assuming that each individual's utility depends only on his own consumption of goods and services" (Halvorsen and Ruby 1981, 18). Other texts are less careful and leave unaddressed the discrepancy between the individual-based discussion of the BCA paradigm's welfare criteria and the commodity-based discussion of the actual measurement of benefits and costs.

AGGREGATING BENEFITS AND COSTS

In order to obtain a final measure of a proposed project's net benefits, an analyst must deal with three problems that I have ignored until now in order to focus on the essentials of measuring benefits and costs at the time that they occur. These problems are posed by benefits and costs that occur at different times, that accrue to different sets of individuals, and that cannot be foreseen with certainty. They have in common the need for *aggregation* of different types of benefits and costs in order to obtain a single summary measure of net benefits.

Aggregation Over Time: Discounting

Most proposed public expenditures and regulations will have effects over a period of years. In many cases, particularly those involving large physical investments, there will be net costs in early years followed by net benefits in later years. Often, a set of proposed alternatives will differ among themselves in the projected pattern of benefits over time. In all of these cases, it is necessary for BCA to aggregate the benefits and costs occurring in different periods to obtain a *net present value* (NPV) for each alternative. NPV is the sum of money that, if received now, would be regarded as equivalent to the entire projected time stream of benefits and costs.

A dollar now is more valuable than a dollar in the future because it can be invested at a positive interest rate in the meantime. Aggregation over time therefore involves *discounting* future effects—that is, multiplying them by discount factors that are less than 1 and that grow progressively smaller for more distant years—in order to determine their present value. The *discount rate*, analogous to an interest rate, shows the extent to which benefits or costs in any given year are valued less than identical effects in the immediately preceding year. Thus, the problem of aggregating over time reduces to the problem of choosing an appropriate discount rate. The higher the discount rate, the lower the net present value.[13]

In the simplest perfectly competitive economy the choice of the proper discount rate would be easy: There would be no distortions resulting from the taxation of capital; a stable price level would eliminate any need to distinguish between nominal and real (inflation-adjusted) rates of interest; and the operation of the market system would establish a single rate of interest that simultaneously reflected each individual's preference for present consumption over future consumption and each firm's rate of return on private investment, thereby ensuring an optimal division of total income between consumption and investment. In the real world, however, things are not nearly so simple: Numerous, and very different, market rates of interest exist side by side as a result of inflation, tax rules, and a variety of capital market imperfections. Furthermore, most proponents of BCA believe that the share of private investment in total income is below the level that would be socially optimal. That is, they believe that the social rate of return on additional investment is greater than the *social rate of time preference* (SRTP) for consumption this year rather than next year, so that the NPV of the entire time stream of present and future consumption would be increased if some of the income currently used for consumption were instead used for investment.

The subject of choosing an appropriate discount rate has been the source of much confusion and disagreement in the BCA literature. By the late 1970s there was general agreement on the theoretically proper way to deal with aggregation over time: The NPV of a project should be obtained by first obtaining net benefits for each year in terms of dollars of consumption of goods and services and then discounting these net benefits using the SRTP. To the extent that a project's costs result in a reduction in private investment or that its benefits result in an increase in private investment in any year, the calculation of that year's consumption benefits should include multiplying the dollar amount of the change in investment by a shadow price for private investment. This shadow price, called the social opportunity cost of capital, is calculated (using the SRTP discount rate) as the NPV of the future consumption benefits that will result from each dollar of private investment.

There is also general agreement, however, that actually implementing this theoretical ideal would require information that simply is not available: The SRTP is not directly observable in any market, nor is it clear how one would feasibly obtain reliable information on the proportion of costs and benefits that would take the form of investment rather than consumption. So the agreement on a theoretical ideal is accompanied by continued disagreement over the best practical guidelines for determining the discount rate to be used in actual applications of BCA.[14]

The lack of a clearly agreed-on practical standard creates the possibility that a BCA will incorporate a discount rate that tends to enhance the attractiveness of the alternative favored by the decisionmaker who commissioned the analysis. Three safeguards are suggested in the texts under review. First, if and only if future benefits and costs are adjusted for expected inflation, should the discount rate be so adjusted; that is, real benefits and costs should be discounted by a real discount rate, and nominal benefits and costs should be discounted by a nominal discount rate. Second, projects competing for the same pool of budgetary funds should, in general, be evaluated using the same discount rate; this rate can be set by a higher-level authority rather than left to the discretion of individual analysts. Third, a *sensitivity analysis* may be performed by calculating a project's NPV using different rates. If the favored alternative changes when the discount rate varies, then additional attention can be focused on the choice of this critical parameter; whereas if the favored alternative is not "sensitive" to the choice of discount rate, this issue need not be a matter of further concern.

Aggregation over People: Distribution

The potential Pareto improvement criterion (PPIC), discussed earlier, disregards the distribution of gains and losses among individuals or groups. It ranks one alternative as superior to another if those who are better off with that alternative are enough better off so that they *could* compensate those who are worse off, even if no compensation is actually paid. This is an adequate basis for evaluating a project's contribution to social welfare only if one of two conditions is satisfied: Either the existing distribution of economic welfare is optimal (so that the impact on social welfare of individual gains and losses is not affected by which individuals gain or lose), or society is able to achieve its distributional goals through other measures (so that any negative distributional consequences of a proposed project can be ignored by BCA on the grounds that it will be effectively dealt with by an offsetting redistributional policy) (Pearce 1983, 6; Musgrave and Musgrave 1984, 175). Because it is clear that "neither of these conditions is satisfied in practice" (Halvorsen and Ruby 1981, 35), there is broad agreement that the PPIC must be supplemented or replaced as BCA's welfare criterion. To put it more positively, because public policy often places special importance on increases in the welfare of particular groups of people (for example, those below a certain income level, in a particular geographic area, in a certain age group, of a particular race, or with special medical needs), BCA, as an input into public policy decision-making, should not ignore distributional effects.

There is, however, a wide range of views on just how distributional matters should be dealt with by BCA. (These views are related to the more general disagreement, discussed previously, between those with a "conventional" approach to BCA and those who favor a "decision-making" approach.) At one extreme are those, such as Harberger

(1971; 1978; 1983) and Mishan (1982a, pt. 4; 1982b), who maintain that BCA per se should be restricted to the use of the PPIC, based on objective, market-based data. Any method for giving special weight to the benefits and costs of particular groups would be, according to this view, arbitrary and unjustifiable. Analysts may—indeed, they should (Mishan 1982a, 191)—identify significant distributional consequences of the alternatives under review in a supplementary section of their report. A view with identical implications for practice bases its conclusion in favor of "describing but not valuing distributional effects" not on any theoretical objection but on the present lack of "a satisfactory methodology for capturing distributional concerns" (Thompson 1980, 181).

The majority of BCA texts reviewed argue, however, that distributional consequences can and should be incorporated directly into BCA.[15] Simply to provide decision-makers with supplementary data on distributional effects is to provide them with more information than they can process effectively, with the likely consequence that it will be either ignored or overemphasized; analysts are better equipped than decision-makers to *integrate* efficiency and distribution considerations in an explicit and systematic way. The most frequently advocated approach is to assign *weights* (reflecting relative contributions to social welfare) to the net benefits of different groups, before adding them all together to provide an estimate of an alternative's aggregate net social benefits. While there are a number of approaches to establishing these weights, and "no technique for dealing with this highly subjective matter is totally satisfactory" (Gramlich 1981, 133), proponents argue that distributional consequences are important enough that substantial effort should be made. To the charge that any set of such distributional weights is arbitrary, their advocates answer that the uniform weights of 1.0 implicit in the PPIC are likewise arbitrary and are also, in fact, biased in favor of perpetuating the status quo. And to the charge of subjectivity, the answer is that matters of social objectives are inherently subjective and explicit use of distributional weights makes these subjective judgments subject to review and evaluation.

Choosing appropriate weights is not the only additional difficulty faced by BCA when it seeks to take distributional effects systematically into account: The informational needs for BCA are also greatly expanded. When concern is limited to the PPIC, all pecuniary effects, or transfers, can be ignored on the grounds that gains to some individuals are exactly matched by losses to others; the benefits or costs resulting from price changes in marketed goods and services can be estimated solely on the basis of observing prices and quantities in the market for that good or service; and the distribution of the burden of the taxes used to finance a project can be ignored. When the distribution of benefits and costs matters, however, none of these simplifications holds:

> To use non-unitary weights is to make CBA a much more difficult and time-consuming exercise.... [For example,] consumers' surplus and producers' surplus, measured from observable market demand-and-supply relationships, are themselves aggregates ... [that] measure *total* gains or losses to consumers as a whole. In arriving at these totals, the use of unitary weights is implicit. To apply a different set of distributional weights requires the analyst to unscramble an omelette of market-generated information (Sugden and Williams 1978, 206–07).

Aggregation over States of Nature: Uncertainty

The discussion up until now has proceeded as though it were possible to specify precisely the future effects of the alternatives being evaluated. In fact, uncertainty about the future is pervasive and substantial. A few examples are sufficient to establish the point: Estimates of construction costs have often proven to be grossly inaccurate; the randomness in patterns of precipitation makes the benefits of having a flood control project impossible to predict precisely; prices of internationally traded goods, such as petroleum, are influenced by unpredictable political and technological developments; and environmental and medical consequences of present choices are dependent on many complex and poorly understood biochemical, ecological, and other relationships.

The BCA paradigm acknowledges the existence of uncertainty and the importance of taking it into account. But the inherent intractability of the problem results in a lack of successful ways for incorporating uncertainty into BCA. The conclusion reached by Pearce (1983, 88) summarizes the discussions of uncertainty in the entire set of texts reviewed: "The overriding impression we are left with is that there is no very satisfactory way of treating either risk or uncertainty in CBA."[16]

On the one hand, BCA texts provide expositions of a theoretically ideal approach that assumes perfect knowledge of both the probabilities of all possible future events and the attitudes toward risk of all affected individuals. On the other hand, the practical advice that the texts offer to practitioners amounts to three main commonsensical guidelines, two of them negative and one positive. First, do not ignore uncertainty; BCA reports should clearly identify and discuss the main areas of uncertainty in the alternatives under review. Second, do not attempt to deal with it by the arbitrary and distorting method of adding a "risk premium" to the discount rate. Third, use sensitivity analysis to show how BCA results are affected by alternative assumptions concerning future costs and benefits—for example, a "best estimate" could be accompanied by an "optimistic estimate" and a "pessimistic estimate." By presenting ranges of estimates and identifying how sensitive the results are to changes in the various uncertain values, sensitivity analysis can indicate those areas where it would be most worthwhile to devote resources to reducing the amount of uncertainty.

BCA AND CRITERIA FOR CHOICE

After the tasks of identifying, measuring, and aggregating benefits and costs have been completed, the BCA analyst must complete the report in a way that will help the decision-maker choose among the alternative proposed expenditure projects or regulatory programs being evaluated. There are two principal aspects of this final phase of BCA. The first, which represents the essential and distinctive contribution of BCA, is presentation of the results of the formal, quantitative calculation of a single summary measure—the net present value, in monetary terms, of each proposed alternative's net benefits. The other is supplementing this summary measure with information about significant consequences of the proposed alternatives that were not incorporated into the central calculation.

When BCAs have been completed for a number of potential projects, there remains the problem of how to use the summary measures of net benefits to decide which proposals to implement. On the assumption that all relevant consequences have been adequately captured in the BCA itself, the correct approach is succinctly stated in what Stokey and Zeckhauser (1978, 137) call "the *Fundamental Rule:* In any choice situation, select the alternative that produces the greatest net benefit." BCA textbooks devote considerable attention to spelling out the practical implications of this deceptively simple injunction in various circumstances—for example, when projects are mutually exclusive and when they are not, and when there is and when there is not a budget constraint. Most important, they demonstrate that the use of the benefit-cost *ratio* to rank competing projects can lead to incorrect results. Unlike total net benefits, the size of the ratio is affected by the arbitrary decision of whether certain undesirable effects are treated as costs or as negative benefits; furthermore, a relatively small project with a high benefit-cost ratio may produce fewer benefits than a larger project with a smaller benefit-cost ratio.

If a multiple-objective approach is used, in a situation where not all benefits and costs are regarded as commensurable, the results of the BCA itself constitute only one part of an analyst's final report. The BCA reports the consequences with respect to the economic efficiency objective (or the PPIC). Analysis of the proposal's consequences with respect to other objectives (environmental or distributional) is carried out and reported separately; there is no attempt to provide one single, overall numerical score for each proposed alternative. In these cases, the analyst can look for *dominant* alternatives (one alternative is said to dominate another when it does better with respect to each of the objectives) but beyond that can do little to argue that one alternative is better than another. In fact, the entire point of the multiple-objective approach is to present the decision-maker with information on each of two or more dimensions rather than to have the BCA process itself reduce everything to a single number. Even in these cases, however, the analyst can quantify the implicit trade-offs that would be implied by favoring one specific alternative over another.

No matter whether a single- or multiple-objective approach is taken, however, the BCA paradigm is clear that there will be relevant factors that cannot be effectively incorporated into BCA. From one perspective this is simply another way of saying that decisions should be made by decision-makers—who are determined through a political process—rather than by analysts. From another perspective, however, it underscores the importance of benefit-cost analysts' systematically providing information in their reports about consequences of proposed alternatives that cannot readily be evaluated quantitatively. Ultimately, choices are up to the decision-makers, but BCA should offer them as much help as it can. Carefully describing the limitations of the quantitative results obtained through the BCA is an important part of doing this.

NOTES

1. To my knowledge, the history of BCA remains to be written. The historical accounts that exist are, like the present one, relatively short sections of larger works with a more general focus. Among the short accounts that proved useful in preparing the present brief historical survey were those of Grubb, Whittington, and Humphries (1984, 125-30); Hammond (1960, ch. 1); Haveman and Margolis (1977, 1-10, 20-22); Marglin (1967, 15-18); Merewitz and Sosnick (1971, 9-12); Pearce (1983, 14-21); and Steiner (1974, 331-42).
2. On the nature and history of the PPBS system, see Lyden and Miller (1972); Merewitz and Sosnick (1971); and Schick (1973). On use of BCA at the state and local level, see Schick (1971). The growing employment of BCA in underdeveloped countries during this period is indicated by the publication of influential manuals by three leading international organizations in the area of economic development—the United Nations Industrial Development Organization (Dasgupta, Marglin, and Sen 1972), the Organization for Economic Cooperation and Development (Little and Mirrlees 1968), and the World Bank (Squire and van der Tak 1975).
3. The most important survey article was that of Prest and Turvey (1965). Influential anthologies included those edited by Layard (1972) and by Haveman and Margolis (1970) (which consisted of selections from a three-volume compendium of papers originally published by the U.S. Congress's Joint Economic Committee 1969) and the four volumes in a series of *Aldine Annuals* on *Benefit-Cost and Policy Analysis* (Harberger et al. 1972; Niskanen et al. 1973; Haveman et al. 1974; and Zeckhauser et al. 1975).
4. The use of BCA in the regulatory area during the 1970s took place in a complex legislative, administrative, and bureaucratic framework; a detailed account is provided by Baram (1980). For a discussion and quantification of the growth of federal government regulatory activity between 1970 and 1977, see Miller and Yandle (1979, 1-4).
5. For the best single source of information and analysis on the Reagan administration's use of BCA in the area of environmental regulation, see Smith (1984).

46 PRELIMINARIES

6. The textbook expositions are: Edward M. Gramlich, *Benefit-Cost Analysis of Government Programs* (1981); E.J. Mishan, *Cost-Benefit Analysis*, 3d ed. (1982a); D.W. Pearce, *Cost-Benefit Analysis*, 2d ed. (1984); D.W. Pearce and C.A. Nash, *The Social Appraisal of Projects: A Text in Cost-Benefit Analysis* (1981); Robert Sugden and Alan Williams, *Principles of Practical Cost-Benefit Analysis* (1978); Mark S. Thompson, *Benefit-Cost Analysis for Program Evaluation* (1980); Robert Halvorsen and Michael G. Ruby, *Benefit-Cost Analysis of Air Pollution Control* (1981); Robert Haveman and Julius Margolis, *Public Expenditure and Policy Analysis*, 3d ed. (1983); Richard A. Musgrave and Peggy B. Musgrave, "Expenditure Evaluation: Principles" and "Expenditure Evaluation; Case Studies," in their *Public Finance in Theory and Practice*, 4th ed. (1984, chs. 8-9); and Edith Stokey and Richard Zeckhauser, "Project Evaluation: Benefit-Cost Analysis," in their *A Primer for Policy Analysis* (1978, ch. 9). The first six of these are textbooks completely devoted to BCA. The seventh is a book-length exposition of BCA in a monograph concerned with its application in air-pollution control, the next a widely adopted book of readings. The remaining two are the BCA chapters in leading public finance and policy analysis texts.
7. Kuhn also emphasizes the importance of textbooks to a "scientific community" (1970, 10, 137).
8. The terms *benefit-cost analysis* (BCA) and *cost-benefit analysis* (CBA) are essentially equivalent (see Chapter 1, note 1). While I consistently use the former in the text of this book, quoted passages retain the terminology adopted by their original authors.
9. For a detailed, technically sophisticated exposition of applied welfare economics, including its relationship to the results of theoretical welfare economics, see Just, Hueth, and Schmitz (1982).
10. This example can offer some indication of the nature of the problems encountered in enumerating benefits and costs. The statement in the text is based on the implicit assumption that the benefits of the improved subway service are being estimated directly (for example, by estimating savings in travel time and the value of this time savings). Because it is precisely these benefits that make tenants near subway stops willing to pay higher rents, to count both the higher rents and the value of travel-time savings would be *double-counting* two different manifestations of the same effect. If the value of travel-time savings was not estimated directly, however, then the increased WTP for rental property near subway stations (measured, as a first approximation, by estimates of increased rental payments) could be validly used in measuring the benefits from the improved subway services.
11. This $20 million is not the total increase in consumers' surplus resulting from the change, but it is the largest part of it. The WTP for an additional

quart of strawberries drops from $2.00 (the original market price) at a consumption level of 100 million quarts to $1.80 (the final market price) at a consumption level of 110 million quarts. And an average WTP of $1.90 per quart for the 10 million more quarts of strawberries purchased at $1.80 results in an additional $1 million of consumers' surplus ($0.10 per quart times 10 million). The reader familiar with demand and supply diagrams may recognize that the increase in consumers' surplus is indicated graphically by the area to the left of that portion of the downward sloping demand curve that lies between the original price and the final price. This diagrammatic representation of consumers' surplus may also help clarify why it does not change unless the market price changes. For explanations of consumers' surplus, including discussion of some subtleties not discussed here, see Gramlich (1981, 29-32), Halvorsen and Ruby (1981, 78-83), Pearce (1983, 25-30), or Sugden and Williams (1978, ch. 9).

12. A brief "proof" of this proposition offers an indication of the kind of economic reasoning that underlies the measurement techniques of BCA. If my WTP for a commodity—quarts of strawberries, say—is higher (or lower) than its market price, then I can make myself better off by buying more of it (or selling some of what I already have). As I continue to buy (or sell) quarts of strawberries, my WTP for one more quart will surely begin to fall (or rise); I will continue the process of adjusting my strawberry holdings until my WTP is just equal to the market price (because only then will I have reached the position where no further purchases or sales can make me better off). If making purchases and sales in this way is possible for all of the individuals in an economy, then it is reasonable to assume that each individual's WTP will be equal to the market price. If making such purchases and sales is not possible, then the market for strawberries is, by definition, not working properly—that is, there is some form of market failure.

13. The issues involved in aggregating benefits and costs over time are discussed in all BCA texts (see, e.g., Gramlich 1981, ch. 6; Halvorsen and Ruby 1981, ch. 4; Pearce 1983, ch. 4; Stokey and Zeckhauser 1978, ch. 10; Sugden and Williams 1978, chs. 4, 15; and Thompson 1980, 153-75). No attempt is made in this short subsection to give citations for individual points or arguments.

14. Gramlich's text is rare in suggesting that the range of possible discount rates consistent with any reasonable theoretical position is very narrow, and in actually providing a numerical value for the range of appropriate discount rates: "All of these subtleties are not likely to make much practical difference.... use of a real discount rate in the 3 to 4 percent range will probably yield present value solutions that come as close to being correct, or at least unbiased, as is possible in this messy area" (1981, 107-08).

15. See, e.g., the discussions of Gramlich (1981, ch. 7); Halvorsen and Ruby (1981, 21-23, ch. 3); Pearce (1983, 3-9, ch. 5); Sugden and Williams (1978, ch. 14).
16. The most extensive discussions of uncertainty and BCA are in Halvorsen and Ruby (1981, ch. 5); Mishan (1982a, pt. 7); Pearce (1983, ch. 6); Pearce and Nash (1981, ch. 5); Sugden and Williams (1978, chs. 5, 12).

II LIBERALS, CONSERVATIVES, AND BENEFIT-COST ANALYSIS
The BCA Debate

3 WHAT'S WRONG WITH BCA
The Liberal Indictment

> All is not well with benefit-cost analysis, and never has been (Dorfman 1978, 268).

As applications of BCA have expanded in recent decades, a substantial body of criticism has emerged in response. This criticism has come from economists and noneconomists and has reflected a wide range of political positions. In the last ten years, BCA has become widely perceived to be a tool for cutting back spending and regulatory programs favored by liberals, and most criticism has come from a liberal perspective. Other economists, however, including some with liberal beliefs and values, have strongly defended BCA and advocated its increased use. Part II will examine this BCA debate by reviewing the arguments made by BCA's critics (in the present chapter) and by its proponents (in Chapter 4). My summary evaluation (presented in Chapter 5) may be briefly previewed at the outset: One is more likely to contribute to improved public policy outcomes in general, and to the advancement of liberal goals in particular, by working for *better* BCA rather than by working for *less* of it.

The intensity of some of the attacks on BCA, and the sweeping nature of the negative assessment of its value in formulating public policy, can be illustrated by citing the congressional subcommittee that concluded that "The limitations on the usefulness of BCA in the context of health, safety, and environmental regulatory decision-making are so severe that they militate against its use altogether" (U.S. House 1976, 515). Similarly, a professor of law has maintained that "It simply does not make sense—either logically or ethically—to apply the techniques of cost-benefit analysis to major questions of public policy" (Junger 1979, 187).[1] Another legal scholar has argued that "regulatory uses of cost-benefit analysis stifle and obstruct the achievement of legislated health, safety, and environmental goals" (Baram 1980, 473). And in 1981 the American Public Health Association (1982, 196-97) adopted a resolution critical of the use of BCA in the public health area, citing its "severe ethical and methodological limitations."

This chapter is an attempt to present a comprehensive, systematic case against BCA, based on published criticisms. No single critic of BCA, to my knowledge, has made all of the points included here, nor should those cited in support of one line of criticism be assumed necessarily to agree with any other line. Also, while the criticisms have generally been made from a liberal perspective and are consistent with liberal values and beliefs, many of the same points have been made by both conservatives and radicals. Taken as a whole, however, the case presented in this chapter reflects a distinctively liberal position on BCA.

JUSTIFICATION OF PREDETERMINED POSITIONS

The most common criticism of BCA is that it is not, in practice, the objective technique that it purports to be. Ida R. Hoos of the University of California contends that in reality, "It is almost always an ex post facto justification of a position already taken" (Pear 1982). Michael Baram, a lawyer who has studied the practice of BCA in considerable detail, maintains that it "is today known as a 'numbers game,' in which analysts choose numbers and 'push the numbers' to reach predetermined outcomes" (1981, 125). Herbert Kaufman of the Brookings Institution has called BCA "a smokescreen" (Tolchin 1983), and a congressional subcommittee concluded that BCA can "provide an effective disguise for subjective advocacy" (U.S. House 1976, 555). The common core of these criticisms is not so much the fact that BCA is used to justify particular positions but that it is being used in this way at the same time that it is presented as a scientific, unbiased method of analysis.

Congressional testimony by Baruch Fischhoff provides a nice illustration of how analysts can act to ensure that they come up with results that support a pre-selected alternative. He tells of a colleague's visiting a

> consulting firm and seeing an analyst hunched over a terminal massaging a computerized analysis. Said he [the analyst], "The analysis didn't come out the way my client wanted it. However, there's quite a bit of wiggle room or ambiguity in almost all of the cost, benefit, and probability assessments. I'm going to alter each a little bit until I get the right conclusion. No one will notice and my client will be happy with this justification for what he was going to do anyway" (U.S. House 1979, 23).

The heroic and imaginative efforts by the Corps of Engineers and the Bureau of Reclamation to achieve acceptable benefit-cost ratios for egregiously ill-conceived water projects are legendary (Baram 1980, 479, 486-87; Roberts 1976). These agencies exist in order to move water from one place to another, and they tailor their analytical work in support of this institutional imperative. One illustration is provided in a careful review of the Bureau of Reclamation's 1967 benefit-cost analysis supporting the proposed Nebraska Mid-State project—the main feature of which was diversion of water from the Platte River for irrigation of crop land (Hanke and Walker 1974). The BuRec's BCA concluded that benefits were 24 percent greater than costs—that is, that the project's benefit-cost ratio was 1.24 (and thus well above the 1.0 level needed to justify the project). Hanke and Walker show that this conclusion depended on several inappropriate assumptions; among the more important of these were (1) using an artificially low discount rate of 3.125 percent; (2) assuming a project life of 100 years, rather than the more common and supportable fifty-year assumption; (3) counting positive wildlife and fish benefits when the project would in fact have resulted in the Platte drying up in over half of the months during the thirty-year period of record (1931-60), thereby destroying the in-stream fishery, eliminating waterfowl habitats for a 150-mile stretch of river, and reducing the survival prospects of such endangered species as the whooping crane, sandhill crane, and bald eagle; (4) valuing increased farm output at support prices that incorporated a substantial federal subsidy; (5) including secondary benefits for agricultural processors that would in fact simply be transfers of economic activity from other regions; and (6) ignoring the costs resulting from the predictable failure of farms in the South and East that would be displaced by increased agricultural output in Nebraska. Hanke and Walker adjusted the BuRec's calculations to take account of several (but not all) of these deficiencies; their final estimate of the actual benefit-cost ratio was 0.23 — that is, that the project's costs would be more than four times as great as its benefits (1974, 341, 343). There is ample evidence to support Stephen A. Marglin's observation that "in American practice (as distinct from theory) it [BCA] often has served as window dressing for projects whose plans have already been formulated" (1967, 18).

A particularly striking example of the relationship between bureaucratic orientation and BCA conclusions is offered by a set of analyses done of the costs and benefits of increased flights to the United States by the Concorde supersonic passenger plane. Studies undertaken by the Environmental Protection Agency, the Council on Environmental Quality, and the Federal Energy Administration all concluded that costs would outweigh benefits. On the other hand, BCAs carried out by the Federal Aviation Administration, the State Department, and the National Aeronautics and Space Administration all concluded that there would be positive net benefits. A detailed examination of the use of BCA in this case concluded that in the individual agencies "The result was not determined by the cost-benefit analysis, but rather was a subjective policy choice in which the locus of decisionmaking authority determined the results of the analysis" (Means 1977, 1038).

The Reagan administration has used BCA as a means of advancing its objective of deregulation. The extent to which its conclusions preceded the carrying out of the ordered BCAs is indicated by the fact that when a rigorous benefit-cost standard was mandated for all major regulatory proposals, the U.S. Office of Management and Budget decreed a blanket exemption for proposals "which relax or defer regulatory requirements, or which delegate regulatory activity to the states" (quoted in Grubb, Whittington, and Humphries 1984, 133). Thus, the new BCA requirement contributed to bringing about the "paralysis by analysis" that has made it difficult to gain final approval of new regulatory measures, without erecting any comparable procedural hurdles for proposals to loosen or eliminate existing regulations (Connerton and MacCarthy 1982, 6-7). In addition, the administration's written materials have echoed the President's emphasis on the costs of regulation while minimizing or ignoring its benefits in terms of a cleaner environment, reduced illnesses and injuries, and improved consumer information. A General Accounting Office study of fifty-seven analyses prepared under the aegis of Executive Order 12291 found that those who carried out the analyses were responsive to the wishes of administration policy-makers: Twenty-three of the analyses contained no estimates of benefits, while only eight contained no estimates of costs.[2]

Examples could be multiplied almost without limit. In the words of the editors of one survey volume on BCA in the area of water pollution (Peskin and Seskin 1975, 30), "Since in most cost-benefit analyses, there is considerable opportunity to make self-serving assumptions. . . . it is fairly easy to doctor the analyses." Whole categories of benefits are routinely ignored by those with an interest in doing so, assumptions and parameter values are regularly chosen in order to reach preferred outcomes, and biased estimates of the entire range of benefits and costs are common. In short, there appears to be good reason to agree with the congressional subcommittee that concluded that:

> The most significant factor in evaluating a benefit-cost study is the name of the sponsor. Benefit-cost studies generally are formulated after basic positions on an issue are taken by the respective parties. The results of competing studies predictably reflect the respective positions of the parties on the issue (U.S. House 1976, 180).

BCA AND DISTRIBUTION

The preceding criticisms deal essentially with the question of honesty—of whether applications of BCA really constitute good-faith attempts to evaluate the relative merits of alternative proposals. Even assuming good faith, however, BCA has been subjected to serious criticisms along several other lines of argument. The first of these holds that the narrow focus of BCA on total benefits and costs results in a neglect of distributional consequences. The central welfare criterion embodied in the BCA paradigm, as we saw in Chapter 2, asks whether those who gain from a project *could* compensate the losers. This is equivalent to asking simply whether total gains are greater than total losses, without in any way taking into account who wins and who loses.

There are at least two distinct reasons for being critical of BCA's failing to take the distribution of costs and benefits into account. The most commonly recognized of these is based on the view that public policy should operate to reduce economic inequality by improving the well-being of disadvantaged groups such as the poor, racial minorities, or residents of underdeveloped regions. Even though there are many cases where making distributional judgments may be difficult or impossible, there are many other cases where it is quite clear that distributional changes represent improvement (or worsening) from the point of view of public policy. A form of analysis that ignores distributional impacts will systematically undervalue projects that improve distribution in this regard and systematically overvalue projects that exacerbate economic inequality. As a result, BCA may be used to provide justification for projects with adverse distributional consequences.

A second reason for BCA to take distributional consequences into account reflects a widespread concern for equal treatment of people who are in approximately equal economic circumstances. (In economics jargon, this is "horizontal equity," in contrast to "vertical equity," or fair treatment of people in unequal economic circumstances.) The relevance of horizontal equity can be illustrated by the following extreme hypothetical example. Consider a proposal to raise property taxes by 50 percent on all properties with odd-numbered street addresses and simultaneously to lower property taxes by 50 percent on all properties with even-numbered street addresses. A conventional benefit-cost analysis of this proposal would conclude that its net benefits were approximately zero, and an analysis of its impact on the overall level of inequality in the size distribution of income would also show no significant effects. Nevertheless, such a proposal would be generally, and rightly, condemned as consisting of an arbitrary and unfair redistribution of income.

The same general point is relevant to proposals that would confer benefits (or impose costs) on the residents of one river basin (even though their income levels may approximate the national average); or on the workers in a particular industry (even though they may have average earnings); or on commuters on a particular route (even though they may represent an accurate cross-section of national income levels). The issue here is not solely an abstract concern for fairness. Potentially affected groups can be expected to monilize politically, and policy-makers are almost certain to become aware that their choices have distributional dimensions. Richard Zeckhauser, noting that policy-makers' concern with the distribution of benefits and costs is, in fact, "almost a preoccupation," has criticized BCA because "by ignoring distributional concerns it severely limits its relevance for policy decisions" (1981, 215, 218).

Each of the major approaches to dealing with distributional matters has been subject to criticism. In the case of those who believe that BCA should be restricted solely to calculation of aggregate benefits and costs and application of the potential Pareto improvement criterion, no more need be said.[3] In the case of those who argue that the formal, quantitative calculation should be supplemented by the presentation and discussion of distributional consequences, critics argue that the main quantitative conclusions of an analysis are what matters in practice. They point out that accompanying qualifications tend to be overlooked and ignored in the desire of decision-makers, politicians, and the media for short, summary, numerical conclusions.

The alternative approach to distributional issues favored by the majority of the BCA texts reviewed in Chapter 2 is to attempt to bring them into the analysis through the use of weights that give extra value to the benefits and costs accruing to specified groups. The crux of the criticism of this approach is that implementing such weighting is so difficult that it will in fact either be done poorly or, more likely, not done at all. The extent of the practical difficulties of including distributional weights in BCA is inadvertently indicated by the abstract nature of the discussions offered by proponents of doing so, by the absence of specific helpful guidance to practitioners, and by the lack of actual implementation of the idea.[4] One striking illustration is provided in the text by Gramlich (1981, 214–17). Although he devotes an entire chapter to distributional considerations, just four chapters later he presents a case study of the application of BCA to a regulatory issue—proposed standards for limiting noise in the workplace—in which he simply ignores distributional issues in an instance where they are clearly central. The benefits of more stringent noise standards would accrue almost solely to the workers, while their costs would fall mainly on employers and/or customers;[5] to simply add all benefits and costs together in this case, as Gramlich does, is to ignore the distributional implications that are one of the essential features of the problem.

In practice, BCAs seldom include serious treatment of distributional issues. Fischhoff notes that "There has been some theoretical work on how to incorporate equity considerations in cost-benefit analyses," but then observes pointedly that "This research has, however, had little impact on the way analyses are performed" (1977, 180). When there is any treatment of distributional issues, it is generally confined to qualifications and additional explanatory passages appended to the main report.

In short, whether distributional concerns are explicitly ruled outside of the scope of BCA's quantitative analysis, or whether they are viewed as deserving explicit treatment in such analysis, the result is approximately the same, and highly unsatisfactory. Economic efficiency remains the center of concern, the de facto criterion remains maximization of national income regardless of the effect on distribution, and losers are left with the cold comfort of knowing that they could, potentially, have been compensated by the gainers.

NEGLECT OF SIGNIFICANT SOCIAL VALUES

Proponents of BCA tend to advocate its use as though the merits of increased reliance on the systematic, quantitative analysis of benefits and costs were self-evident and noncontroversial—as if the approach taken by welfare economics were the only valid approach to social decision-making. There are, however, several grounds for arguing that the approach of BCA is procedurally inappropriate because it operates to subordinate other important standards for decision-making in the area of public policy. A number of critics of BCA have forcefully employed such arguments, based on "logics other than that of cost-benefit analysis" (Fischhoff 1981, 183). These arguments fall into four broad, and somewhat overlappings, categories.

Ethical Dimensions of Public Policy Choices

The essence of the case against BCA on ethical grounds has been succinctly stated by Eric Ashby: "BCA is ... an *inappropriate* technique. It sets out to answer the question: what is *efficient* for society? But this is not what the public asks about environmental issues nowadays; they ask: what is *good* for society." (1980, 1178). The most developed "ethical critique" of BCA has been offered by Steven Kelman (1981), who argues that BCA's basis in utilitarian ethical theory (the theory, essentially, that an action ought to be undertaken if its benefits will exceed its costs) provides an incomplete and often inappropriate guide to correct choices. Kelman does not reject BCA out of hand, but he concludes that in the area of environmental, safety, and health regulation "it is not justifiable to devote major resources to the generation of data for cost-benefit calculations or to undertake efforts to 'spread the gospel' of cost-benefit analysis further" (1981, 33).

Kelman argues that more persuasive, nonutilitarian ethical theories assign moral significance to duties and rights as well as to consequences, so that "there may be many instances where a certain decision might be right even though its benefits do not outweigh its costs" (1981, 33). He goes on to point out that the very act of attempting to place monetary values on certain types of nonmarketed consequences may have substantial negative impact on widely shared social, political, human, or environmental values. To regard something as "priceless" or "of infinite value" is not the logical absurdity that welfare economists make it out to be but is a socially meaningful way of saying that something is specially valued. Attempts to quantify the value of such things threaten to erode or destroy this special status. Of course, things "of infinite value" must sometimes be sacrificed, but the process of individual or social choice appropriate in such circumstances involves a kind of deliberation and decision quite different from reliance on the quantitative comparisons of BCA.

One thing that is normally regarded as priceless is human life, yet attempts to calculate a monetary value for a life are often made as part of BCAs in areas such as health care, environmental protection, and workplace and consumer safety regulation. These efforts to assign a monetary value to human life epitomize, for many critics of BCA, the fundamentally amoral, ethically blind nature of technocratic quantification run amok (see, e.g., Babson 1979 or Marx 1983). (Criticisms concerning the results of these calculations will be discussed below; the criticism here is of the propriety of attempting any calculations at all in this area.)

Another fundamental ethical issue, the problem of intergenerational comparison of benefits and costs, is less widely recognized. How does one compare the significance of extra lives lost one or two generations in the future, or of additional persons undergoing extended periods of intense suffering, or of more people being able to experience a canoe trip along a river preserved in its natural state, with the significance of corresponding consequences in the present? BCA's attempts to quantify the value of such consequences in monetary terms, and then to make interperiod comparisons by means of a discount rate, tend to deny the very existence of the ethical problems involved.

When the issue is one of valuing normal consumption goods, the use of a discount rate to calculate the present value of even distant future consumption seems reasonably appropriate (largely because the discount rate also approximates the amount of additional future consumption that could be obtained by investing now an amount equal to the present value of that future consumption). But in other cases, particularly when the consequences being evaluated are morbidity or mortality or irreversible environmental changes, the ethical propriety of using a discount rate to compare benefits and costs in different time periods is highly questionable. Is the value of saving a human life now really to be regarded as equivalent to saving eleven and one-half lives fifty years from now—or 132 lives a century in the future—as is implied by using a discount rate of 5 percent? Is one person gazing in awe at the majesty of the Grand Canyon in 1990 to be regarded as having the same value, from the point of view of public policy, as 117 gazing visitors in 2040, or 13,776 visitors in 2090? Such equivalencies result from the use of a 10 percent discount rate. Particularly in areas of health and safety and environmental regulation, many of the most important benefits are likely to be felt primarily after a considerable period of time, and to a large extent by those not yet born at the time decisions are taken. To talk of "future generations" is far more than an empty figure of speech; 30, 50, 75, or even 100 years is certainly not too long a period to consider in such cases. These are the considerations that Baram (1980, 487) has in mind when he states that "Ultimately, the discount rate is an ethical problem that transcends economic and legal perspectives."

Rights, Entitlements, and Due Process

Criticism of BCA from the standpoint of moral philosophy shades into argument from the point of view of jurisprudence. The critique of lawyer Michael Baram emphasizes the importance of "constitutional guarantees of due process, equal protection, property rights, and representative government" and their erosion when the role of quantitative analysis is expanded beyond its appropriate limits (1980, 488). Baram argues that

> Our constitutional framework for governmental decisionmaking involves balancing many factors. It does not mandate the use of an economic framework, and indeed establishes a framework for decisionmaking which ensures that no single factor such as economics will dominate. The varied and often conflicting needs and desires of many segments of our society must be weighed against fundamental individual rights in order to establish ultimate societal values and reach an optimal governmental choice. This process is subverted when cost-benefit analysis is the basis for decisionmaking (1980, 525).

The issue that Baram is addressing here is no mere theoretical possibility. We have seen how Executive Order 12291 imposed a benefit-cost test on all major proposals for new or strengthened regulations. The earlier insistence by some parties that new regulations must be justified by a favorable benefit-cost analysis resulted in litigation that reached the U.S. Supreme Court in the year following publication of Baram's article. In its widely noted decision in a case concerning the cotton-dust standard established by the U.S. Occupational Safety and Health Administration (OSHA), *American Textile Manufacturers Institute v. Donovan* (1981), the Court ruled that OSHA's statutory mandate to set workplace health standards assuring, "to the extent feasible," the right of employees to "safe and healthful working conditions" is not subject to a benefit-cost standard. An analysis of that decision in the *Ecology Law Quarterly* summarized the import of the Court's decision in this way:

> The Secretary of Labor is not required to perform a cost-benefit analysis before promulgating permissible exposure levels of toxic materials and harmful physical agents. Indeed, the Court implied that the Secretary may not limit the stringency of such standards solely because the anticipated costs exceed the anticipated benefits (Karpf 1982, 89).

The themes of this argument and of the ethical one are combined in the critique of A.J. Culyer, who contends that the allocation of "certain crucial primary goods" should not be subject to considerations of economic efficiency but should be regarded instead as basic individual rights, whose proper allocation is subject to a different set of principles. These "primary goods" are "those goods necessary to any normal individual's ability to plan his life in society, whatever that plan may be: health, the legal enforcement of his rights, protection of whatever property is his, opportunities for the development of his intellect, and so on." If the allocation of primary goods is made subject to BCA, Culyer argues, "what may well be shattered is a relatively just organization of society.... a too thorough-going application of the principles of efficiency has within it the potential for doing vast damage to the quality of life in so-called free societies" (Culyer 1977, 147, 148, 152).

The Political Process

A third major type of criticism of BCA's focus on economic efficiency has been voiced primarily by political scientists. Viewed as a political process, they argue, decision-making in the area of public policy is a potential means of incorporating a broad range of issues and interests. To the extent that BCA operates to narrow or replace that political process with quantitative analysis of the single issue of economic efficiency, or maximum net benefits, there are reasons for concern.

On the one hand, many of the most important aspects of public policy decisions are simply not susceptible to meaningful quantitative analysis; they are better brought to the attention of politically responsible decision-makers through the entire range of traditional political activities. Thus, Pearce and Nash identify criticisms of BCA based on the fear that it involves an attempt to substitute "rationality" for "politics"; that BCA "has been designed to *replace* political decision-making with a 'mechanistic calculus'"; and that "BCA cannot embrace the wider considerations which the political system can deal with" (1981, 16–17).

On the other hand, there are critics of BCA whose "main concern is that the use of analysis transfers power for societal decision making to a technical elite, in effect disenfranchising the lay citizenry"

(Fischhoff 1981, 183). This can be expected not only to result in a loss of the information and perspectives brought about by public discussion and debate but also to skew the results of government decisions. Wealthy and powerful groups can be expected to find ways to make their interests known during the BCA process, but those who are less comfortable with formal and quantitative procedures, less able to hire experts to represent them, and more dependent on traditional channels of political influence will almost certainly fail to have their interests adequately represented in this more closed and technocratic procedure. In short, BCA tends to preclude effective representation of the interests of many of those most importantly affected by the decisions being made (Ashford 1981; Baram 1980; Fischhoff 1977).

Criticisms based on political process are related to those based on the value of legally established procedural standards governing public decision-makers. Baram has argued persuasively that the results of benefit-cost analyses have frequently been used in violation of the procedural standards established by the Administrative Procedure Act and that BCA results are used to undermine the rights of all interested parties to be fully informed of, and able to comment on, all materials that are taken into account in the rule-making processes of regulatory agencies. While there is no inherent reason why BCAs could not be properly entered into the decision-making process in a timely and public manner, in actual practice practitioners and proponents of BCA have used their results in attempts to short-circuit and undermine the existing procedures (Baram 1981, 125-26).

A. J. Culyer (1977) and Eric Ashby (1980) go on to argue that a narrow, biased, closed, and unrepresentative political process will undermine public faith in prevailing political institutions. Ashby has written, for example, that "a decision is only one of the outcomes. ... The most critical outcome ... may be a serious weakening of confidence in the institutions of government. ... What matters just as much [as the decision] is the process by which the decision is reached" (1980, 1180).

Environmental Values

Finally, environmentalists have argued that environmental values are not commensurable with those benefits and costs that can be evaluated in monetary terms. The survival of an animal species, the preservation of wilderness areas, the avoidance of manmade ecological change all have values that cannot be accurately measured by people's willingness to pay for such consequences—and that exist independently of this willingness to pay. For example, a major BCA of proposals to clean up the Delaware River "attempted to calculate the benefit *accruing to fisherman* as a result of an increased population of fish in the estuary. One looks in vain to the economist to provide a value for the benefit *accruing to fish*, which have no money to sacrifice" (Ackerman et al. 1974, 139, emphasis in original). For many nonenvironmentalists this point, based on a rejection of the usual anthropocentric framework whereby things have value only to the extent that one or more persons values them (a framework explicitly adopted by welfare economics), is difficult to understand, let alone accept. It is analogous to the attitude toward the natural world in general, and land in particular, of many Native Americans.

Peter Junger has argued that BCA's conclusions "will be consistently biased against . . . preventing further environmental degradation. . . . When the issue is whether increased economic productivity (as determined by the existing price structure) imposes environmental costs that exceed the benefits of the increased production, it is perverse and dangerous to decide that question by an analytical technique that pursues, as its sole goal, increased economic productivity" (1979, 180).

In a thoughtful critique of BCA and other "policy sciences," Laurence Tribe has touched on many of the preceding themes. His conclusions bring together several strands of the arguments developed in this section:

> The policy sciences' intellectual and social heritage in the classical economics of unfettered contract, consumer sovereignty, and perfect markets . . . inclines them . . . toward the exaltation of utilitarian and self-interested individualism, efficiency, and maximized production as against distributive ends, procedural and historical principles, and the values (often nonmonetizable, discontinuous, and of complex structure) associated with personal rights, public goods and communitarian and ecological goals (Tribe 1973, 42).

INACCURATE VALUATION OF BENEFITS AND COSTS

Another major line of criticism directed at BCA is that, even within its narrow focus on economic efficiency, BCA cannot validly quantify benefits and costs: Some important types of benefits cannot be accurately measured or meaningfully quantified; BCA's quantitative approach is inherently biased against less tangible—but not necessarily less important—consequences; and the theoretical framework that is used to justify its reliance on market-based prices as indicators of economic welfare is deeply flawed. It follows that BCA's numerical results are not a useful guide to decision-making.

Imprecise Measurement of Intangible Effects

Some critics of BCA have no principled objection to attempts to measure intangible benefits and costs but argue that these attempts have in practice produced inaccurate and misleading numbers and can be expected to continue to do so. Given the present state of the art, they contend, estimates of a wide range of environmental, safety, and health effects simply cannot be calculated with sufficient confidence and precision to provide a reasonable basis for informed and responsible public choice.

Perhaps the most notorious example of this is the attempts to calculate a value for saving a human life. There is continuing debate about the proper approach to calculating such a value. The "discounted future earnings" approach attempts to measure the value of the future consumption that would be made possible by an individual's productive employment during the rest of his or her life. While this approach may be the easiest to implement and seems to be the most widely used in practice, it is inconsistent with general BCA methodology by not being based individual willingness to pay, and it has the unattractive (not to say obscene) consequence of valuing the lives of women less than those of men, valuing the lives of blacks less than those of whites, valuing the lives of older people less than those of younger people, and valuing at zero the lives of those who are retired or are too severely handicapped for paid employment.

An alternative approach to the valuation of saving a life is to reformulate the problem in terms of the value of reducing the probability of death from a specific cause—and to investigate what individuals themselves are willing to pay for reducing the chances of their own death. But determining these values through interviews is subject to all of the problems inherent to the interview approach in general, including strategic answering, poorly considered answers to hypothetical questions, and a general inability to understand and deal appropriately with small probabilities. And determining these values by examining existing market premiums for dangerous work is subject to problems of imperfect information by workers, lack of free choice in the sense of lack of opportunities for safer employment, and self-selection by risk-preferrers for risky jobs.

Neither method is able to incorporate the value of saving a life, or lowering the risk of death, to people other than the person saved. And yet almost every person has relatives and friends who would experience loss on that person's death (and thus be willing to pay some positive amount to prevent that death), and most people would be willing to pay something to know that the lives of unknown strangers were being saved.

The actual state of life valuation in BCA is indicated by some of the findings reported in John D. Graham and James W. Vaupel's recent survey of empirical estimates in this area:

> Surveys of expressed willingness-to-pay for small reductions in the probability of death have yielded values of a life from $500,000 to $8 million (in 1978 dollars). Nine recent labor market studies of wage premiums have produced a somewhat narrower range of values spread roughly evenly from $300,000 to $3.5 million.... [In a set of 24] benefit-cost analyses that explicitly assigned dollar values to lives saved ... 15 used a foregone-earnings value, 7 used a willingness-to-pay value, and 2 used values that were claimed to be consistent with both ... approaches. Four of these analyses used ranges of values; the other 20 picked point estimates ranging from $55,000 to $7 million.... Only 7 of the 24 benefit-cost studies, however, contain any sensitivity analysis at all.... Beyond this, most of the studies are afflicted with a variety of sins of omission and commission (1983, 177).

While the problem may be most extreme for the valuation of human lives, there are similar difficulties for a wide range of benefits and costs, particularly in the environmental, health, and safety areas. A review of three ambitious benefit-cost analyses that were undertaken by the Environmental Protection Agency in response to Executive Order 12291 concluded that "despite the substantial effort involved in these [BCAs], they are not helpful for regulatory decision-making or policy formulation.... the fundamental problem remains the impossibility of applying benefit-cost techniques in areas for which the most critical benefits still cannot be calculated" (Grubb, Whittington, and Humphries 1984, 145, 148).

Regulatory costs often consist primarily of compliance costs—that is, the cost to producers of reducing emissions to a specified level or the cost to employers of meeting a specified physical standard for workplace health or safety. These costs are not, strictly speaking, intangible, but often the only source of information about them is the producers and employers who would be forced to bear them. These firms have a strong incentive to provide information that will make costs appear high and to withhold information that will make costs look low. Another source of upward bias in compliance cost estimates is the neglect of the "technology-forcing" role of new regulations: Even standards that might in fact be quite difficult to meet with existing technology may lead to the development of new technology that enables the standards to be met at substantially lower cost (Ashford 1981, 130-31). For example, a review of the costs to industry to achieving compliance with OSHA's vinyl chloride standard indicated that these costs were only 7 percent of prospective industry estimates ($127 million rather than $1.91 billion), largely because of technological innovation (Connerton and MacCarthy 1982, 19-20; for an account claiming an even more dramatic divergence of prospective and retrospective estimates in this case, see Green and Waitzman 1979, 201-02). In addition, there is "emerging evidence that benefits can also arise from regulation-induced technological change" (Ashford et al. 1980, 13).

A congressional committee concluded after its study of the use of BCA in the areas of health, safety, and environmental regulation that "When quantification cannot be achieved with a large degree of confidence in its accuracy ... the role of BCA must be eliminated or reduced" (U.S. House 1976, 555). Some critics have suggested that a far superior procedure would be first to decide, by an appropriate means, on the goal to be achieved and then to use *cost-effectiveness* analysis to compare the costs of alternative ways of achieving this goal; in this way, the necessity to directly compare benefits and costs in terms of a common unit can be avoided—although it must be noted that this alternative approach will work only if there is just a single benefit for which quantitative assessment is so difficult (see, e.g., Baram 1980, 524; 1981, 127-28).

Overemphasis on Readily Measurable Consequences

If including unreliable estimates of hard-to-quantify effects leads to distorted and unreliable results, what happens when those effects are (as is often the case) omitted? The critic's answer can be expressed very simply: The effect of a quantitative analysis is to upgrade the influence in the outcome-determination process of those consequences that can be quantified—and therefore to slight the importance of the intangible, harder-to-measure aspects of the problem under review. (This criticism is similar to that previously directed against appended discussions of distributional effects.)

Both busy decision-makers and popularizing journalists welcome the specificity of a single summary number. Regardless of how carefully the introduction, textual discussion, or concluding section of a BCA may emphasize the importance of intangible factors that were omitted from its quantitative analysis, readers and writers in a hurry tend to focus on "the bottom line"—that is, in this case, on the single number that best summarizes whether a specific proposal should be adopted or, more generally, its ranking relative to alternative proposals. A congressional committee agreed with the expert witness who testified that "There is a kind of Gresham's Law of decision-making: quantified effects tend to dominate consideration, even if the unquantified effects are believed to be more important." The committee concluded that "Whenever some quantification is done—no matter how speculative or limited—the number tends to get into the public domain and the qualifications tend to get forgotten.... The number is the thing" (U.S. House 1980, 7, 10).

An editorial in the *American Journal of Public Health* noted that because "it is easiest to draw policy conclusions from simple comparisons," benefit-cost analysts "often collapse numerous health benefits into an aggregate measure, discard effects whose magnitude is not well understood, and emphasize effects more readily expressed in dollars over those without a clear market value" (Boden 1979, 1210). Moreover, a study prepared for the U.S. Senate Committee on Government Operations found that "Even those who profess to be motivated by non-monetary values and concerns exhibit a tendency to emphasize the quantitative" (Ashford 1980, 20). Because there is no reason to believe that more readily measurable consequences are also more important, this bias toward the tangible will tend to produce decisions with a bias that is both systematic and serious.

Taken together, this subsection and the last seem to present BCA's proponents with a "damned if you do and damned if you don't" argument concerning BCA's treatment of intangibles. Omitting them to focus on more readily quantifiable consequences is criticized because they are important and should be fully taken into account; including them in the quantitative analysis is criticized because there is no way to quantify them with reasonable accuracy. This is precisely the point that the critics wish to make: When intangibles are an important part of the effects of the proposals under review, BCA is unable to offer helpful and accurate guidance to decision-makers. Their conclusion is not that BCA should be done differently, but rather that it should not be done at all in such circumstances—that public policy evaluation and decision-making should proceed on other grounds.

Flawed Theoretical Foundations and Unreliable Estimates

As a field of applied welfare economics, BCA is based on theoretical welfare economics. In particular, its use of market-based prices to measure costs and benefits and its acceptance of individual willingness to pay as a standard for valuation derive their justification from this underlying theory. Serious deficiencies in this foundation raise serious doubts about the validity of the superstructures of applied welfare economics, including BCA, that have been erected on it.

This is not the place to present a general survey of the failings of theoretical welfare economics as a guide to public policy making.[6] But it is appropriate to note both that the failings are serious—Graaff has remarked that "there is no doubt that if the usefulness of CBA were to be judged solely by the validity of its logical structure it would fail miserably" (1975, 243)—and that they have had almost no effect on the spreading use of BCA. The proponents and practitioners of BCA have simply ignored the criticisms of its theoretical foundations and have gone on with their applications of the technique. As Pearce and Nash observe, "One of the most interesting features of the history of CBA is that it secured its most significant development and advance at a time when the welfare economics on which it was based had come under increasing critical scrutiny.... In the eyes of many economists in the 1950s the problems were held to be so severe... that welfare economics was truly dead as a discipline with practical application" (1981, 2).[7]

I shall, however, examine two particular theoretical issues that are serious enough to cast doubt on the validity of the conclusions reached by applications of BCA to public policy problems: the existence of significant market failures and the dependence of willingness to pay on the existing distribution of income.[8] BCA's techniques for estimating benefits and costs are based on the use of market information, even for valuing consequences that are not themselves marketed commodities. The theoretical justification for this practice lies in the argument of theoretical welfare economics that — when a number of assumptions are fulfilled so that there is no "market failure" — competitive markets will operate to establish prices that will bring about a situation from which it is impossible for any individual to increase his or her welfare without making at least one other individual worse off. In other words, when public and private decision-makers act on the basis of competitively determined market prices, the economy will (as if guided by Adam Smith's "invisible hand") produce Pareto optimal outcomes — that is, outcomes to which no other possible outcomes are Pareto superior.

However, the assumptions that guarantee the absence of market failure are both strong and unrealistic. They include perfect information, lack of monopoly power, and absence of externalities. When these assumptions are not satisfied, the theoretical basis for ascribing optimality properties to market prices no longer exists. This point is particularly significant because government expenditures and regulatory activities are — according to welfare economics — justified precisely in those cases where there is market failure. Thus BCA, which relies on market prices (and other market-generated information) in order to value benefits and costs, is employed in exactly those situations where theoretical welfare economics itself asserts that these prices do not have optimality properties. This provides good reason to be skeptical of the results when BCA is applied to proposed expenditures or regulations.

An important but much-ignored portion of the literature of theoretical welfare economics—the "theory of the second best," first rigorously established by R.G. Lipsey and Kelvin Lancaster (1956-57)—demonstrates that when one or more of the assumptions necessary to prevent market failure are violated somewhere in the economy, then applying the criteria of theoretical welfare economics elsewhere in the economy will not necessarily bring about increased welfare. As summarized by a leading text in microeconomic theory, the theory of the second best "has important implications for welfare economics, since it means that, if some parts of the economy are misbehaving in the sense that they are not fulfilling the conditions [necessary for Pareto optimality], there is no reason to believe that welfare would be greater if other parts of the economy were to be convinced (or forced) to fulfill these conditions" (Mansfield 1982, 462). The theory of the second best suggests the need for a comprehensive approach to improving resource allocation throughout the economy. BCA is, however, an analytical tool designed for use in connection with the piecemeal approaches involved in individual expenditure and regulatory proposals. Accordingly, the theory of the second best implies that BCA's reliance on market-derived information will lead to distorted results.

Another major reason for skepticism concerning the optimality properties of the results of BCA calculations follows from the facts that both market prices and the WTPs of individuals depend on the distribution of income and wealth and that there is general agreement that the present distribution is not optimal. Two specific implications of the dependence of benefit and cost estimates on income and wealth distribution are worth noting briefly.

The first of these, the possibility of "reversals," was originally pointed out in another well-known but generally dismissed contribution to the literature of theoretical welfare economics (Scitovsky 1941; for a more recent explanation, emphasizing the significance for BCA, see Graaff 1975). Consider a project that would result in a change from economic situation A to situation B. It is possible both that this change could meet the potential Pareto improvement criterion, in that the gains of the gainers exceed the losses to the losers, *and*, once situation B was reached, that a change from B back to situation A could also satisfy the PPIC. Such a reversal is possible because the evaluation of each of these changes takes place at the prices prevailing in its initial situation, and the change in question could redistribute income among people with differing preferences in a way that results in changed prices. Graaff maintains that although "the implications for cost-benefit analysis are quite devastating . . . , cost-benefit practitioners are often reluctant to take the idea of reversals seriously." He specifically quotes Mishan's textbook's dismissal of reversals as merely a "disconcerting theoretical possibility" and characterizes it as "no more than an exercise in wishful thinking" (1975, 238–39; Graaff cites the passages of the 1972 edition of Mishan's text that correspond to Mishan 1982a, 165–68).

An additional problem is created by the dependence of willingness to pay—BCA's agreed-on conceptual standard for valuing benefits and costs—on ability to pay, which in turn depends on the distribution of income and wealth. For relatively small and frequently purchased items the effect of unequal abilities to pay is not an important consideration. In the case of milk or blue jeans, people will adjust their level of purchases so that, at the margin, their willingness to pay is approximately equal to the market price. But for large consequences, especially those that are not marketed, willingness to pay will be constrained by ability to pay. As a result, the values estimated for such important items as reducing the probability of death, saving a neighborhood or a rural area from demolition and development, or obtaining a good education for one's children will tend to be systematically underestimated to the extent that the individuals affected (or, more precisely, whose WTP is measured) have low ability to pay. In this way, BCA's reliance on willingness to pay distorts the values that applied welfare economics is able to assign to benefits and costs.

FLAWED AND COSTLY IMPLEMENTATION

The criticisms of BCA in the preceding three sections are primarily directed at the "textbook ideal"—that is, the criticisms have been based on the assumption that BCAs would be carried out in accordance with the principles and practical guidelines contained in recent textbooks written by BCA proponents. The final set of criticisms concerns the extent to which the implementation of BCA—despite good-faith attempts—falls short of this ideal.

Problems of Coordination

One of the significant claims made in support of increased use of BCA is that it will bring about improved resource allocation. Whatever the flaws in valuing the lives that might be saved by government spending or regulation, a typical argument goes, it surely makes little sense to save lives through regulating the emissions of industry A at a cost of $5 million per life saved, while passing up opportunities to save lives through imposing more stringent emission control standards on industry B, where lives can be saved at a cost of only $600,000 each. Or if water resource projects are evaluated using a discount rate of x percent while educational projects are evaluated using a lower discount rate of y percent, there will be a tendency to spend too much on education and too little on water resources. In short, much of the potential gain from applications of BCA can be expected to result from the use of common valuations and parameters in calculating the net benefits from proposed spending and regulatory programs. The use of such common values is advocated by a number of the texts reviewed in Chapter 2.

In practice, however, there is a woeful lack of coordination and consistency among applications of BCA even within a single agency or applications area, to say nothing of throughout the federal government. The previously cited study of life valuation by Graham and Vaupel (1983) shows a bewildering diversity of methods, assumptions, and results contained in the twenty-four BCA's reviewed. Michael Baram's study of regulatory applications of BCA in accordance with the mandate of Jimmy Carter's Executive Order 12044 emphasized this problem with respect to BCAs done by the Environmental Protection Agency—"without meaningful congressional or agency guidance on critical methodological issues" (1980, 499)—and by the Council on Wage and Price Stability (COWPS) in the Office of the President:

> COWPS lacks a uniform policy for dealing with many methodological limitations of cost-benefit analysis that it encounters when preparing regulatory analyses.... Each analyst selects a discount rate and estimates critical factors, such as the economic valuation of health and environmental benefits and the allocations of costs and benefits to different society sectors, without any meaningful guidelines.... a clear need exists [for] coordination of review functions and generic treatment of persistent methodological problems (Baram 1980, 510–11, 515).

Little if any improvement was found by a detailed review of the BCAs undertaken in the early 1980s in response to the mandate of Ronald Reagan's Executive Order 12291. The reviewer observed that although "the overall process of managing and coordinating the multitude of cost-benefit analyses prepared in different federal agencies is critical to E.O. 12291's objective of fostering efficient regulation," their research revealed that the Office of Management and Budget (OMB), the body responsible for providing central direction, failed to do so:

> OMB has not sent the agencies any detailed rules and procedures to ensure minimal consistency among [BCAs].... Not only did OMB fail to issue detailed instructions on methodological approaches, it also failed to issue information on "national parameters" necessary to ensure consistent evaluation. [OMB did specify use of] a 10% real rate of discount... [but] nothing was forthcoming from OMB on the value of life, the shadow value of labor or investment, macroeconomic conditions, population projections, or future relative prices for energy or raw materials.... The current situation is in some respects similar to the period in the 1940s, when different agencies and analysts conducted cost-benefit analyses without any central direction or guidance (Grubb, Whittington, and Humphries 1984, 130–32).

Widespread Failure to Meet Standards of Good Practice

Even if there were uniform standards or guidelines for the conduct of BCA, there are good reasons to doubt that BCAs actually will be carried out in accordance with them. Doing BCA well is complex and difficult, not a matter of merely following some set of cookbook-like formulas. Even the best BCAs manage their problems only by adopting heroic simplifying assumptions and ignoring large numbers of relevant consequences. The estimation of consumers' and producers' surpluses, for example, depends on having reliable estimates of the relevant market demand and supply curves, information that is often unavailable. A short catalog of areas where it is difficult for even honest and competent analysts to avoid going astray would include identifying consequences without either double-counting or inclusion of pecuniary effects; determining when the calculation of a shadow price to replace a market price is feasible and appropriate; judging when and how to adjust data that contains clear biases;

undertaking sensitivity analyses; and coping with limited and uncertain information.

These sorts of considerations are important because they support the argument that the many failings of BCA in practice cannot simply be dismissed by BCA proponents as the result of abuse, misuse, or incompetence by some practitioners. Insofar as BCA is being examined as a technique for practical implementation in the process of public policy decision-making, rather than as an abstract theoretical ideal, it is appropriate to take into account what one can realistically expect BCA in practice to be like. And the only realistic expectation, critics contend, is that issues of definition, measurement, estimation, and valuation will systematically be dealt with in a manner that is flawed and that will tend to produce distorted and unreliable results. A. Myrick Freeman reports that he learned from reviewing the state of the art of empirical estimation of air and water pollution control benefits "that many—if not most—of the studies on which national estimates were based were flawed conceptually and theoretically" (1979, xii). And two sympathetic observers concluded that "Even those who in principle favor analysis have to admit that analysis in practice is so devilishly demanding that the most diligent, intelligent, and well-intentioned practitioners often go astray" (Graham and Vaupel 1983, 177).

Implementation Costs May Exceed Benefits

The final point in this catalog of criticisms of BCA presents a paradox by asserting that the use of BCA would itself fail to pass a benefit-cost review. The paradox—that those who attack BCA appear to commend its use in evaluating the technique itself—may be resolved if the critics are interpreted as using the term *BCA* in two different ways: consciously using the same term as BCA proponents to give their claim the added force of irony, while substantively suggesting that attempts to utilize BCA on a large scale certainly have substantial budgetary and opportunity costs that should not be omitted from any assessment of their desirability. While this point may seem obvious once made, it is often not recognized, as both critics and proponents focus on the question of whether or not BCAs can be expected to provide unbiased, reliable quantitative guidance to decision-makers. Even if BCA were judged, on balance, to provide helpful information, however, there could still be grounds for concluding that the implementation of BCA involved too great a use of time, money, and other scarce resources to represent a positive net contribution to social, political, and economic welfare.

NOTES

1. Professor Junger's depth of feeling on this issue is indicated by the fact that he had earlier been moved to write the longest article I have ever encountered—333 pages!—to detail the failings of BCA (Junger 1976).
2. This "relative neglect of benefits" has been documented in some detail by Grubb, Whittington, and Humphries (1984, 136-38).
3. This is the position taken, for example, in a 1975 discussion of BCA by J. de V. Graaff, author of a classic critique of theoretical welfare economics (1967): "The cost-benefit analyst concerns himself only with the problem of efficiency. He leaves it to others to decide whether or not any resulting inequity is important enough to call for a correction. His job is done when he has assured them that, even if everyone were to be restored to his previous level of indifference, there would still be a surplus available for distribution" (1975, 235). And Ronald Reagan's Executive Order 12291 (sec. 2(b)) directs without qualification that "Regulatory action shall not be undertaken unless the potential benefits to society from the regulation outweigh the potential costs to society."
4. For example, several texts discuss the idea, apparently originating with Weisbrod (1968), that past legislative decisions could be examined to determine implicit weights, before concluding that the idea is interesting but not useful in practice. On the one hand, because legislatures are inconsistent, empirical studies have been unable to find consistent weights. On the other hand, if legislatures were always consistent and did make decisions actually incorporating their genuine distributional preferences, there would be no need for employing any analytical tool to help them do better.
5. Gramlich's remark in passing that workers would bear the costs in terms of fewer jobs and lower wages (1981, 216) is hardly convincing coming from an advocate of valuing benefits and costs on the basis of the expressed preferences of individuals—since it is workers and their representatives who are pushing for lower noise standards and employers and business-oriented regulators who oppose them.
6. The classic critical analyses of theoretical welfare economics from within mainstream economics are those of Little (1967), Graaff (1957), and Lipsey and Lancaster (1956-57).

7. An illuminating and candid account this process is provided by the 1981 Presidential Address to the Association of Environmental and Resource Economists by John Krutilla, one of the pioneers in the application of BCA in the field of water resources. Krutilla offers a clear nontechnical review of, in his words, "(1) the nature of the criticism advanced to justify the low esteem welfare economics was accorded [in the 1940s and 1950s], (2) the more or less weak formal response to the weight of theoretical criticism, and (3) the unaccountably robust growth of applied welfare economics in the face of severe theoretical criticism" (1981, 2).
8. Steve H. Hanke (1981) provides another serious criticism of BCA's reliance of the standard methodology of mainstream microeconomic theory. He demonstrates that in situations where project outputs are not sold (and/or inputs are not purchased) at market-clearing prices—which assures that they will go to (or come from) those who place greatest (least) dollar value on them—the use of conventional consumers' surplus measurements will yield inaccurate indicators of benefits (and/or costs).

4 IN DEFENSE OF BCA
Responses to Liberal Critics

Proponents of BCA concede that many of the points made by BCA's liberal critics are well taken. They acknowledge that advocates of BCA sometimes oversell its potential and ignore its limitations. They do not deny that proper implementation of BCA is difficult. And they admit that the historical record of BCA applications merits serious criticism. Nevertheless, they argue that there are three basic reasons why the preceding liberal criticisms fail to provide a legitimate, persuasive case against BCA: Many of the criticisms compare BCA to an imaginary ideal way of evaluating proposed public policies rather than to the actual alternatives to use of BCA; many of the criticisms are based on a misunderstanding of the limited role that proponents envision for BCA; and many of the criticisms are of abuses and misuses rather than of the technique itself. In short, BCA's defenders contend that when it is properly understood, honestly and competently applied, and correctly interpreted, BCA can make an important contribution to improved public policy in the areas of public expenditure and regulatory policy.

This chapter reviews the responses of BCA proponents to their critics. Although not organized as a point-by-point rebuttal of the points made in Chapter 3, it responds to all of those criticisms. Like the earlier case against BCA, this chapter's defense is a synthesis of arguments made by numerous writers, no one of whom has made all of the points included here.[1]

THE BOTTOM LINE: LACK OF A BETTER ALTERNATIVE

Mainstream economists have been conditioned to think in terms of existing alternatives. In this respect, they are like the University of Chicago freshman who went home for Thanksgiving and, when a former high school chum asked "How are you doing?" responded "Relative to what?" Indeed, mainstream microeconomics essentially *is* the analysis of maximizing behavior by households and firms confronted with alternative possibilities for buying and selling. It is, therefore, entirely natural that economists should insist that BCA itself be evaluated and judged in relation to its alternatives. Although they may acknowledge that BCA has many serious defects, most economists support its continued use in the belief that no feasible alternative is superior.

This pattern was well established by the time of Prest and Turvey's classic survey article whose concluding section first summarized "a formidable range of difficulties which might give the appearance of being a technical if not an actual knockout" but then immediately asserted that "before we throw in the towel we have to ask some further questions. First of all, is there a better alternative?" (1965, 73).

Examples of this point could be multiplied almost without limit for, as Peter Self has observed, "Invariably when CBA is under discussion, someone will say: conceding all the snags, what better or more rational way of making a public decision is there?" (1977, 196). One of the strongest and most succinct statements was offered in an early text by Ajit K. Dasgupta and D.W. Pearce: "Criticisms of cost-benefit analysis are only admissible if they can demonstrate that alternative prescriptive procedures are in some way superior" (1972, 16). Gramlich concludes a survey of serious problems involved in benefit measurement by enjoining "the discouraged evaluator [to] always remember that there is not much in the way of an alternative. . . . Policy decisions must be made. If they are not made on the basis of objective analysis that makes the best possible estimates under the circumstances, they will be made on some other even more arbitrary and inconsistent basis" (1981, 78). Finally, in what is probably the single most widely cited defense of BCA, Alan Williams places central importance on this line of argument:

Unfortunately, the valid criticisms are applicable *a fortiori* to the only alternative techniques of analysis.... I ask once more for suggestions as to a practical alternative.... Even if all of [one critic's] strictures on BCA were valid, however, the sad thing is that he has nothing to offer in its place.... In contemplating CBA, I prefer the philosophy embodied in the answer Maurice Chevalier is alleged to have given to an interviewer who asked him how he viewed old age: "Well, there is quite a lot wrong with it, but it isn't so bad when you consider the alternative" (1972, 537, 556–58).

Although some defenders of BCA are content to rest their case here, most attempt to characterize the nature of the inferior alternatives that they believe would prevail in place of continued (or expanded) use of BCA. They emphasize two contrasts between BCA and these hypothesized alternatives. The first is that the formalized, explicit nature of BCA increases the extent to which decision-makers can be held accountable for their decisions and reduces the effect of behind-the-scenes personal, bureaucratic, or political factors. With respect to the distributional consequences of regulatory decisions influenced by BCA, for example, Robert Crandall has argued that "no one should be deluded into thinking that those who manage regulatory decisions today without the guidance of formal cost-benefit analysis... are in the process of moving resources from rich to poor. When political considerations guide the regulation of industry, the poor are not likely to be heavily represented" (1981, 105).

The second contrast is between the systematic analytic framework provided by BCA and arbitrary, impressionistic, ad hoc, or other ill-informed approaches to decision-making. When decision problems are approached rationally and systematically, when attempts are made to identify all of the consequences of the alternatives under review and to quantify the value of these effects as much as can reasonably be done, it is much more likely that no important features of a problem will be overlooked. Trade-offs between different types of consequences will still be implicit in the resulting decisions. But without the discipline and insights offered by the BCA approach, these implicit trade-off rates are likely to be inconsistent both with each other and with economic efficiency.

It is in this general context that BCA's defenders deal with the specific criticisms of its underlying theoretical foundations. The theoretical soundness of the criticisms is acknowledged, but their practical relevance is denied. Unless and until a satisfactory replacement is found, the concepts and techniques of applied welfare economics are regarded as providing the only game in town. Therefore is is necessary to make compromises with complete theoretical purity. In this regard, the conclusions reached by one of theoretical welfare economics' sharpest critics, J. de V. Graaff, deserve special attention. I noted earlier Graaff's contention that "There is no doubt that if the usefulness of cost-benefit analysis were to be judged solely by the validity of its logical structure, it would fail miserably." However, the quoted passage continues in quite a different vein:

> But when asked whether or not, in the view of the man in the street, cost-benefit analysis is likely to make a more sensible selection of projects than conventional profit-and-loss accounting, one must give a more cautious answer. At least it takes a wider view and tries to bring to account intangibles and externalities which we all know to be important.... And if one ... asks if cost-benefit analysis can aid administrative decisions in the public sector, the answer must be that it can. The mere fact that costs and benefits are enumerated and that some attempt is made at evaluating them must lead to more informed appraisal, better appreciation of wide-ranging indirect effects and greater sensitivity to public opinion. In short, whether you believe the result or not, you always know more about a project when you have done an analysis (1975, 243).

In sum, proponents of BCA contend that an alternative would almost by definition be less visible, less systematic, less rational, more arbitrary, and more political. They argue that when BCA is compared to the less formal and explicit decision-making procedures that seem to be the only realistic alternatives, rather than to some unattainable abstract ideal that would always identify and produce the optimal result, BCA looks good.

UNDERSTANDING BCA'S LIMITED ROLE

BCA's defenders respond to many of the sharpest criticisms of BCA by arguing that the charges are based on misunderstandings of its relatively modest purpose. In particular, they contend that BCA is not intended to determine decisions or to be used to the exclusion of other approaches, but rather that it is intended to provide one useful input into decision-making. Advocates of BCA deny any implication that public policy decisions should be based solely on the criterion of economic efficiency; and they agree that those consequences of a policy that cannot be quantified and evaluated in monetary terms should nonetheless be taken into account in choosing among alternative proposals. While some proponents of BCA have at times ignored its limitations, sought to have it play an inappropriately large role in determining decisions, or oversold its value, these actions are not consistent with the true principles of BCA. The critics have merely succeeded in tearing apart a straw man, albeit one that some practitioners of BCA helped them to construct.

The first and most important point made in this regard is that BCA is merely one input in the outcome-determination process. The role of BCA is to provide better information to decision-makers, to encourage systematic thought about alternatives, consequences, and values, and to increase the explicitness of the evaluative process and the accountability of those who actually make decisions. Decision-makers must still use their judgment to combine the economic efficiency results of BCA with the results of evaluations according to other relevant standards—whether these standards are concerned with ethics, jurisprudence, politics, distributional justice, or ecology. Quantitative information provided by BCA constitutes a highly useful input into the process of balancing, or trading-off, among different types of objectives—a necessary process whenever there is no dominant alternative that is best with respect to each individual standard.

Similarly, proponents of BCA point out that they do not seek to replace the "political process" with "technocratic rationality." They seek instead to increase rational inputs into the decision-making process, in the form of more and better information concerning the consequences of alternative choices. In any case, the current problem is not to keep rationality from pushing politics aside, but to get rationality into its rightful place. Whatever one believes about the proper balance, there are strong grounds for believing that rationality now plays too small a role in shaping public policy. A continuation or expansion of BCA is thus a move in the right direction; only if and when this move has proceeded substantially further than it has to date will the debate about undermining the political process become relevant to current practices.[2]

A related point made by defenders of BCA is that those who have undertaken BCAs have a particularly keen sense of the limits on measuring and quantitatively evaluating important types of benefits and costs. Good analysts recognize these limits and the consequent limits of BCA itself in problems where such nonquantifiable consequences are the major part of the problem. However, the fact that some things cannot be accurately measured or appropriately evaluated in monetary terms does not imply that nothing should be. Careful and creative analysts can carry out appropriate quantification, and even imperfect quantification may be better than none as long as the analyst is explicit about what has been done. Furthermore, the defenders of BCA argue that it is not inevitable that quantifiable benefits and costs will be given disproportionate weight in reaching decisions. With awareness of the potential for this to happen, decision-makers can avoid overemphasizing the quantifiable aspects of a problem. When the genuine limits to quantification are ignored, or when the nonquantitative aspects of an issue are pushed aside in the decision-making process, that is bad practice and should be criticized by BCA critics and proponents alike.

With respect to environmental consequences in particular, defenders point out that the *Principles and Standards* for evaluation of water resources projects, promulgated by the U.S. Water Resources Council (1973), require that in addition to the traditional calculation of economic costs and benefits, a project evaluation must separately analyze environmental effects (and, where they are important, regional economic effects and impacts on social well-being as well). Executive branch decision-makers may recommend projects, but they must also submit the information on the different categories of consequences to the Congress—enabling it, too, to make political judgments on the appropriate trade-offs among competing goals. Grubb, Whittington, and Humphries's previously cited review of the implementation of Reagan's Executive Order 12291 stresses the importance of the trend toward multiple-objective approaches during the 1970s. They argue that E.O. 12291's mandated sole reliance on BCA's calculation of net economic benefits represents a big step backward: "In ignoring the development of multiobjective approaches, E.O. 12291 is perhaps twenty years out of date and ignores the fact that previous attempts to impose economic efficiency as the single policy objective have been short-lived" (1984, 124-25, 157).

For all of the reasons reviewed here, BCA's defenders argue that BCA should be understood and accepted, together with its limitations, as a valuable aid to the process of formulating public policy. It should not be rejected for failing to be a complete and self-contained methodology for determining public policy choices. I shall give the last word on this matter to Baruch Fischhoff, who has written critically about BCA, but who nevertheless concludes that "the benefits of cost-benefit analysis can substantially outweigh the costs [when it is] properly done and used." Fischhoff emphasizes the importance

> for analysts themselves to point out the limits of their craft. ... A public that recognizes these limits will turn to the analyst not for ironclad solutions to problems, but for otherwise unobtainable understanding of their intracacies. If the analysts' best efforts at quantification prove inadequate this would be seen as a sign, not of failure but of the fact that some questions of quality cannot be incorporated into analyses, but must be studied in their own right and combined with the insights produced by cost-benefit studies (1977, 194-96).

EXPOSING MISUSE AND ABUSE OF BCA

Alan Williams, an articulate and persuasive defender of BCA, has written that "Cost-benefit analysis is one of the techniques most prone to misunderstanding and misapplication in the hands of the uninitiated (not to mention the unscrupulous!)" (1972, 536). This observation is certainly consistent with the many instances of misuse and even intentional abuse of BCA identified above. But it does not provide valid grounds for opposing the application of BCA to aid public sector decision-makers. Proponents insist that such abuse and misuse is neither inevitable because of some inherent aspect of BCA itself nor specific to BCA as opposed to alternative approaches to evaluating proposed public policies. They also argue that BCA's very nature as a formal, explicit analytical technique facilitates exposing abuse and misuse and provides a means of increasing the accountability of analysts and decision-makers.

BCA forces the advocates of a particular course of action to go beyond empty rhetoric and vague appeals to the promotion of public welfare. By making assumptions explicit and open to critical scrutiny, BCA provides a means of making decision-makers more responsible, and holding analysts more accountable, than does a less formal method. In spite of the inevitable attempts by proponents of particular proposals to use BCA in abusive and distorted ways in support of their favored alternatives, BCA can contribute importantly to promoting the public interest relative to special interests.

Clarity about assumptions and methods reduces the opportunity for decision-makers and analysts to "tilt" the analysis in a direction favorable to their own narrow interests or those of a favored interest group.

In a pluralistic political process, characterized by divergent interests and differing positions, BCA can play a useful role even though it is not a neutral or objective way of resolving such differences (there is no such thing). Just as legal advocates competing in a juridicial setting can provide a means to aid in the discovery of truth and justice even though each individual advocate seeks to promote only his or her own side of a case, so too can use of BCA methodology by contending advocates assist in discovery of what alternative is most in the public interest. This use of BCA can introduce greater rationality into an adversary, pluralistic political process and thereby partially offset the otherwise too large role of "politics" in the negative, narrow meaning of the term.

The best historical example of how BCA can operate to promote the general public interest over narrow special interests is provided by its role in the area of water resources development, the first area of significant BCA applications. The BCA paradigm as an element of applied welfare economics took shape as a result of attempts to assert the national interest in an area traditionally dominated by political support for projects from the regions that would benefit and by the bureaucracies that would be in charge of building them—the U.S. Army's Corps of Engineers (the Corps) and the Interior Department's Bureau of Reclamation (BuRec). As noted in Chapter 2, the Bureau of the Budget played a key role in the processes of encouraging consistent procedures, promoting evaluation of benefits and costs from the viewpoint of the entire nation, and monitoring the attempts of the Corps and the BuRec to tilt BCA studies in their preferred direction. The argument here is that the "real BCA" was that being used for these ends by the Bureau of the Budget and its allies, not that being conducted by the Corps and the BuRec.

Certainly, the success of this effort has been, and continues to be, limited, as those agencies and others continue to distort BCA for their own ends—but the relevant question is, How are things different from what would have happened in the absence of BCA? While it is impossible to be sure of any conclusion based on a counterfactual historical premise, an examination of the historical record indicates that BCA has played a role in promoting an outcome of which liberals would generally approve: reducing the number of ill-conceived pork-barrel water resources projects adopted. Robert Dorfman, closely involved in the effort to improve BCA in the water resources area, has concluded that "it is beyond doubt that many thousands of projects were scrubbed and many more were improved because of the necessity of showing that the benefits of each project were great enough to justify the cost, in some sense" (1978, 270). Aaron Wildavsky, another student of BCA, has also emphasized the importance of BCA "in getting rid of the worst projects. Avoiding the worst where one can't get the best is no small accomplishment" (1966, 380). A more recent effort to apply centralized BCA in an effort to stop water projects ill-advised from the point of view of the economic welfare of the nation as a whole—Jimmy Carter's attempt to use BCA analyses as part of an attack on a sizable number of pending water projects in the late 1970s—was notably unsuccessful, but it indicates an important use of BCA on the "public interest" side of this issue. Thus, BCA proponents argue, the badly flawed BCAs done by the Corps and the BuRec should not be taken as evidence of the bias of BCA toward legitimizing weak proposals. Rather, these flawed analyses have regularly provided critics of those proposals with opportunities to make damning arguments against their authorization—opportunities that would not have been available in the absence of the requirement that each proposed project be justified by an explicit BCA (*Business Week* 1979).

The same point has been made in the context of the application of BCA to regulatory policy. While there can be little doubt that the Reagan administration attempted to make use of BCA in its campaign to weaken and reduce health, safety, and environmental regulation, there is considerable basis for doubting that BCA was in fact an effective vehicle for promoting this objective. Grubb, Whittington, and Humphries have observed that "Of course, benefit-cost analysis is inescapably susceptible to political manipulation; but as an analytic technique it does have its own rules and standards and thus provides a method for opponents of deregulation to object legitimately to political decisions" (1984, 158). Fischhoff has emphasized a similar point by arguing that "Properly done and used, [BCA] can open up the business of technology assessment and regulation to the public. It forces government and industry to consider societal costs and benefits in their planning and to do so in a way that allows the public to criticize their analyses" (1977, 194).

A similar line of defense responds to criticism of BCA's poor implementation. Although it is undeniably difficult to implement BCA well on a broad scale, there is no obvious reason why it cannot be done. For example, the criticism that the Office of Management and Budget has not offered adequate guidelines to bring about consistent, high-quality applications of BCA throughout the federal government in response to Executive Order 12291 is well taken; but the most sensible response would seem to be a call for appropriate central guidance—not a conclusion that the entire effort should therefore be abandoned. Movements in the direction of more central coordination and direction were in fact being made until the 1980s A BCA manual could certainly be prepared and competent treatment of a number of problems in accordance with procedures and guidelines in the manual could be insisted upon—although it is unrealistic to expect generally good practice in the absence of guidance and pressures from above.

In short, proponents of BCA argue that the BCA pardigm includes standards and criteria for good analyses; that abuses and misuses of BCA are just that, and should be criticized and avoided; that the fact that BCA often is abused does not mean that it need be; and that BCA can and should be done honestly. Sugden and Williams provide a good summary statement of the core of this argument:

> The more explicit a decision-maker is called upon to be in justifying his decisions, the more difficult it is for him to act against the interests of the people to whom he is accountable. . . . In a sense, cost-benefit analysis carries a stage further the function of traditional financial accounting. The obligation on the part of privately owned firms and public agencies to keep financial accounts is a very effective deterrent against embezzlement and fraud by managers, public officials, and politicians. The obligation to justify public decisions within the framework of cost-benefit analysis discourages a much subtler form of abuse of responsibility—that of taking decisions on behalf of others by using criteria that these others would not approve (Sugden and Williams 1978, 239-40).

NOTES

1. This defense was able to draw very little from the BCA texts reviewed in Chapter 2—because these texts have very little to say about criticisms of BCA. For the most part, they do not acknowledge the possible existence of

criticisms of BCA that deserve to be taken seriously; on the few occasions when criticisms are noted, they are dismissed quickly and complacently (Halvorsen and Ruby 1981, 8–9; Pearce 1983, ch. 1; Pearce and Nash 1981, 12–20). The only significant exception to this generalization is an essay by Alan Williams that offers an extended defense of BCA against three strands of criticism (1972; included in Haveman and Margolis 1983)

2. Congressional testimony by Charles L. Schultze when he was director of the U.S. Bureau of the Budget offers the perspective of one frustrated partisan of greater rationality in the formulation of public policy:

> On the basis of my experience in government . . . this fear of the statisticians and analysts taking over ranks about 28th on my list of fears, perhaps just below my fear of being eaten alive by piranhas. I have many fears of government, but this is not one of them (quoted in Hinrichs and Taylor 1969, 6).

5 EVALUATING THE BCA DEBATE

An openminded reader of the arguments presented in the previous two chapters must recognize that BCA's critics and proponents both make many valid points and that no simple judgment is possible. BCA is neither wholly good nor wholly bad. Any reasonable conclusion as to its worth will be qualified, and grounds for further discussion will inevitably remain. Unless someone is willing to argue that BCA should be used in every possible instance of public decisionmaking, it must be admitted that alternatives are in at least some cases superior. And it then becomes reasonable to inquire as to what set of public policy issues are properly subject to BCA—rather than to seek any overall positive or negative verdict on BCA in the abstract. Recognizing all of these caveats, this chapter nevertheless offers some general conclusions about the outcome of the BCA debate.

In so doing, I will rely on the definition of BCA presented in Chapter 2, in particular the understanding of BCA as

> a formal procedure for comparing the costs and benefits of alternative policies [that] differs from more informal comparisons of costs and benefits in two principal ways. First, the terms *cost* and *benefit* are defined more narrowly than in general English usage. Second, the formal procedure and basis of comparison rely on specialized techniques and principles, most of which are derived from economic theory (Peskin and Seskin 1975, 1).

As understood here, BCA produces a single quantitative measure of net benefits (i.e., benefits minus costs) expressed in monetary terms. This summary measure, accompanied by descriptive analysis of other consequences not included in its quantitative valuation, is intended to provide one important input into the decision-making process rather than to determine the outcome of that process. That is, BCA as I shall evaluate it must be clearly recognized as a decision-making *tool* as opposed to a decision-making *rule* (a distinction emphasized by Ashford 1979, 76).

Assessing BCA, so understood, is both more difficult and more relevant a task than would be required for other conceptions of BCA that are sometimes encountered. If, on the one hand, BCA is taken to mean no more than an approach to evaluating alternatives that attempts systematically to identify and consider all positive and negative consequences (as its proponents sometimes disingenuously suggest), then who could find any of the criticisms of Chapter 3 persuasive against it? On the other hand, if BCA is interpreted as a procedure for determining policy decisions solely on the basis of the results of formal, quantitative analysis (as its critics sometimes suggest), then who could seriously defend its use in the formulation of public policy? The interpretation of BCA offered in this book, however, provides a subject for serious consideration, one about which reasonable and informed people can disagree and that is worthy of the attention it is receiving here.

THE POSITIVE POTENTIAL OF BCA

A first major conclusion from the BCA debate is that BCA is, in many instances, an appropriate and useful tool capable of improving public sector decisions. To be sure, BCA in practice has not always had this effect in the past, and it will not always be helpful in future applications. To have a generally positive effect on the determination of public sector outcomes, BCA must be understood and used as a means of aiding decision-makers rather than as a way to justify choices already made on other grounds, to delay the decision-making process, or to substitute technical analysis for politically responsible judgments.

The great potential benefit from the use of BCA is its ability to provide increased understanding of the consequences of proposed public policies. When the analysis is done properly—always a major qualification—those responsible for making decisions find their task the more manageable (but still far from trivial) one of integrating a summary measure of net benefits with other aspects of the decision-problem that are not commensurable with the quantifiable economic effects. The value of BCA will vary inversely with the importance of these incommensurable aspects in the case at hand, and BCA will in fact be inapplicable in cases where such factors are dominant. Nevertheless, there is a broad class of decision-problems where economic effects are important enough to warrant careful, formal, quantitative analysis.

The quantitative results provided by BCA can be expected to contribute to promotion of the public interest in better decisions in two major ways. First, they furnish helpful information for the decision-makers themselves. Less obviously, they also furnish a means of increasing the accountability of the decision-makers. These two contributions may be expected often to be in conflict, as decision-makers welcome the first but resist the second. It is significant that these two contributions provide a basis for favoring the use of BCA, properly applied, whether one favors or opposes the values and political objectives of incumbent decision-makers. To take the most extreme case, if I myself had decision-making responsibility, I would want to make use of BCA in helping me to choose more effectively among the available alternatives; I would press to obtain the information and insight that BCA is capable of providing to aid in furthering the public interest as I understand it. In the polar opposite situation, if decision-making responsibility were in the hands of those whose political values and programmatic agenda were clearly opposed to my own, I would urge the use of BCA to increase the accountability of these decision-makers and thereby reduce their ability to implement their political agenda simply by exercising political muscle.

This conclusion—that the use of BCA could assist us to promote our objectives if we had political power but could hinder the effectiveness of our political opponents in the same circumstances—may appear at first to be contradictory. The apparent contradiction can be explained, however, once it is recognized that political differences are based on disagreements about matters of fact as well as matters of value. It is therefore reasonable for me to believe that the relatively objective analysis and public scrutiny provided by BCA would provide support for the sorts of programs that I favor while it would expose the weaknesses of the sorts of programs favored by my opponents. And at the same time, my political opponents could also favor the use of BCA, believing that it would tend to provide support for their positions and programs.

When the nature and purpose of BCA are understood in the way that I have argued that they should be, then it is clear that most of the criticisms put forward by BCA's liberal critics are directed against misuse or abuse of BCA, not toward the technique itself. This point is explicitly recognized by several of those offering the most forceful and persuasive criticisms (Ashford 1979, 64; Baram 1980, 526; Fischhoff 1977, 194). The authors of the very vigorous criticism of the analyses carried out by the Corps of Engineers and the Bureau of Reclamation in the water resources area have generally argued not that BCA should be abandoned as a method but that it needs to be done better (see, for example, Haveman 1973 and Roberts 1976).

Other criticisms are based on incorrectly understanding BCA's role as involving the attempt to determine decisions rather than to provide one input into the decision-making process, and to eliminate rather than merely complement the consideration of political, distributional, environmental, ethical, cultural, and other factors. Such misuse should be criticized as such rather than regarded as legitimate grounds for criticizing BCA itself. A third group of criticisms argues that the use of BCA, while sometimes appropriate, is often inappropriate in the areas of safety, health, and environmental regulation. One can agree with the general thrust of this line of criticism—as I do in a subsequent section—while still concluding that BCA is in many instances a useful tool.

In judging the value and impact of BCA, it is important to remember the political, economic, and institutional framework within which decisions on public policy are made. At most, BCA is just one input into the ongoing political process where individuals, groups, and organizations seek to promote their interests. In many cases, the balance of political forces is such that the nature of the resulting outcome is virtually ensured. When the Senate majority leader feels strongly about a water project in his home state, or the speaker of the House of Representatives pushes hard for a subway extension in his own district, no formal analysis of economic impact is likely to matter much at all. It is in cases where the outcome is somewhat open—either because of uncertainty about the actual effects of alternative decisions or because no alternative is backed by a clearly dominant political coalition—that BCA may play a significant role. And to the extent that BCA operates to produce better information for both decision-makers and other interested parties, it is reasonable to believe that the impact of properly conducted and effectively presented BCA will be to help identify and thereby increase the probability of adoption of those alternatives with the greatest net benefits—that is, that will make the largest contribution toward increasing social welfare. In short, more active use of BCA could result in movement toward realizing a principle that Ronald Reagan's former budget director David Stockman enunciated but failed to live up to—"curtailing weak claims rather than weak clients" (Greider 1982, 13).

THE PRO-LIBERAL IMPACT OF BCA

There is a widespread current impression, largely a result of the Reagan administration's adoption of BCA as a tool in its campaign against health, safety, and environmental regulation, that BCA itself is somehow inherently conservative and that its increased use should therefore be opposed by liberals. However, the conclusion that liberals should oppose the use of BCA because of the way that it has been used by the Reagan administration is no more logical than would be a conclusion that liberals should abandon the use of 3 × 5-inch note cards simply because of their misuse by the President. On the contrary, both the internal logic of the BCA paradigm and the historical record of its applications provide reasons for liberals to conclude that its increased use is likely to promote the objectives that they espouse.

One group of liberal objectives—promotion of general interests versus special interests, competence versus incompetence, honesty versus corruption—is broadly shared by nonliberals. The way that increased use of BCA could be expected to serve these "good government" objectives was discussed in the final section of Chapter 4. The present section develops the further argument that more and better BCA can also promote more specifically "liberal" goals—such as expanded public programs to provide improvements in housing, transportation, education, and other areas of social life; reduced economic inequality; enhanced environmental protection; and increased health and safety for working people. (This does not imply that conservatives would necessarily oppose BCA. As I argued above, an important part of the differences between liberals and conservatives consists of disagreements about factual matters: It is entirely possible for a liberal to believe that a thorough, objective evaluation would show that, for example, stricter workplace noise standards are justified, and for a conservative simultaneously to believe that such an evaluation would show that existing noise standards are already too strict.)

One central liberal belief is that the operation of private markets will often fail to bring about outcomes that promote people's social and economic welfare—indeed, that "market failures" often create or exacerbate social problems—and that public, governmental expenditures or regulations are often needed to bring about improved outcomes. (This liberal belief stands in strong contrast to the conservative belief that private markets generally work quite well, and that government efforts to improve on market-generated outcomes will often end up making things worse rather than better.) BCA is a technique designed explicitly for application in cases where private markets are failing; one of its most essential features is the attempt to take into account total costs and benefits, including externalities, rather than just those effects "internalized" through the operation of the market system that would be taken into account in a narrow financial appraisal. BCA involves using empirical, quantitative investigation in order to identify what form and extent of public intervention is justified. Thus, while BCA does indeed make considerable use of market-generated information, it is based on a recognition of the need to go beyond the faith in the market that tends to characterize conservative views. It brings organized, collective rationality to bear on social and economic problems. If liberals are right about the prevalence of market failure, and about the potential of governmental action to bring about improvements, then proper use of BCA will produce reports whose conclusions support such action—that will, in short, tend to support the liberal position.

There are also good reasons to believe that more and better use of BCA will tend to support the liberal preference for improving the circumstances of less wealthy and powerful groups in society. Whether weights are incorporated into the analysis or, more often, distributional consequences are identified and discussed apart from the summary measure of net benefits, these consequences are made explicit in a properly done BCA, thereby making it harder for decision-makers to ignore unfavorable distributional effects when reaching their final decision. Even BCA's use of willingness to pay as the criterion for evaluating benefits and costs—inherently weighted in a one-dollar, one-vote manner that is inegalitarian compared to the one-person, one-vote standard of a democratic political system[1]—has the virtue of including all "dollar votes," including those made by people whose preferences might be ignored in more traditional, "political" ways of reaching decisions (this argument is made by Stokey and Zeckhauser 1978, 151).

The arguments about the favorable distributional impact of BCA are based on a comparison not with ideal egalitarian decision-making, but with real-world decision-making processes that are greatly influenced by behind-the-scenes pressures from special interests with wealth and power. It is in this relative sense that the distributional consequences of greater use of BCA can be expected to be progressive—that it can contribute to "curtailing weak claims rather than weak clients." As before, this conclusion depends on BCA's being conducted in an open and accessible manner that facilitates rather than forecloses participation by all interested groups.

The case that BCA can support liberal objectives is not only a theoretical one. BCA first began to be applied on a substantial scale following the Flood Control Act of 1936 (during Franklin Roosevelt's New Deal); related techniques began to be seriously applied in the Department of Defense in the early 1960s (under Secretary Robert MacNamara during the Kennedy administration); and expansion throughout the federal government was mandated in the mid-1960s (during Lyndon Johnson's presidency). In other words, each of the major expansions of the role of BCA prior to that initiated by Ronald Reagan took place during a liberal, Democratic administration. Historical analysis at this level of generality can hardly be conclusive, but it should at least give pause to the facile identification of BCA as an essentially conservative methodology.

Furthermore, an examination of the record of BCA applications in recent years indicates that in many instances BCA has played a significant role in bringing about the adoption or continuation of programs favored by liberals. For example, Whittington and Grubb note that some BCAs "of social programs have been widely accepted and have been credited with saving programs from legislative attack— particularly in the WIC program of nutritional supplements for women and infants, the Job Corps program for training the disadvantaged, and early childhood education programs like Head Start" (although they observe that the BCA results obtained their effect "in conjunction with political support" for these programs) (1984, 69). The same authors found, in their examination of the implementation of Executive Order 12291, that benefit-cost analyses have

> been used in some cases—for example, the proposed beef grading standards, auto bumper standards, pension benefits, and the Channel Island-Point Reyes Marine Sanctuary—to support positions contrary to the deregulatory bias of the Reagan administration.... The case of passive safety restraints in automobiles provides the best example of this process: The decision of the National Highway Traffic Safety Administration to eliminate requirements for passive safety restraints was successfully overturned in federal district court (and upheld by the Supreme Court) on the grounds that the available evidence—including that in the RIA [Regulatory Impact Analysis]—contradicted the government's decision (Whittington and Grubb 1984, 66).

Even those who have been among the most vocal and effective critics of the use of BCA in the areas of health, safety, and environmental regulation have cited and/or undertaken numerous studies showing that regulation in these areas does have substantial positive net social benefits. This is only natural; those who support expanded regulation do so because they believe that, in at least some sense, its benefits are greater than its costs—so it is entirely reasonable that they should believe that when BCA is honestly and competently done it will tend to support this conclusion. For example, in the course of their strong arguments against the way that BCA in practice has been used to support deregulation in the areas of health, safety, and environmental protection, Green and Waitzman cite numerous studies of the benefits of regulatory programs in these areas that support their position that such regulation has positive net benefits (1979, 223-80).[2] The actual thrust of their argument, therefore, can be best interpreted as being against the misuse and abuse of BCA; they demonstrate their belief that BCA done properly can provide useful support for arguments favoring a pro-consumer, pro-worker, pro-regulatory position. Similarly, while Nicholas Ashford has criticized the use of BCA in the regulatory area, he has also led a group that provided a major survey of studies demonstrating substantial identifiable and quantifiable benefits from safety, health, and environmental regulation (Ashford et al. 1980).

Finally, it is important to recognize that a pro-liberal impact of BCA is neither automatic nor immutable. In particular, it is not sufficient simply to offer a definition, however accurate, of what BCA is and then to assess the impact of BCA, defined in this way. The actual nature of BCA is constantly being determined by current theory and practice; it is not decreed by scholars. An important issue in the ongoing struggles between liberals and conservatives in the area of public policy concerns precisely the nature and meaning that BCA will have in the period ahead. A number of controversies within the framework provided by the generally accepted BCA paradigm (e.g., in Chapter 2 I briefly noted disagreements concerning the handling of distributional issues, the treatment of discounting, and the relative merits of the conventional and decision-making approaches to BCA) have come to be disputes organized along essentially liberal versus conservative lines. Thus, one important focus for liberals engaged in the struggle to promote better BCA involves contesting conservative efforts to redefine it in ways more favorable to their own goals.

PROMOTING BETTER BCA

The positive conclusions of the preceding sections were conditional on BCA's being done better than it has been done. They represent an endorsement of efforts to bring about improvements in the practice of BCA. What might such efforts involve?

The very first criticism of BCA presented in Chapter 3 was directed at BCA's being falsely presented as an objective technique, when in fact it is generally manipulated in order to reach predetermined conclusions favored by those sponsoring and/or conducting the analysis. While the techniques of BCA themselves may be unbiased, so many value-laden assumptions are needed in the course of carrying out a BCA that it would be naive and unrealistic to accept the outcome of any BCA as indicating the results of an unbiased process. BCA's defenders have argued, correctly in my view, that BCA can be a force for increased openness and accountability in the decision-making process, but this effect is not automatic. An alternative potential effect of increasing use of BCA is just the reverse of this openness: "driving politics deeper into the technical analysis, veiling the real choices from the public eye" (Hanke and Walker 1974, 344). The principal task in the effort to bring about better BCA is establishing the kinds of actual and potential scrutiny that will increase the likelihood of detecting and correcting conscious or unconscious bias in carrying out the analysis.

A set of suggested measures assembled by Michael Baram offers a number of promising means of working toward this end (1980, 491-92, 516-17, 527-31). These include designing and implementing both internal efforts by individual agencies and more effective oversight by higher levels within the executive branch, by Congress, and by the courts. For example, "an agency should promulgate generic rules to limit ad hoc arbitrary assumptions" (1980, 517). Such agency rules should be formulated in light of guidelines supplied by legislation, by interagency committees, or by OMB; both the content and enforcement of these rules should be subject to review. One of Baram's suggestions was that the Office of the President issue a new executive order, amending Carter's E.O. 12044 and mandating, among other things, that higher-level executive review as well as individual agency analysis "function in open proceedings, provide full public access to the information they use and ... follow all requirements of the Administrative Procedure Act.... All RARG proceedings and materials germane to any agency's final regulatory action [should] be incorporated in the agency record of decision, available for public, congressional and judicial review" (1980, 528). The contrast between the thrust of Baram's suggested revised executive order and Reagan's E.O. 12991, which has no counterpart to E.O. 12044's section 2(c) on "Opportunity for Public Participation," offers support for the contention that the Reagan administration's initiative involved a movement toward worse practice of BCA, not simply more of it.

The fact that BCA tends frequently to reflect particular interests is not, on reflection, particularly worrisome in itself—any more than is the fact that attorneys presenting their cases to a court of law tend to reflect the interests of their clients rather than an impartial analysis of the matter being adjudicated. The legal idea that truth may be best discovered through an adversary proceeding offers an alternative perspective on how BCA's positive potential for improving public decision-making might best be furthered. The biases in particular applications of BCA would not represent a major problem if other BCAs incorporating the biases of opposing groups were also being conducted, or if those with opposing biases could critically examine the BCA and present their comments to the relevant decision-makers. To the (very considerable) extent that this is not now the case, there is a tendency for BCA to become one more means by which those with wealth and power are able to influence governmental decision-making in their favor.

Some efforts could therefore be devoted to ensuring that all groups with significant interests in the outcome of a decision—including the general public—are represented in the process by which BCA is used. This requires that BCAs, including all of the assumptions and valuations incorporated into them, be publicly available and that clear channels for public input such as open hearings and opportunities for submission of written comments be systematically provided. It may also require taking specific steps—analogous to the provision of public defenders for persons unable to afford private attorneys—to ensure that all groups with a major interest in the outcome of a proposed decision are able to retain the services of a qualified analyst to work on their behalf. Fischhoff has emphasized the desirability of protecting the interests of the general public by "hiring public defenders [who] would be entrusted with scrutinizing all reports . . . from the public's point of view. These public defenders should be paid as well for their criticism as the cost-benefit analysts are paid for producing their reports" (1977, 195).

In short, if BCA's very real potential for abuse and misuse is to be effectively countered, efforts to make government applications and reviews of BCA as objective and professional as possible could be usefully complemented by efforts to identify potentially interested groups and to facilitate their effective representation in an adversary-type process of analysis and review.

One additional major way of promoting better BCA involves efforts to make the careful identification and description of the *distribution* of benefits and costs be a standard component of BCA reports. Critics of BCA have been correct in denouncing it for more often than not simply ignoring, in practice, the distributional consequences of alternatives being evaluated. At the same time, those who have emphasized the theoretical and practical difficulties of incorporating distributional effects directly into BCA's summary quantitative measure of net benefits have also been correct. The best solution therefore appears to be identifying and quantifying distributional impacts separately, in a manner that indicates these effects should receive attention commensurate with that given to the summary measure of net benefits. This would be an important means of making BCA a less distorting and more relevant tool for public policy evaluation. (Similar points are made by Zeckhauser 1981, 215-18.)

Like the other measures for promoting "better BCA" that were discussed just above, incorporating the identification of distributional consequences into BCA reports would require a difficult effort, the success of which would not be guaranteed. The argument here is based on judgments—informed by the information and arguments presented in Chapters 2 through 4—that the probability of achieving a reasonable degree of success in all of these efforts is high enough, and the value of doing so is substantial enough, that undertaking the necessary effort is warranted.

TWO QUALIFICATIONS

My conclusion that BCA's impact on the determination of public policy is potentially positive does not take the form of a *carte blanche* endorsement of expanded applications of BCA. I wish now to offer two major caveats and to note the grounds they provide for being less than fully confident that BCA will in fact fulfill its positive potential.

When Not to Use BCA

First, although BCA can be fruitfully applied to a broad range of the problems that confront public sector decision-makers, it is not appropriate to all such problems. When pervasive uncertainties and intangible factors (such as human life and health, ecological effects, ethical implications, political consequences, or cultural and aesthetic issues) dominate the problem at hand, BCA has little to offer. The underlying issue here was captured nicely in the metaphor of "horse-and-rabbit stew" that was used in summarizing the debate on similar matters at a conference more than two decades ago (and subsequently adopted as a chapter title in a leading BCA text (Mishan 1982a, ch. 22): The problem is compared to that of

> appraising the quality of a horse-and-rabbit stew, the rabbit being cast as the consequences that can be measured and evaluated numerically, and the horse as the amalgam of external effects, social, emotional, and psychological impacts, and historical and aesthetic considerations that can be adjudged only

roughly and subjectively. Since the horse [is] bound to dominate the flavor of the stew, meticulous evaluation of the rabbit would hardly seem worthwhile. (Dorfman 1965, 2).

This analogy suggests merely that there is little value in such efforts. In fact, however, BCA's applications in such situations may actually be counterproductive. They can convey a false sense of knowledge and precision and can cause too much attention to be focused on the relatively unimportant parts of the problem under review. This is the point that Merewitz and Sosnick are making when they assert that "when intangibles are important, benefit-cost analysis may do more harm than good. If analysis is preoccupied with tangible, measurable benefits, it may divert attention from elements that cannot be quantified" (1971, 269). The real problem may not be that of horse-and-rabbit stew but rather that of the proverbial drunk who a friend saw one night crawling around under a streetlamp, intensely scrutinizing the sidewalk. The friend inquired as to what was happening, learned that the first man had lost his house key, and joined in the search. After several minutes of fruitless searching, the second man asked the first if he was absolutely certain that the key had fallen into the area that they were minutely going over for the seventh time. "Oh, no," replied the drunk, "it fell into the bushes over there." Looking up in exasperation, the friend demanded, "Then why in the world aren't we looking where you dropped it?" With a patient sigh, the drunk explained: "Because there is no light over there." When the analysis of proposed public policies is guided more by the nature of existing analytical techniques than by the nature of the problem to be analyzed, its opportunity cost is likely to be similarly substantial.

There are no established guidelines to determine those cases where intangible effects are so dominant that BCA is best not used. As a result, there are legitimate grounds for concern that BCA proponents will apply it in cases—particularly in the areas of safety, health, and environmental regulation—where its use will do more harm than good. Many of the strongest critics make their case against the mandatory use of BCA in these areas (whether imposed by statute, by executive order, or by other means), rather than against its selective application in cases where the degree of uncertainty and the significance of intangible effects are relatively minor. My positive general conclusion concerning BCA requires the important qualification that its application not be pushed beyond its appropriate boundaries—

and that legitimate attempts to quantify a subset of a proposal's effects not be allowed to be used as a proxy for an evaluation of the entire proposal.

A Residual Worry

A second major caveat is perhaps best characterized as a nagging doubt or a troubling residual worry. I have emphasized that my conclusion is conditional on BCA's being done better—and my belief that this is an attainable goal. Nevertheless it seems prudent to continue to wonder if the misuses, abuses, and improper applications of BCA are, in practice, really capable of being reduced to a minimal level. This may be much more easily said than done, as Baram has pointed out:

> The literature on cost-benefit analysis is curious in that a typical article will candidly treat the limitations of cost-benefit analysis and warn against overreliance upon its use, but thereafter describe its possible use in a particular situation and finally urge adoption of the results (1980, 481).

The limits in practice to reform of BCA may be so severe that hopes of significantly reduced abuse and misuse would be disappointed even in the event of a major effort at reform and improvement. Given a realistic view of who will be doing BCA, the political and bureaucratic context in which it will be undertaken, and the inherent attractiveness of having "hard," quantitative results, abuses and misuses may be unavoidable. The theoretical framework of applied welfare economics may almost inevitably produce a mindset that overemphasizes the quantifiable. On all this, the implications of Baram's just-quoted observation suggest possible limits on what may be realistically expected in practice. Doing BCA properly, and keeping it in its proper place, may in fact be much more difficult than its mainstream proponents are willing to acknowledge, with the result that there is a tendency to evaluate an idealized conception of BCA rather than a conception that is actually possible of realization. In short, there remains a nagging doubt that BCA can actually be implemented in a way that will avoid enough of the myriad potential pitfalls to make it worthwhile, that recognition of its limitations will go beyond lip service, and that certain biases are not inherent in the technique itself. Although I believe, on balance, that my overall positive judgment on BCA is justified, this second major caveat is justified as well. The question should remain an open one.

THE LIMITS OF THE BCA DEBATE

The description of BCA in Chapter 2 emphasized that it is one element of applied welfare economics and, as such, is situated within the intellectual and political framework provided by contemporary mainstream economics. The BCA debate summarized in Chapters 3 and 4 has taken place largely within that framework. Contributions to the debate did come from outside of the disciplinary boundaries of economics—from political scientists, legal scholars, environmentalists, psychologists, and others. Nevertheless, these contributions, too, were based on a general acceptance of the broader set of understandings, shared by conservatives and liberals, that constitute the mainstream view of the U.S. economic and political system.

Chapter 5 has evaluated the BCA debate from the general public policy perspective provided by this mainstream framework and also from the specific point of view provided by liberal beliefs and values. It is perhaps not surprising that the proponents of BCA should prevail in this evaluation, when proponents and critics alike accept the overall framework of mainstream values and beliefs—the same general framework of which BCA is a part. Within this framework, criticisms of BCA are correctly seen as limited, rather than as fundamentally threatening to BCA itself, and the possibilities for alternatives to BCA are also correctly perceived to be limited. In particular, because BCA is essentially a pro-liberal technique, it is not surprising that liberal criticisms of it don't cut very deeply—and that the most cogent and devastating attacks on BCA in practice can be persuasively answered by responding that the problem lies with the abuse and misuse of BCA, and/or with its application to a problem for which it is inappropriate, rather than consisting of any basic flaw in BCA itself.

But the conclusions offered here are called into question if the mainstream worldview, accepted by all participants in the BCA debate, is itself called into question. We saw in Chapter 1 that there is at least one major alternative conceptual framework for approaching the analysis of the U.S. economic and political system—that of radical political economics. It thus becomes necessary, as part of any comprehensive analysis of the theory and practice of BCA, to investigate what conclusions might be reached when BCA is examined within this alternative conceptual framework.

NOTES

1. Graaff's critical appraisal of BCA, published in the *South African Journal of Economics*, includes a striking euphemism for his country's highly undemocratic political system: He contrasts the market, "where all votes are weighted by purchasing power," with the ballot box, "which gives *one voter one vote*" (1975, 243-44; emphasis added) — a formulation that neatly avoids any need to acknowledge that the franchise is limited to the white minority.
2. The studies cited were concerned with estimating the benefits of government regulations rather than with comparing benefits and costs. What Green and Waitzman (1979) demonstrate is that the estimated benefits are greater than even the highest cost estimates published by critics of social regulation.

III A RADICAL CRITIQUE OF BCA THEORY AND PRACTICE

6 RADICAL POLITICAL ECONOMICS, THE CAPITALIST STATE, AND BCA
An Overview

The analysis presented in the following chapters is based on a rejection of the *public policy perspective* that is shared by all of the participants in the BCA debate reviewed in Part II. That perspective, which is central to the intellectual framework that mainstream economics provides for all areas of applied welfare economics, views the goal of public policy as the promotion of the public interest. BCA is examined and evaluated as one particular tool—one specific set of analytical techniques—designed to assist public policy-makers in their efforts to bring about the greatest contribution to social welfare. For those whose work on BCA is guided by this perspective, scholarly inquiry focuses on two main questions: First, in what circumstances can the application of BCA be expected to make a positive contribution to informed choice among proposed expenditures or regulations and thereby to increased social welfare via improved public policy? Second, how can the techniques and procedures of BCA be improved, refined, and extended in order to enhance its ability to fulfill this role?

From the public policy perspective such questions are part of an essentially *prescriptive* approach to questions of governmental decision-making: The goal is not so much to understand BCA in the broadest sense as to discuss the pros and cons of its contribution to the decision-making process. Thus, the public policy perspective involves an uncritical acceptance of prevailing institutional arrangements rather than any attempt to analyze their nature, origin, or consequences. This acceptance is usually implicit, although Stokey and Zeckhauser note that "policy analysis is a discipline for working within a political and economic system, not for changing it" (1978, 4).

Part III, in contrast, will analyze BCA from a *radical political economics perspective* (which I will often refer to simply as a *radical* one). From this perspective, the public policy perspective is seen as incapable of providing more than a limited and distorted understanding of BCA. The limitation comes from its narrow focus, which excludes any analysis either of the forces that led to the emergence and spread of BCA, or of the factors that determine the role that it plays in particular applications (that is, the approach is ahistorical and apolitical). The distortion stems from the public policy perspective's basis in naive and misleading conceptions of the nature and role of government and of the determinants of human welfare.

When the radical political economics perspective is employed to address questions of public policy in general, or of BCA in particular, the focus is not on the task of providing information and advice to policy-makers, nor is the concern primarily with improving the quality of public policy outcomes. The aim, rather, is to develop a broad critical understanding of the question under study—in its historical, institutional, ideological, and political-economic contexts. The goal of radical political economists is to develop and communicate such understanding as one important contribution toward building and strengthening broad-based popular movements that will struggle to bring about fundamental changes in prevailing social and economic arrangements. A primary purpose of the present examination of the theory and practice of BCA is to demonstrate that analysis based on the radical political economics perspective offers a more illuminating account of the nature and role of BCA in this country during the last half century than the mainstream perspective is capable of providing.[1]

Whereas previous chapters have drawn on and analyzed the extensive literature on BCA that has been written from a mainstream perspective, the chapters that follow constitute what is, to my knowledge, the first attempt to present an extended, systematic analysis of BCA from the perspective of radical political economics. As a result, the investigation raises more questions than it has been able to investigate thoroughly, the analysis that follows is at times more suggestive than definitive, and the hypotheses presented are plausible but not always proven. The present study is offered with the hope that it will stimulate additional research into the matters that it addresses—and that the potential explanatory power latent in the radical approach not be denied or underestimated because of flaws in this particular study.

THE STATE IN CAPITALIST SOCIETY

Mainstream economists regard government (they are not likely to use the term *state*) as an essentially neutral entity that seeks to promote the common interests of society's members and to mediate among groups whose interests may conflict in particular situations but are not fundamentally opposed. Government action is called for in cases where private market outcomes diverge significantly from those that would best promote social welfare (e.g., to reduce negative externalities by limiting pollution; to create positive externalities by providing public education; to provide public goods such as police and fire protection; or to minimize the exercise of monopoly power).

The perspectives of liberals and conservatives are equally ahistorical, and both take as given the basic social relations and institutional structures of capitalism. The major division between the conservative and liberal branches of the mainstream involves divergent views concerning the seriousness of existing market failures and the extent to which government actions can be expected to bring about improved results. Liberals tend to believe that the government can act to benefit everyone; conservatives tend to believe that it is incapable of benefiting anyone (except, perhaps, those within the government apparatus itself and special interests who obtain subsidies at the expense of the general public); neither views the determinants or results of government policy in a class framework.[2]

For the most part, mainstream economists simply assume that government will pursue the goal of promoting social welfare and that the goal of economic analysis is to provide policy-makers with helpful information and analyses. This view of government—which Samuel Bowles has critically characterized as "the view that beneficial social change can come through expert and enlightened advice to the powerful" (1974, 132)—is longstanding among economists. James Buchanan has observed that "[The] charge that much of the discussion in fiscal theory proceeds on the implicit and unrecognized assumption that society is ruled by a benevolent despot remains almost as true today as it was [when it was articulated by Swedish economist Knut Wicksell] sixty years ago" (Buchanan 1960, 4). As if to verify the continuing validity of this observation, one prominent contributor to the BCA literature has written that "In an open, non-dictatorial, and rationally governed society all government expenditures are made ultimately in pursuit of a single objective, the improvement of human welfare or well-being in that society. This lofty goal is above dispute" (Freeman 1977, 239). At a more popular level, the naivete of the prevailing mainstream view of the state was nicely captured in the statement of the *Boston Globe*'s editorial writers that "If government serves any function beyond national defense, it is to seek to assist the disadvantaged in society" (December 12, 1981).

In contrast, radical views of the state in capitalist society are based on recognition of the class nature of capitalism—that is, the division of capitalist society into major groups with fundamentally opposed interests, based on their positions in the economy. The state both reflects and helps to shape the balance of class forces within society. Insofar as the capitalist class is the dominant class, the state operates to promote capitalist class interests.

The capitalist class has two main needs to which the state responds. The first is the need for assistance in sustaining the process of capital *accumulation* that constitutes the very heart of capitalism. The state furnishes this assistance by, on the one hand, directly providing such support as transportation and communications infrastructure and, on the other hand, helping capitalists to respond successfully to a variety of economic difficulties that can interfere with the profitability of their activities. The second need is for the *reproduction* (stabilization, continuation, and elaboration) of the basic social arrangements of capitalism that make capital accumulation possible. In contributing to the fulfillment of this second need, the state's efforts are aimed largely at bringing about the acceptance of a class society by the subordinate classes within it, especially by the working class. The state seeks to promote social cohesion through the legitimation of existing institutional arrangements.

Accumulation and reproduction are interests of the capitalist class as a whole. In its efforts to promote these interests the state needs not only to oppose the efforts of the working class (and other subordinate classes) to promote its class interests, but also to oppose the particular interests of capitalist class fragments (which may be individual capitalists or capitalist firms, or may be larger groupings organized by industry, geography, or other criteria). Because of these contending interests, there is no guarantee that the state will always be successful in promoting the needs of the capitalist class as a whole. Furthermore, the inherently contradictory nature of the process of capitalist development means that even successful measures that are taken by the state can be expected to be self-limiting, in the sense that their very success engenders the development of counter-forces that will ultimately undermine them. In short, the capitalist state operates in a setting that is characterized by both continuing conflict with other forces and continually evolving historical circumstances.

Within the last two decades there has been a great deal of theoretical work by Marxists, and by others with a class perspective on society, devoted to understanding how, why, and to what extent the state accomplishes the task of meeting the needs of the capitalist class. While I believe that the preceding paragraphs provide a summary of general views that are broadly shared by those who have carried out this work, there have also been important controversies. Several attempts have been made to group or classify the multiple contributions to the literature. The categories most commonly adopted include: *instrumental* approaches, which emphasize the state as an instrument through which the capitalist class acts to promote its interests; *structural* approaches, which emphasize how the nature of capitalist economic institutions compels the state to act in the interests of the capitalist class, regardless of the views or affiliations of those who actually occupy positions of authority within the state; *class struggle* approaches, which emphasize that the state is an "arena" where capitalist class forces contend with other forces; and *hegemonic* approaches, which emphasize the role of the state in creating and maintaining values and beliefs that sustain popular acceptance of capitalist arrangements.[3]

This variety goes back to the very earliest work on the state within the Marxist tradition—that of Karl Marx and Friedrich Engels themselves. Bob Jessop's examination of their writings led him to observe that "they offered a variety of theoretical perspectives which co-exist in an uneasy and unstable relation" and to suggest that "It is this very plurality of viewpoints and arguments that provides the basis for the subsequent diversification of Marxist state theories" (1982, xii). The two most thorough surveys of recent Marxist writings on the capitalist state both emphasize that no "general" (Jessop 1982, 211) or "universal" (Carnoy 1984, 255) theory of the capitalist state is possible because of the multiple factors that contribute to determining state action and the varying historical conditions within which capitalist states act. They both argue that there is value in each of the major approaches that they review. In the same spirit, Bertell Ollman's brief "Theses on the Capitalist State" contends that each major approach offers insight into one aspect of the capitalist state "conceived of as a complex social relation of many different aspects," while none can claim to offer a satisfactory, comprehensive account: "Each of these one-sided interpretations of the state brings out something important about the capitalist state—about its appearance, structure, functioning (including contradictory functioning), ties to the rest of capitalism, and potential for change—just as it hides and distorts much else" (1982, 41, 42).

In spite of their great diversity, however, these radical theories of the state in capitalist society are all based on certain fundamental views that differ sharply from the mainstream perspective: that the nature of the state reflects the nature of the capitalist mode of production; that the state is part of a broad process of interaction of class forces; and that the state occupies a central place in an overall system of class domination. As Carnoy summarizes, "The State is both a product of relations of domination and their shaper" (1984, 250).

There is, in general, no need to choose among the contending radical approaches; it is entirely reasonable to believe that multiple determinants of state action are operating simultaneously, often in a mutually reinforcing way. Why does the administration of Governor Michael Dukakis of Massachusetts, a Democrat, adopt generally probusiness policies during the period that this book is being written? An instrumental analysis would examine the major role of business interests in financing the governor's election campaigns and would examine the organized groups through with the business community makes its views clearly known. A structural analysis would emphasize that maintaining a "good business climate" is necessary to bring about the level of investment required to prevent an economic downturn and associated fiscal and political crises within Massachusetts (i.e., to avoid a "capital strike"). A class struggle approach would examine the interplay of class and nonclass forces on particular issues and observe the general, although far from exclusive, dominance of capitalist groups. A hegemonic approach would emphasize the extent to which the general notion that "what is good for Massachusetts business is good for the people of Massachusetts" has become widely accepted.

The proper task for an investigation of this phenomenon from the perspective of radical political economics is to develop a concrete analysis of the factors actually at work in this particular historical situation, drawing on the entire range of available interpretations in order to develop a realistic, full, and coherent approach. Theoretical propositions offer a necessary guide for approaching the examination of social reality, rather than a sufficient basis for reaching predetermined conclusions,

Particular attempts to employ a radical approach to understanding the causes and consequences of actions by the state must take into account the specific historical circumstances involved, including the particular stage and state of the process of capital accumulation. In the case of the use of BCA by the U.S. government, it is important to recognize that the Great Depression of the 1930s and the period of World War II brought an institutional restructuring that laid the basis for the extended period of capital accumulation and general prosperity that followed. Part of this restructuring was the emergence of an enlarged and transformed role for the government in the economy, involving a major increase in the level of government spending and a commitment to macroeconomic policies that would maintain sufficient aggregate demand to avoid another major depression. But the postwar expansion was, like all those before it, self-limiting, in the sense that its very successes generated forces and conditions that undermined its continuation.

The increased role of the state, which had been a part of the solution to the crisis of the 1930s, became by the 1970s a part of the problem—one element of the newly emerging economic crisis. Part of the capitalist response to the new period of prolonged crisis has involved efforts to redefine and alter the role of the state in U.S. capitalism. The ascendancy of generally liberal approaches during the long postwar expansion, which reached its zenith in the 1960s, was replaced by the ascendancy of generally conservative forces by the early 1980s. This is not the place for a detailed account of the development and ongoing nature of the current economic crisis.[4] It must be understood, however, that any serious attempt to apply the radical approach to analyzing the state in U.S. capitalist society during this period will involve exploring the mutual influences between the activities of the state and the general status of the process of capitalist development.

UNDERSTANDING BCA: A RADICAL PROSPECTIVE

From the radical political economics perspective, the use of benefit-cost analysis can be seen as one element of the U.S. capitalist political and economic system. The questions to be addressed, then, concern how BCA fits—and how it fails to fit—into this broader system: how it has taken shape in response to needs that have emerged during the process of capitalist development and how, in turn, its operation and outcomes have had an impact on the capitalist development process.

BCA emerged and developed in particular historical circumstances. Its growth accompanied the growth of the government's role in the economy: The 1930s saw big increases in public works spending (and initial use of BCA); the 1960s witnessed a major expansion in domestic social spending (and the spread of BCA into that area); and the early 1970s brought an unprecedented amount of social regulation (followed by the expansion of BCA into that area as well). As spending and regulating grew, their size and composition became increasingly controversial. BCA's development reflected both capitalist class efforts to shape and control this growth in its own interests and conflicts that resulted when these efforts engendered resistance.

The development of BCA has served to promote capitalist class interests in two basic ways. The first is directly related to BCA's ostensible purpose of influencing the choices made among alternative proposed expenditure and regulatory policies: From the capitalist point of view, the *selection function* of BCA is to contribute to the identification and adoption of those expenditures and regulations that are most conducive to continuation of profitable capital accumulation. The second is less obvious, but crucial nevertheless: BCA's *reinforcement function* is to contribute to reproducing the existing set of institutional arrangements by legitimizing certain economic beliefs and encouraging certain patterns of political behavior. By fulfilling these two functions, BCA has promoted capitalist class interests both vis-à-vis the particularistic interests of specific capitalist class fragments and vis-à-vis the interests of the working class and other noncapitalist groups.

Like other elements of the capitalist state, however, BCA is not always successful in serving capitalist interests: Contradictions inevitably develop, circumstances change, opposing forces achieve some successes. These countertendencies have limited and undermined the success of BCA in promoting capitalist interests and may even result in future applications of BCA having impacts that favor interests other than those of capitalists.

Each of the following chapters of Part III explores in detail one of these three themes: accumulation/selection, reproduction/reinforcement, and contradiction. Before proceeding, however, two brief comments may be helpful. First, it should be clear that radical and liberal interpretations of BCA are not opposed on every particular; indeed, they are often complementary. A number of arguments in the following chapters take up deficiencies of BCA that liberals have criticized during the course of the mainstream BCA debate reviewed in Part II—but the different frame of reference of radical political economics leads to different analyses and conclusions. I hope to demonstrate that a radical analysis is superior in providing insight into the nature and role of BCA; that it contributes to improved general understanding of the operation of the state in capitalist society; and that the application of radical political economic analysis in one particular area illuminates what is distinctive about this approach to explaining the way that the world works.

Second, my focus is on application of the radical political economics perspective and thus does not include other analyses that might also be termed "radical." In particular, a critique of BCA that focuses on its reliance on utilitarian standards of valuation would be quite radical in the etymological sense of going to the root. Such a critique would, indeed, complement a critique from the point of view of radical political economics by undermining the claimed—more often, simply assumed—legitimacy of a utilitarian approach to public policy. Pursuit of this critique is, however, beyond the scope of our present inquiry.[5]

NOTES

1. The contrasting nature of the public policy perspective and the radical political economics perspective was introduced in Chapter 1, where I also discussed my choice of the terms *radical* and *radical political economics* to characterize the perspective (or paradigm) employed in Part III. Among the best of the numerous attempts to explicate the radical political economics perspective in relation to that of mainstream economics are those of the *Review of Radical Political Economics* (1971); Gordon (1977); and Franklin (1977).
2. For an excellent characterization and discussion of mainstream (liberal, corporatist, pluralist) theories of the state, see Carnoy (1984, ch. 1, 246-50).
3. The enormous literature on Marxist and other radical theories of the state in capitalist society has recently been surveyed and critically analyzed in two very useful books: Of these, that of Martin Carnoy (1984) is both more accessible and more oriented to writings by U.S. authors and about the U.S. state; that of Bob Jessop (1982) is more difficult and abstract in its treatment and concentrates on the Western European literature, deliberately omitting U.S. contributions. Bertell Ollman's brief "Theses on the Capitalist State" (1982) compresses a number of useful insights into very few pages.
4. For my own analysis of the nature and development of the current economic crisis, see Campen (1981) and Campen and MacEwan (1982), which provide numerous references to the radical literature on economic crises.
5. The basic value judgments incorporated into BCA, that social welfare is nothing but an aggregation of individual welfares and that individuals are the best judges of their own welfares, reflect the fundamentally utilitarian nature of welfare economics in general and of BCA in particular. That is, they are based on the premise that the best course of action is the one that will produce the greatest total amount, somehow defined, of perceived satisfaction (or well-being, or welfare, or happiness, or utility). This is not the only possible standard for judging public policy, and a number of critics, as we saw in Chapter 3, have suggested that it is an inappropriate one. For example, government actions can be evaluated in terms of their conformity to specified normative standards of proper behavior (e.g., no torture, no exploitation, equal treatment before the law). In such a nonutilitarian framework, support for, say, the Bill of Rights would be based on a judgment that the rights protected are truly fundamental, rather than on any quantitative assessment purporting to show that maintaining these rights is the course of action that will maximize satisfaction.

The interested reader is referred to Amartya Sen's *Choice, Welfare and Measurement* (1982), especially to Part IV (Essays 13–16), the corresponding portion of the Introduction (pp. 25–31), and the extensive bibliographic guidance provided there. For an application of the argument to BCA in particular, one might begin with Sagoff (1981).

7 SERVING THE POWERFUL
The Selection Function of BCA

During the middle decades of the twentieth century, governmental expenditures in the United States rose tremendously. Between 1927 and 1967, the dollar volume of total government spending rose from $11 billion to $264 billion; more significantly, while it equaled just 11 percent of gross national product (GNP) in 1927, by 1967 its share of GNP had grown to 33 percent. The expansion of federal government expenditures was particularly dramatic: from $3 billion (3 percent of GNP) to $158 billion (20 percent of GNP) during this forty-year period (U.S. Bureau of the Census 1975, 224, 1114, 1127). This enormous growth in public expenditures provides the essential context for understanding the rise of the theory and practice of BCA.

It is beyond the scope of this book to offer an analysis from the radical political economics perspective of the massive growth and changing composition of public expenditures.[1] The focus here will be on an examination of the role played by BCA. The radical perspective does not accept the mainstream understanding of BCA as a means of helping the makers of public policy identify those alternatives whose selection would make the greatest contribution to social welfare. Rather, it emphasizes the proposition that BCA operates to help identify and justify expenditures and regulatory policies favoring the long-term, classwide interests of the capitalist class. This is the *selection function* of BCA.

The selection that I am referring to here is not that resulting from capitalists applying overt political power in favor of specific outcomes, although that is certainly an important factor at work in determining the composition of public expenditures. My concern is with the selection that takes place in response to the straightforward application of BCA techniques and criteria. Such selection occurs because of the way in which these techniques and criteria have been designed. While BCA claims to be promoting the "public interest" or the "general good" over the demands of "special interests," the "good" being promoted is "general" only to the capitalist class and not to society as a whole. Alternatives that promote the interests of other classes—or of individual capitalist class fragments—are automatically at a disadvantage.

The present chapter examines in detail two particular ways in which BCA has functioned to promote the selection of pro-capitalist alternatives. The first way involves insulating public policy-making from popular political pressures, by enlarging the role of experts and expertise and promoting an ideology that emphasizes efficiency and social harmony. In this, BCA is part of a more general effort that has been going on throughout the twentieth century. Under the guise of promoting the public interest, individuals and institutions representing the most class-conscious elements of the capitalist class played a dominant role in shaping and implementing BCA during the period between World War II and 1970.

The second way stems from the narrowly focused objective function used in BCA. The emphasis on goods and services, to the exclusion of important "noneconomic" consequences of public budgetary and regulatory choices, tends to support and legitimize the selection of those social outcomes that are most compatible with capitalism's core processes of commodity production and capital accumulation.

BCA AND THE RISE OF RATIONALITY IN GOVERNMENT

From the early years of the present century, class-conscious individuals, drawn primarily from the monopoly-corporate segment of the capitalist class, have sought in a variety of ways to remove decision-making about public affairs from the "political" realm and to entrust it to experts who would evaluate and decide "efficiently" in the "public interest." Their efforts were greatest in the first quarter of the century and in the period following World War II. During each of these periods, capitalists and their representatives worked to direct and control a significant expansion of the scope and level of governmental involvement in the economy.

Through this process—which I shall refer to as the "rise of rationality in government"—these members of the dominant class have largely succeeded in promoting their own class interest as the general interest of all members of society. Under the banner of promoting such objectives as "efficiency," "scientific management," and "the public interest," this profoundly antidemocratic development has in fact operated to increase the role and enhance the authority of "experts," thereby reducing popular involvement in determining the direction of public affairs. It has facilitated indirect capitalist class dominance of policy outcomes through the operation of a whole set of institutions and organizations concerned with the policy planning process.

The movement for promoting the rise of rationality in government has had many manifestations. Among its fruits have been the Municipal Reform Movement in the first decades of the century, numerous corporate-funded policy research institutions, the United States's bipartisan postwar foreign policy, several pieces of major social legislation, the basic shape of U.S. educational policy, and the increased centralization of power at all levels of government, most especially in the executive branch at the federal level.[2]

The emergence of the theory and practice of BCA was also a logical and institutional outgrowth of this general development. BCA developed under the guidance of individuals and institutions drawn from the corporate sector of the capitalist class—and without input from most people who would eventually be affected by it. The criteria adopted for evaluating the costs and benefits of policy alternatives, not surprisingly, were ones tending to result in outcomes favorable to capitalist interests.

This aspect of BCA's selection function sometimes involves helping capitalists to identify what alternatives best promote their interests, which can be a very complex problem. At other times it involves helping them in promoting the alternatives that they already favor (e.g., the Reagan administration's use of BCA to promote deregulation). The form that BCA takes and the way that it is used have varied in response to the stage and state of the capital accumulation process itself.

I will begin by examining the rise of rationality in government as a general phenomenon, discussing in turn the goals and ideology that lay behind it and the nature of the individuals and institutions who promoted it. Against this background, I then consider the ways in which the emergence and development of BCA in the middle decades of this century were one aspect of this more general development. Finally, I suggest that the changed economic environment that emerged in the early 1970s has called into question BCA's ability to continue fulfilling its selection function successfully.

Motivation and Ideology

The efforts to rationalize public affairs arose in response to the changing circumstances of the twentieth century. As large corporations became more dominant in U.S. society, two related developments led businessmen to promote the rise of rationality as a means of increasing their control over government decision-making. First, the increasing size and interdependence of the business sector required ever greater government spending to promote the stabilization, coordination, and continued expansion of the ever more complex capitalist economy. Second, capitalists realized that existing procedures for determining public expenditures, and other public policies, were becoming less responsive to the needs of the economy as a whole (as seen from their perspective). They worried that these needs would be subordinated to either the needs of particular capitalists or the needs of working people, and they feared that the political process would serve these other interests if they did not intervene to shape the policy-making process. Samuel Bowles notes that

> An extension of state activity in the interests of amelioration of explosive social conditions, repression of dissident groups, and coordination of an increasingly interdependent economy brought with it the possibility of this newly empowered state falling under popular control and ultimately being used against the capitalist elite and its allies in the professional classes. The modern liberal solution was to welcome the extension of state power and simultaneously to insulate the implementation of state action from popular control (1974, 130).

A major theme of James O'Connor's discussion of "political power and budgetary control in the United States" is that "by itself, interest group politics is inconsistent with the survival and expansion of capitalism" (1973, 67) and that class-conscious activity in this area by corporate capitalists was motivated by the realization of their need to curb the political power—most important, the influence over state budgetary policy—of particular interest groups. Samuel P. Hays agrees, explicitly and emphatically, in his analysis of "The Politics of Reform in Municipal Government in the Progressive Era":

> These business, professional, and upper-class groups who dominated municipal reform movements... objected to the structure of government which enabled local and particularistic interests to dominate.... The movement for reform in municipal government, therefore, constituted an attempt by upper-class, advanced professional, and large business groups to take formal political power from the previously dominant lower- and middle-class elements so that they might advance their own conception of desirable public policy (1964, 161-62).

The advocates of increasing rationality in government affairs argued for their objective in terms of an ideology that saw an underlying harmony of interests among all social groups and emphasized the importance of efficiency and expertise in the process of advancing these interests. All of the major themes of this ideology rested on the fundamental assertion of social harmony, the claim that conflicts among the various elements of society were based on a failure to understand that everyone could be better off if they all cooperated in working to carry out the suggestions made by experts. Corporate liberal ideology argued that it was silly and destructive to fight over the division of the pie, when cooperative behavior could result in an enlarged pie with bigger slices for everyone. Gabriel Kolko reports that progressivism's efforts to rationalize business conditions "operated on the assumption that the general welfare of the community could be best served by satisfying the concrete needs of business," and he notes "the nearly universal belief among political leaders in the basic justice of private property relations as they essentially existed" (1967, 3).

Furthermore, this ideology also maintained that the general interest would be greatly advanced by applying in the public sector the techniques of management and decision-making developed in the business world. James Weinstein concludes his survey of the municipal reform movement by noting that "Developed and led by business groups, the movement [succeeded in] rationalizing city government and institutionalizing the methods and values of the corporations that had come to dominate American economic life" (1968, 115). Several decades later, the Committee for Economic Development (we shall see shortly the CED's central role as a corporate liberal policy planning body) acted on its "preoccupation with the application to public administration of the lessons learned in private management" and established a "Committee for Improvement of Management in Government" whose major purpose was to increase the extent to which the government made use of "sound business practices" (Schriftgiesser 1967, ch. 20; quotes from p. 189).

Samuel Haber (1964) and Harry Braverman (1974) have shown that the management techniques developed during the early twentieth century in private business included, above all, "scientific management," which strongly emphasized separating conception from execution and shifting planning and decision-making power into the hands of experts. Similarly, those who promoted the rise of rationality in the public sector believed strongly that evaluation and choice ought to be as much as possible entrusted to those best informed and best qualified—that is, to experts.

The rise of rationality was, perhaps more than anything else, an effort to depoliticize public issues—to insulate the government from the public, delimit the area for public debate and discussion, and reduce the role played by popular pressures in governmental policy- and decision-making. Given the assumption that there were no important conflicting interests, it followed that politics must be about frivolous and insignificant matters and could only reduce the efficiency of the policy-making process in promoting the general welfare. Since political conflict could only be destructive, it was right that it should be transcended. David Eakins characterizes the viewpoint of "Progressive Era 'corporate liberal' reformers" in this way:

> Fact-finding and policymaking had to be isolated from class struggle and freed from political pressure groups. The reforms that would lead to industrial peace and social order, these experts were coming to believe, could only be derived from data determined by objective fact-finders (such as themselves) and under the auspices of sober and respectable organizations (such as only they could construct). The capitalist system could be improved only by a single-minded reliance upon experts detached from the hurly-burly of

democratic policymaking. The emphasis was on efficiency—and democratic policymaking was inefficient (1972, 163–64).

Expertise, scientific method, professionalism, rigor, detachment from partisanship or special interest—these were the alleged advantages from the depoliticization of public policy-making. A close student of the period states that "The rhetoric and symbolism of the years from the last part of the 19th century until the Great Depression were filled with images of science and technology, efficiency and system, and 'businesslike' alternatives and policy-making by experts" (Hays 1972, 1). Those with expertise could promote the interests of various nonexpert segments of society whose direct participation in a political process would only be counterproductive. One businessman advocating the reform of municipal government "told a labor audience [that] the businessman's slate represented labor 'better than you do yourself'" (Hays 1964, 160).

A final theme of the ideology underlying the efforts to increase the role of rationality in government was an inclusive perspective—a belief that it was generally advantageous to deal with problems on as general and comprehensive a basis as possible. Thus, a commission or city manager form of municipal government was preferable to a local government consisting of ward representatives, for it would respond to the interests of the city as a whole. Similarly, at the state and national levels, the executive branch, headed by a president or governor elected at large, would have a more inclusive perspective than the legislative branch, consisting of representatives elected by particular geographic (and, hence, often ethnic or economic) constituencies. And within the federal structure, higher levels (e.g., national as opposed to state) would be able to approach problems in a more comprehensive framework. There is much truth in the adage that "Where you stand depends on where you sit." The corporate liberal reformers wanted power in the hands of those "sitting" in centralized locations, believing that their resulting "stands" would best promote the capitalist class interest in the well-being of the system as a whole.

In short, the ideology of the advocates of the rise of rationality in government was a deeply antidemocratic one, resulting in the conception of a public policy-making process that was almost totally depoliticized, that left little room for government *by* the people. The ideology not only failed to recognize the value of direct public participation, it encouraged attempts to limit the role of political organizations, of public debate, and even of elected representatives in the determination and implementation of public policy. William Appleman Williams has argued that "the two irreducible forms of functioning government are benevolent despotism and democracy" (1966, 7). It should be clear that the advocates of the rise of rationality in government envisioned the former.

Proponents and Organizations

Despite some of the rhetorical claims made on its behalf, the rise of rationality in government was far from an automatic response to exogenous developments in administrative and managerial techniques. To an important extent, it was the result of the efforts of men and organizations representing the most class-conscious segment of the capitalist class, seeking to advance their own long-term interests. In the words of historian James Weinstein, there was "a conscious and successful effort to guide and control the economic and social policies of federal, state, and municipal governments by various business groupings in their own long-range interest as they perceived it" (1968, ix-x).

The proponents of the rise of rationality in government were primarily "corporate liberals," drawn predominantly from the big-business sector of the capitalist class. Other proponents were well-meaning middle-class reformers, generally sharing in the ideology described above. Businessmen from the more competitive sector of the economy tended to be conscious only of the particular interests of their own company, industry, or region, and to place little importance on working to promote the common interest of the entire class in the systemwide needs of capitalism.[3]

The present interpretation suggests that the interests of workers were most opposed to capitalist class interests—and workers did in fact oppose many of the reforms. Haber observes that "efficiency had its opponents and detractors. Organized labor was foremost among these" (1964, 52). Similarly, Hays demonstrates that "the leading business groups in each city and professional men closely allied with them initiated and dominated municipal movements. . . . Lower- and middle-class groups not only dominated the pre-reform governments, but vigorously opposed reform" (1964, 159, 162).

The fact that the members of the monopoly sector of the capitalist class had a common interest in the expanded reproduction of the social system did not by itself ensure that they would be able to determine the specific policies and actions best suited to advance this general goal or that they would be able to get together and act collectively in pursuit of their common interest. Determining the policies most favorable to capitalist interests and achieving collective support for them are genuine problems—but they are problems that were, to a considerable extent, dealt with effectively by twentieth-century U.S. monopoly capitalists.[4] The mechanism was remarkably straightforward: the most class-conscious among them took the lead in establishing, financing, and directing an interdependent set of academic centers, governmental units, policy analysis institutions, business organizations, and foundations. These bodies devoted themselves precisely to the tasks of generating policies that would promote the long-run interests of the capitalist class as a whole and of mobilizing the support necessary to have these policies adopted and implemented by the public sector. There has been, and still is, a large and diverse panorama of such organizations, ranging from the Council on Foreign Relations to the Advertising Council.[5]

The organizations that played a particular role in promoting the rise of rationality in government took several forms: policy research institutions (such as the Brookings Institution, Resources for the Future, the Rand Corporation, and the New York Bureau of Municipal Research and its counterparts in other cities);[6] business organizations (such as the National Civic Federation at the beginning of the century and the Business Council and the Committee for Economic Development in the post-World War II period); private foundations (notably the Ford, Rockefeller, and Carnegie Foundations); projects, programs, and centers at leading universities (such as the State-Local Finances Project at the George Washington University and the recent spate of programs and centers in "Public Affairs" and "Public Policy"); and even units within government (such as the Bureau of the Budget within the Executive Office of the President). The various organizations are distinct, but they tend to cooperate closely, to keep each other well informed, and to circulate personnel among themselves—and between themselves and corporate hierarchies—in a steady stream.[7]

Together, this set of organizations has been accurately characterized by Domhoff as "policy-planning and consensus-seeking organizations of the power elite . . . the central units in the policy network [through which] the various special interests join together to forge general policies which will benefit them as a whole" (1974, 7, 6). The organizations have been involved in three major ways: advocating depoliticized procedures for evaluating and choosing public policies, particularly budgetary choices; conducting such policy analyses themselves; and selecting, training, and socializing the public sector's future experts.

Domhoff notes that studies on "the financing and leadership of these organizations . . . show beyond a doubt that they are underwritten and directed by the same upper-class men who control the major corporations, banks, foundations, and law firms" (1974, 7). The issue of financing and control is important because of the widespread belief that it is really the experts themselves who are important in shaping the analyses of alternative social policies that emerge from the policy-analysis and planning organizations. Not so, Domhoff points out: "the upper-middle-class experts thought by some to be our real rulers are, in fact, busily dispensing advice to those who hire them" (1974, 8). He makes the same point at length in an earlier essay:

> Members of the upper class and their high-level corporation executives finance and control the universities, foundations, institutes, and associations which train and are repositories for the experts. This control over the sources of expertise implies at the very least the power to select, train, and encourage those who will become experts. . . . Members of the power elite have financed, encouraged, and utilized the experts trained in the universities, foundations, institutes, and associations of which they are trustees and directors (1968, 273, 275).

These organizations were central to the rise of rationality in government—beginning with their role in the municipal reform movement, and continuing with their successful efforts to establish the federal Bureau of the Budget and to repeatedly expand its powers at the expense both of public debate and of the Congress and the various component parts of the executive branch, which tended to be more responsive to local and particularistic interests. Some of these same organizations were actively involved in the promotion of BCA.

The Case of BCA

The BCA paradigm contains a view of social welfare similar to that contained in the ideology that accompanied the rise of rationality. BCA, too, is based on the assumption that the basic institutions of society are to be taken as given and that the goal of public policy is to promote common interests within this established social framework. Accordingly, it too regards the interest of the capitalist class in the stabilization and expansion of the existing economic system as an interest of society as a whole—and sees competing claims by particular groups of capitalists, by poor or working people, or by others as "political" or "special" interests that conflict with the general "public" interest. For example, in its applications in the water resources area following the Flood Control Act of 1936, "BCA was originally a way to emphasize the public interest in projects inspired by local political interests" (Grubb, Whittington, and Humphries 1984, 158). The thrust of the theory as well as practice of BCA has been to remove the evaluation and choice of alternative proposed public expenditures from the realm of "politics," to entrust it as much as possible to expert practitioners, and to centralize governmental power in (and within) the executive branch.

Several of the organizations discussed above as prime movers for "the rise of rationality in government" played important roles in the development, promotion, and implementation of BCA. Among these are the Committee for Economic Development (CED), the Brookings Institution, Resources for the Future, the Ford Foundation, the U.S. Bureau of the Budget, and the Rand Corporation. An elite university-based and foundation-funded program, the Harvard Water Resources Program (financed by the Rockefeller Foundation), was actively involved in the development of theory and the critical evaluation of BCA practice in the water resources area in the late 1950s and early 1960s; its major publication, *The Design of Water Resource Systems* (Maass et al. 1962), was very influential.

BCA first saw large-scale use outside of the water resources area in the Department of Defense in the early 1960s. Defense Secretary Robert McNamara (former president of the Ford Motor Company) brought in a number of top analysts—including Charles J. Hitch, Alain Enthoven, and Henry S. Rowen—from Rand, where they had spent years developing managerial and analytical techniques for evaluating and controlling military expenditures. Their explicit goals included subjecting the narrowly based demands made by the separate military services to rational centralized control, based in the Office of the Secretary of Defense. The results in the Pentagon were regarded as so successful that in the mid-1960s an effort was made to apply the same techniques throughout the executive branch of the federal government. This effort was coordinated by Rowen, who was made an assistant director of the Budget Bureau and head of the Program Evaluation Staff, a special unit created within BOB. BCA was one part of the more general effort, largely subsumed under the rubric of the planning-programming-budgeting system (PPBS), to promote "rationality" and centralize power in federal government budgetary decision-making. PPBS met with only partial success, primarily because of the resistance of those governmental bureaucracies, congressional power centers, and special interest groups that stood to lose from its implementation.[8]

The explicit concern of the Committee for Economic Development—probably the most important single corporate liberal policy planning group on domestic matters during the postwar period (see Schriftgeisser 1960 and 1967; Domhoff 1971, ch. 6)—with the advancement of BCA is shown in their 1966 Research and Policy Committee Statement on National Policy, *Budgeting for National Objectives*. This report's entire thrust was in support of further rationalization and centralization of budgetary practice: "We recommend that cost-benefit and cost-effectiveness techniques be applied and utilized intensively by the agencies and the Bureau of the Budget" (CED 1966, 38).

The Brookings Institution has been centrally concerned with the federal budgetary process ever since its precursor, the Institute for Government Research (headed by Robert Brookings) played a crucial role in the formulation and passage of the Budget and Accounting Act of 1921, which established the Bureau of the Budget. One indication of Brookings's interest in and support of the spreading application of BCA was its sponsorship of two major academic conferences and subsequent publication of the resulting collections of papers on *Measuring Benefits of Government Investments* (Dorfman 1965) and *Problems in Public Expenditure Analysis* (Chase 1968).

Finally, it is worth noting that the governmental units most involved in the promotion of BCA, and that themselves made the most use of it, were those concerned with centralizing decision-making power into the hands of high-level government executives. Most prominent in this regard, of course, has been the U.S. Bureau of the Budget, reorganized in the early 1970s into the Office of Management and Budget, which more than any other governmental unit has considered public expenditures from the perspective of the needs of the system as a whole.

The rise of BCA and the application of market criteria to public budgetary choices was at least partially a response to the emergence of an expenditure-determination process that was threatening to capitalist class interests—an openly political process wherein groups (and, potentially, classes) fought for their interests. As the potential power and control of working-class and particularistic capitalist elements became increasingly evident, the replacement of this political process by a process that relied heavily on experts and on the application of "objective" (i.e., market) criteria was a real contribution to the interests of the capitalist class. The greater the extent to which BCA is applied, the less is the scope for the operation of "political" forces that might tend to favor either working-class or particularistic capitalist interests. For example, Robert Haveman, a leading theorist and practitioner of BCA, has argued that aggressive and effective use of BCA in the areas of natural resource and environmental quality programs can serve to "redress the balance between private interests and the public interest" by reducing the extent to which special interest groups are able to get their way at the expense of the public as a whole (1973, 876).

Murray L. Weidenbaum, who was an important early participant in and observer of the rise of BCA, spells this out quite clearly: "Perhaps the overriding value of benefit/cost analysis has been in demonstrating the importance of making fairly objective economic analysis of proposed essentially political actions and perhaps narrowing the area in which political forces may operate" (in Lyden and Miller 1968, 176). In fact, however, the role of BCA is not less political than the other forces that Weidenbaum has in mind, even though it may appear less so because it operates more indirectly: The "general" interests supported by BCA's concern with efficiency and social welfare reflect not *less* politics, but rather *different* politics, than those of the particularistic interests that he characterizes as "political."

The argument being made here about the selection function of BCA is just the reverse of the more common contention of liberal critics of BCA—that it offers a means by which special interests are able to get their way. As we saw in Chapter 3, the BCAs undertaken by the U.S. Army Corps of Engineers and the Interior Department's Bureau of Reclamation are frequently cited as examples of biased studies, manipulated by the choice of assumptions and of discount rates, that have served to promote the interests of the Corps, the BuRec, and their "special interest" client groups in particular geographical areas in gaining approval for as many water projects as they can. There can be no doubt that these agencies—like other proponents of particular categories of projects, both inside and outside of the federal government—attempted to use the analyses in this way or that they succeeded to some extent, particularly in the early years of BCA when there were relatively few outside people equipped to challenge their analyses. On balance, however, and over the long run, the net impact of BCA has been, as I argued in Chapter 4, precisely the opposite: It has reduced the ability of the Corps, the BuRec, and other particular groups to get their way. It is important to note that BCAs are subject to review by the most centralized agencies of government—at the federal level, by what used to be the Bureau of the Budget and is now the Office of Management and Budget. In addition to their own capacity for undertaking as well as reviewing BCAs, these central agencies also can call on academic economist practitioners and theorists of BCA whose interest is in the integrity of the discipline and of their professional credentials; these academics hold a conception of the "public interest" that is generally similar to that of the class-conscious capitalists.

Proponents of BCA frequently cite its "neutrality," arguing that it merely provides a tool that can be used as an input to any of a variety of political processes. While there may be some validity to this claim in the abstract (for the use of organized human intelligence to deal with social problems does not in itself necessarily favor any class or group), the particular form of BCA that evolved in this country shared the antidemocratic nature of the more general rise of rationality and expertise. The sophisticated and often technical nature of the BCA process effectively disqualified, intimidated, and excluded most citizens from participation.

Instead of offering an arena in which different interests can openly contend, BCA has worked to select projects according to the general needs of the capitalist system as indicated by market criteria (the following section will have more on this point) and high-level executive branch political determinations. The theory and practice of BCA also contribute to capitalist class interests by increasing the *acceptability* of the public expenditure and regulatory decisions that are made. Even in those cases where BCA has little or no impact on the actual content of decisions, the apparent use of experts and of sophisticated scientific decision criteria gives the decisions an aura of objectively and of scientific validity that they would not otherwise have. To the extent that people are respectful of—or intimidated by—expertise, quantitative analyses, and technical jargon, the reported recommendations will tend to confer legitimacy on budgetary decisions.

There were, of course, limits on the extent to which the proponents of BCA had their way and to which BCA was actually significant in shaping and legitimizing public expenditures. Particular interests do frequently prevail in the selection of public expenditures. But to the extent that BCA was implemented and had an influence, it tended to promote the long-term capitalist class interest in stabilizing, rationalizing, legitimizing, and expanding the existing economic and social structure. The increased use of BCA within government was accompanied by the same ideology, promoted by the same organizations, and responded to the same capitalist needs, as the more general rise of rationality in U.S. government. In this way, BCA served the powerful.

After the Rise: Postcript and Preview

As the quarter-century period of relative prosperity that began in the late 1940s gave way to a new (and still continuing) period of economic crisis, an altered set of economic and political forces brought a halt to what we have termed the rise of rationality in government. The conservative political and ideological ascendancy that emerged in the context of this economic crisis has had major impacts on the role played by the state in contemporary U.S. capitalism—and the use of BCA during the past decade and a half has reflected these more general developments.

Slower economic growth and reduced international competitiveness, on the one hand, and the related rightward shift of domestic political forces, on the other hand, have resulted in the previous period's concern for channeling and guiding the growth of government economic activity being superseded by a desire to contain and reverse that growth in both the budgetary and regulatory areas. The kind of rationality discussed in the preceding pages has to a considerable extent given way to an extreme pro-market ideology (rather than recognizing "market failure" and attempting to calculate what markets would have produced in its absence, this newly ascendant ideology simply assumes away the existence of that market failure). At the same time, the role of experts and systematic policy analysis attempting to identify the long-run interests of the capitalist class as a whole has been eclipsed by the exercise of political power by particular class fragments and fractions. Even the most superficial analyses of recent budgetary outcomes are forced to conclude that both areas of increase (such as military procurement) and areas of decrease (domestic social spending) are based on little more than the exercise of political muscle.

In this context, BCA no longer plays a significant role in helping to *identify* those expenditure options that are most in the long-run interests of the system as a whole, as viewed from a capitalist class perspective. Instead, its role has become much more to help to *justify* expenditure and regulatory measures already favored by powerful interests. Meanwhile, this growing misuse and abuse of BCA has to some extent been countered by forces opposed to conservative initiatives, who have used the methods and techniques of BCA to expose its misuse by conservatives and to promote more liberal and progressive alternatives.

These developments, which reflect the contradictions that emerge in the process of capitalist development and which illustrate the general point that the state undergoes changes as the capital accumulation process unfolds, will be analyzed in more detail in Chapter 9. They have been briefly characterized here to stress that the preceding analysis of the emergence and growth of BCA deals with a specific historical period and offers an incomplete basis for understanding the nature and significance of the use of BCA during the two final decades of the twentieth century.

THE MATERIALISTIC BIAS OF BCA: REINFORCING MARKET LOGIC

The foregoing discussion has focused on how BCA and related developments have helped the capitalist class to exercise power over expenditure and regulatory decisions—especially on the way BCA has insulated these decisions from other political pressures. In addition, the selection of alternatives favorable to profitable capital accumulation is aided by the analytic logic of BCA itself. This is especially true of the BCA paradigm's narrowly defined welfare function and its willingness to pay valuation criterion, which produce serious distortions and biases in the analysis and evaluation of potential changes in individual welfares. BCA's focus on economic welfare as measured by people's market-revealed willingness to pay for consumption goods and services reflects an overemphasis on commodities. As a result, BCA fails to take into account other welfare-relevant aspects of alternatives under review.

Public expenditures and regulations can have an extremely wide range of consequences—cultural, psychological, social, political, moral, environmental, and economic among them. BCA does seek to take into account the costs and benefits resulting from "public goods" as well as "private" ones, and this inclusion allows BCA to evaluate much that is excluded from the profit-oriented calculations of private firms. Yet BCA's objective function still limits the analysis to a single subset of consequences—those termed "economic." This narrowness leads to serious distortions not simply because the excluded factors are important, but also because they are inseparable from the "economic" ones.

For example, in the course of his comprehensive analysis of the many consequences of alternative systems for handling the gathering and distribution of human blood for transfusion, Richard M. Titmuss strongly criticizes the attempt to separate out and deal primarily with the "economic" consequences of public policy. He notes that economic analyses of blood transfusion issues have excluded ethical considerations and the whole fabric of values in society, interpersonal relationships, the spirit of altruism, and the question of human freedom; "economists," he concludes, "may fragment systems and values; other people do not" (1970, esp. pp. 11-14, 195-201).

The focus on "economic" consequences is one aspect of what Herbert Gintis, following Marx, has exposed as the "commodity fetishism" of neoclassical welfare economics. He points out that although neoclassical welfare economics ignores them, "the historical development of community, environment, culture, the social relations of everyday life, the structure of and relations among social classes—all ... have direct impact on individual welfare" (1974, 428; see also Gintis 1969; 1970). Gintis has gone beyond criticism to the constructive development of a radical model of individual welfare that provides a framework for including much that is excluded from mainstream welfare economics:

> A radical model of welfare posits that well-being flows from the individual *activities* undertaken in social life. The contribution of an activity to individual welfare depends on (a) the personal *capacities* (physical, cognitive, emotional, aesthetic, and spiritual) the individual has developed to carry out and appreciate the activity, (b) the *social contexts* (work community, family, environment, educational institutions, etc.) within which the activity takes place, and (c) the commodities available to the individual as *instruments* in the performance of the activity (1972b, 273; the model is elaborated in Gintis 1972c).

The BCA paradigm, on the other hand, posits objective functions that include only goods and services—essentially, only what Gintis calls instruments. Yet the alternatives evaluated by BCA are likely to have effects on capacities and social contexts as well, and there is no reason to believe that these effects will be perfectly correlated with the effects on instruments. Thus the general direction of the distortions and biases in the theory and practice of BCA is toward valuing only those commodified goods and services that can be exchanged in the marketplace. In other words, this materialistic bias favors precisely what the capitalist system is best at providing—commodities. As a result, BCA calculations tend to favor the selection of alternatives that are consistent with, rather than challenging to, capitalism's systemic imperative for capital accumulation.

This result should not be surprising, because it reflects the mainstream assumption of BCA's designers that they were trying to remedy cases of "market failure." It is the normal functioning of markets and other capitalist institutions, rather than the conscious application of political power by capitalists, that is of primary importance in generating outcomes that favor capitalist interests. Thus, if for any reason markets themselves cannot be used in an area of output determination, a primary capitalist strategy is to structure the choice process and decision criteria so that the outcome is the same as would have been reached if the markets had been functioning. BCA, using essentially market criteria in search of such outcomes, forms a natural part of this strategy. Samuel Bowles reinforces the point being made here when he notes that, "In practice, public expenditure criteria tend to reintroduce in veiled form the very same market criteria which govern resource allocation in the private sector" (1974, 130).

The following subsections are concerned with three particularly important aspects of individual welfare that the BCA objective function, following market criteria, tends to exclude from consideration: effects on production activities as opposed to consumption ones; effects on individual development as opposed to the satisfaction of existing preferences; and effects of participation in decision-making as opposed to consequences stemming from the decisions made.[9]

Concern with Consumption, Exclusion of Production

The BCA objective function is based on the implicit assumption that what is important to an individual's welfare is his or her consumption of goods and services (broadly defined to include public goods). People are thought of as consumers—not as individuals who engage in productive activities as well as in consumption and whose welfare depends on the nature of their work activities as well as on the goods and services they consume.

Public expenditures and regulations not only affect productive activity directly (e.g., regulation of workplace safety) but also have important indirect effects on productive activity. Educational expenditures, for example, prepare people for certain kinds of work and not for others, while expenditures on transportation, housing, community development, health, and other areas provide the infrastructure essential for the maintenance of the structure of capitalist production, and provide people with benefits that contribute to their being able to tolerate and accept the work they have to do (Bowles and Gintis 1976; O'Connor 1973, chs. 4-6). Nevertheless, BCAs fail to value the effects of proposed alternatives on the nature of productive activities. Analyses of increased school class size, for example, focus on the effects on children's learning while ignoring impacts on the nature of teachers' working lives.

The importance of productive activity for individual welfare hardly needs emphasis. Quite apart from their effects on individual development (discussed in the next subsection), work activities are centrally important both quantitatively (work itself typically occupies approximately one-third of an individual's waking hours, not including associated travel, preparation, and recovery time) and qualitatively (productive, creative labor or the lack of it is a fundamental determinant of an individual's self-conception and sense of well-being). Stephen Hymer and Frank Roosevelt (1972) have emphasized the importance that radical political economists place on the productive sphere of economic life—and the neglect of this area by mainstream economists. In ignoring productive activity as a contributor to individual welfare, therefore, the BCA paradigm is squarely in the tradition of mainstream economics. The direction of the resulting bias in the quantitative results of BCA clearly favors increased production of commodities.

Concern with Satisfying Existing Preferences, Exclusion of Individual Development

Mainstream welfare economics in general, and the BCA paradigm in particular, take individual preferences as given and consider the extent to which these existing preferences are satisfied. This fundamental assumption is seriously flawed. Preferences are in fact significantly influenced by economic factors in general and by the consequences of public expenditures in particular. The next chapter will discuss in some detail the causes and consequences of the endogenousness of preferences; our argument here is simply that individual development—changes in preferences and personal attributes—is a legitimate, important, and welfare-relevant consequence of public expenditure and regulatory decisions that is ignored by BCA.

People develop in accordance with the activities in which they engage. In turn, this development determines their capacities for engaging in and obtaining welfare from other activities and, thus, influences their total welfare. Everyone—except, it would seem, mainstream economists in their professional role—is aware of this, and many people are engaged, more or less self-consciously, in some effort of self-development, change, growth, or personal improvement. In the words of Herbert Gintis, "A basic motivation of economic activity is that of promoting personal development through the acquisition of certain behavioral patterns and capacities in production and consumption. By ruling out this phenomenon, neoclassical welfare theory is guilty of a crass fetishism of commodities:

well-being comes to depend on what an individual *has*, rather than what he or she *is*, or can *do*" (1975, 2-3).

Writing over a century ago, John Stuart Mill argued that the effects of governmental actions on personal development are more important than their impact in terms of satisfying existing preferences. For Mill, as Carole Pateman explains,

> The criterion to be used to judge political institutions in this light is "the degree to which they promote the general mental advancement of the community." . . . [Mill] is against a benevolent despotism, which as he points out, could, if it were all-seeing, ensure that the "business" side of government were properly carried out, because, as he asks, "What sort of human beings can be formed under such a regime? What development can either their thinking or their active faculties attain under it? . . . Their moral capacities are equally stunted. Wherever the sphere of action of human beings is artificially circumscribed, their sentiments are narrowed and dwarfed" (Pateman 1970, 28-29; the passages by Mill are from his *Representative Government*).

Concern with Consequences, Exclusion of Process

Gintis's radical model of welfare incorporates the central insight that an individual's welfare grows out of the activities in which he or she engages—rather than simply being a function of the goods and services available as instruments for these activities. This activity orientation is important to an adequate model of human welfare—and it is absent from the objective function of the BCA paradigm, which would have us consider just the goods and services made available to individuals by public expenditures—rather than the processes through which they are made available or the activities that the expenditures enable people to partake in. The importance of productive activities is one instance of this general point. Another is the process of analysis and decision itself. Participation in analysis and decision-making is not only important instrumentally, as a means of reaching better decisions. In its own right, participation or nonparticipation affects individuals' welfare.

This is analogous to the way preparation and eating of food are not merely means of providing one's body with essential nutrients but are themselves welfare-relevant activities. The contribution, of course, can be either positive or negative: People's welfare can be decreased by participation in an activity that is unpleasant for them, by knowing that they have been excluded from an activity that they would like to take part in, or simply by having knowledge that an important set of decisions is being made in a certain matter. Conversely, people's welfare can be increased by participating in a pleasant activity, by knowing that they have the opportunity to participate in the activity if they choose to do so (even if they do not choose to exercise the option), or simply by knowing that important decisions are being made in a way that they approve of.

The independent importance of processes of deliberation and decision has been emphasized by Robert Paul Wolff. His argument can be applied directly to the case of BCA; it concerns

> that collective deliberation upon social goals and collective determination of social choices which used to be known as direct democracy, and which I shall call rational community. Rational community is not merely the efficient means to such desirable political ends as peace, order, or distributive justice. It is an activity, an experience, a reciprocity of consciousness among morally and politically equal rational agents who freely come together and deliberate with one another for the purpose of concerting their wills in the positing of collective goals and in the performance of common actions.... To be sure, good consequences for each and for all may flow from the dialogue; and there may be men sufficiently impoverished in their political imagination to suppose that such instrumental value is the only merit of rational community. But men may take an interest in the existence of the dialogue itself, and if they do, they will strive to create a political order whose essence just *is* that dialogue (1968, 191-92).

In an early contribution to an influential volume in the BCA literature, Stephen Marglin suggested that social welfare might depend not only on the total level of net benefits and on their distribution, but also on the process by which the distribution of benefits was determined: "The size of the economic pie and its division may not be the only factors of concern to the community—the method of slicing may also be relevant" (1962, 63). This potentially important point has never, to my knowledge, been developed in the literature—to say nothing of being incorporated into the BCA paradigm or being used in any way in the practice of BCA. In this way, also, the BCA paradigm's objective function excludes matters highly relevant to individual, and hence social, welfare.

NOTES

1. See O'Connor (1973), Gough (1979), and Foley (1978).
2. The argument and approach of this section draw on the work of a number of students of reforms in the twentieth-century United States. Many of the results of this work are admirably surveyed and synthesized by G. William Domhoff (1968, 1971, 1974, 1979, 1980, 1983). Among the important studies are those of Bowles and Gintis (1976) on education; Eakins (1966, 1972) on corporate liberal policy research institutions; Haber (1964) on the ideology of efficiency in the progressive era; Hays (1964) on the municipal reform movement; Kolko (1967) on the regulation of business and industrial conditions; O'Connor (1973, ch. 3) on government budgeting; Weinstein (1968) on the rise of corporate liberal ideology; and Williams (1966), whose influential conceptualization of U.S. history provided a framework for much of the work cited here.
3. The evidence for the proposition that it has been primarily corporate capitalists, rather than their brothers from the competitive sector, who have been the dominant members of the U.S. ruling class and its power elite has been summarized clearly and in considerable detail in the series of works by G. William Domhoff cited in the preceding footnote. Domhoff's useful definitions of the key concepts of ruling class and power elite are worth noting here:

   > By a ruling class, I mean a clearly demarcated social upper class which (a) has a disproportionate amount of wealth and income; (b) generally fares better than other social groups on a variety of well-being statistics . . . ; (c) controls the major economic institutions in the country; and (d) dominates the governmental processes of the country.
   >
   > By a power elite I mean the "operating arm" or "leadership group" or "establishment" of the ruling class. This power elite is made up of active, working members of the ruling class and high-level employees in institutions controlled by members of the ruling class [1974, 5].

4. The existence of common interests does not, of course, lead automatically to behavior that promotes those interests. Mancur Olson, Jr. devotes one chapter of the influential book that was most responsible in bringing this general proposition to the attention of the economics profession (1968, ch. 4), to the question of the working class's ability to act collectively in pursuit of its common interests. Olson argues that Marx was naive and wrong because he failed to recognize that the working class would not automatically unite in a common struggle to overturn the capitalist economic system. The flaws in Olson's interpretation of Marx, and in his understanding of the mechanisms that have frequently produced effective collective action by working people is not my present concern (see Roemer 1978; Booth 1978; and Edel 1979). Instead, I wish to point out that Olson fails to

consider the other side of the coin at all—that he gives no attention to the fact that the capitalist class has been successful in sustaining its rule, in perpetuating the capitalist system, and in promoting its interests within the capitalist order. Class-conscious efforts by capitalists and their representatives have in fact been important in shaping political and economic outcomes—including the evolution and use of BCA. A considerable body of evidence persuasively demonstrates that capitalists don't just sit back and let things happen, that they don't trust any sort of "invisible hand" to effectively guide and coordinate the actions of individual capitalists each pursuing their own narrow, particular interest. Nevertheless, the success of the capitalist class in solving its problem of collective action is a phenomenon that Olson is either unaware of or deems unworthy of attention. His nontreatment of this whole issue is a telling example of the way in which bourgeois social science works to ignore and to obfuscate interesting and important aspects of social reality whose clear portrayal might be damaging to capitalist interests.

5. The best general survey and guide to the literature about these organizations may still be Domhoff (1971, chs. 5-6), who draws heavily on the unpublished dissertation of David Eakins (1966); see also Domhoff (1983, 84-107, 131-43; 1979, ch. 3).

6. See Irvine Alpert and Ann Markusen (1980) for an illuminating analysis of "Think Tanks and Capitalist Policy," based in part on personal experiences at Brookings and at Resources for the Future.

7. The fact that important executive positions in government have frequently been filled by corporate leaders should also be noted. Even though they play such an important role in the socialization and selection of their hired experts and executives, capitalists themselves often opt to assume high government positions (Salzman and Domhoff 1980; see also Weinstein 1968, 96, 103).

8. On the nature and history of PPBS, see the very useful collections of documentary, pedagogical, promotional, and analytical material prepared by Lyden and Miller (1968; rev. ed. 1972), the U.S. Congress's Joint Economic Committee (1969), and the U.S. Senate's Committee on Government Operations (1970). Allen Schick (1973) and Stanley Botner (1970; 1972) provide helpful interpretations of the "demise of federal PPB." Schick has also examined the efforts to introduce PPBS at the state level (1971).

9. Note that the categories of effects emphasized in this radical critique extend beyond the types of omission from the BCA objective function emphasized by the liberal critics of BCA whose arguments were reviewed in Chapter 3.

8 PERPETUATING CAPITALISM
The Reinforcement Function of BCA

Chapter 7 demonstrated a number of ways in which benefit-cost analysis has aided the process of selecting government policies favorable to capitalist accumulation. An equally fundamental interest of capitalists is in the continuation, or reproduction, of the basic institutional arrangements of their economic system. Both the process through which BCA is conducted and the welfare criterion that it employs tend to perpetuate the institutional structure of capitalism. BCA must be understood in terms of this *reinforcement function* as well as in terms of its selection function.

The BCA paradigm presents selection as the central goal of BCA but does not include explicit recognition of the need for anything like a reinforcement function. It is based on a generally implicit acceptance of existing institutional arrangements. The formulation of Otto Eckstein deserves repetition: "The economist must interpret the desires of the policy people whom he is serving and express them in an analytical form as an objective function. He then seeks to maximize this function, *given* the empirical relations in the economy and *the institutional constraints* that may be appropriate to the analysis" (1961, 445; emphasis added). For proponents and practitioners of BCA, the continued existence of the capitalist system is never in question—it is simply taken as "given," as a set of "institutional constraints."

In fact, however, capitalist institutions are not fixed or immutable. Like all other sets of social, economic, and political institutions, they emerged historically to replace earlier institutional arrangements, and the question about their future replacement by some other set of institutions is not whether it will happen but when, and how, and by what. Moving away from this grand historical level, anyone who recognizes the coexistence of capitalism's pervasive inequality and many destructive consequences for the great majority of the population, on the one hand, and of a formally democratic political system characterized by widespread suffrage, on the other hand, must ask how the system is able to maintain itself. This is not viewed as a problem from the mainstream public policy perspective, which denies or fails to recognize the negative consequences of the capitalist system. But from the perspective of radical political economics, the successful perpetuation of capitalist institutions is problematic and requires explanation.

A thorough discussion of the multiple means by which capitalist institutions tend to be reproduced is well beyond the scope of the present inquiry. Part of the explanation lies in capitalism's relative success in generating economic growth and a general rise in the material standard of living. In addition, the operation of socializing institutions, of ideology, and of the media are each important, as are the conscious efforts of those with wealth and power. Furthermore, the organization of the market system itself provides what Charles E. Lindblom (1982) has analyzed as a sort of "prison" that limits not only the range of acceptable public policies but also the range of acceptable thinking about alternative possible economic and social arrangements. Perhaps most important, as I noted in Chapter 6, the state operates in a number of ways to maintain and reproduce the economic arrangements that promote the long-run interests of the capitalist class.

BCA fits into this larger picture. In an area potentially challenging to a market-based system—analyzing situations characterized by "market failures" and considering governmental alternatives—the theory and practice of the BCA paradigm are as if designed with the goal of capitalist reproduction clearly in mind. At the most general level, the public policy perspective of BCA helps to obscure the class nature of capitalist society and of its prevailing political institutions. BCA is consistent with the rest of the broad range of mechanisms that operate to reproduce capitalist institutions, rather than to undermine, question, or challenge them. This chapter will examine two major ways in which BCA's reinforcement function is accomplished.

First, the depoliticized nature of the BCA process reinforces the institutional structure of capitalism. The people who will be affected by expenditure and regulatory decisions play only a passive role, in contrast to the active roles played by experts, analysts, and decision-makers. In this way, what I term "the social relations of BCA" correspond to the alienated social relations of production that are at the heart of the capitalist system. This correspondence contributes to the stability of the existing social structure. In the implementation of BCA, people do not have experiences of participation, politicization, or empowerment that might tend to call into question those social relations of production.

Second, the welfare criteria incorporated into the BCA paradigm reinforce the more general pattern of market-based outcomes in the society as a whole. The theory and practice of BCA—based as they are on measuring individuals' welfare by their own preferences as revealed in market choices—reinforce the dominant ideology of consumer sovereignty. By contributing to a principal ideological mechanism for making the capitalist system appear reasonable and legitimate, BCA reduces the likelihood of popular discontent not only with the pro-capitalist patterns of expenditures and regulation selected by BCA, but also with the more general set of outcomes that is justified on the same grounds. When this legitimating function of BCA is subjected to careful scrutiny, however, it is seen to be based on a foundation of widely shared *mis*beliefs.

The various functions of BCA are, of course, part of a single institutional and ideological fabric, which I am separating into different strands solely in order to facilitate analysis. Therefore issues discussed in this chapter will overlap with those discussed in the previous one, but with a different emphasis. For example, both chapters discuss BCA's depoliticization of public policy determination. The focus of Chapter 7 was on how this influences the specific policies that are adopted, while the focus of Chapter 8 will be on how it tends to preserve the broader set of political, social, and economic institutions of which BCA is a part. Put another way, Chapter 7 emphasized the question of whose interests are or are not represented in the decision-making process, while Chapter 8 will emphasize the impact on the experiences, personalities, and expectations of those who are excluded from participation. With regard to the question of individual preferences, Chapter 7 dealt with the willingness to pay (WTP) criterion's relative overvaluation of preferences conducive to pro-capitalist outcomes. Chapter 8's argument will be that even if a much broader range of preferences could be evaluated in a more balanced way, the WTP criterion would still support the false ideology of consumer sovereignty, thereby discouraging citizens from pursuing alternatives to existing economic arrangements.

THE SOCIAL RELATIONS OF BCA: EXPERTS AND ALIENATION

The prevailing BCA paradigm envisions a process of evaluation and decision-making that relies on expert analysts and politically responsible decision-makers. Participation by others is generally limited to providing information about preferences, although even this role is rare as analysts prefer the "objective" data obtained by inferences about preferences based on market behavior. The BCA paradigm considers and deals with people only as isolated individuals. There is no notion that individuals might come together to discuss, evaluate, debate, and decide through any sort of collective process.

Like other social processes, the public policy decision-making process in which BCA plays a role produces more than its ostensible product—in this case, more than decisions. Most important, it produces people, in the sense that individuals' experiences shape their personal development, their consciousness, their expectations, their beliefs, and their preferences. A process of evaluation and decision-making that most individuals read about in the newspaper but do not play a personal role in—that treats their preferences as objects to be isolated and quantified—is a process that will reinforce tendencies toward passivity and apathy. It will reinforce regarding social experience as something that happens to one rather than something that one helps to create; it will push people toward being passive observers rather than active and involved human beings. Such personality attributes tend to decrease rather than increase human welfare.

The principal argument of the present section is an extension and elaboration of this observation. The structure of social relationships that people encounter in the area of public policy evaluation and choice has consequences for personal development, consequences that conform to the needs of the capitalist system. The social relations of BCA correspond to, and therefore help to reinforce and reproduce, the social relations of capitalist production (and, at the same time, correspond to the social relations that prevail in other areas of social life). This is not to claim that the social relations of BCA independently shape people, but that these relationships have arisen—under the influence of what Samuel Bowles and Herbert Gintis have called "the long shadow of work" (1976, 125)—in support of the social relations of production. Thus, they contribute to the reproduction of the prevailing social system rather than provide a source of ideas and experiences that might tend to undermine that structure.

One of the foundations of radical political economics is the observation that at the base of all past and present social systems are the relationships that people enter into with each other in the course of providing the material means of their existence. Under capitalism, these *social relations of production* can be characterized most fundamentally as based on a social division of labor that embodies domination and subordination in the process of producing surplus value for the benefit of capitalists. Capitalist work organization is, with rare exceptions, nonparticipatory and highly undemocratic: Workers do as they are told by their bosses. This is one important way in which labor under capitalism is alienated labor.

Such social relations are not only unpleasant for the great majority of workers, they are also unnatural and conflict with basic human desires for meaning, cooperation, and control over one's own life and activities. Thus, a central problem that must be solved by capitalists is the creation and maintenance of a labor force willing and able to work in a wage-labor system characterized by capitalist social relations of production. The ways that capitalists have dealt with the problem, and the responses by workers, comprise much of the history of capitalism. Although there have been changes through time in the organization of capitalist workplaces, and variations today among the means used to control workers in different segments of the labor force, the fundamentally nonparticipatory and antidemocratic nature of capitalist social relations of production has been a constant (Edwards 1979; Gordon, Edwards, and Reich 1982).

Samuel Bowles and Herbert Gintis (1976, ch. 5) have analyzed the way that educational institutions operate to shape people so that they will be prepared to take their places as workers within such hierarchical enterprises. In their investigation of the role played by schooling in the reproduction of the labor force, they argue that the relationships between students and teachers, among students, and between students and their schoolwork all provide students with a massive body of personal experience that shapes their consciousness—their ideas of what is necessary and what is possible—in ways that prepare them for lives as workers in the structured inequality of capitalist workplaces. This is so, Bowles and Gintis contend, because the social relations of education *correspond* in important ways to the social relations of production. They argue that twentieth-century U.S. education has taken its particular form in response to the needs of employers—and they explain the mechanisms through which corporate capitalists have dominated the process of formulating educational policies favorable to their long-run interests (similar to the mechanisms used in promoting the rise of rationality in government, discussed in Chapter 7). In an article coauthored with Peter Meyer, Bowles and Gintis summarize the core of their argument in this way:

> Both inequality and repressiveness in the educational sphere ... are best understood as reflections of the social relations of hierarchy and subordination in the capitalist economy.... The key which unlocks the secret of social relations of U.S. education lies in the capitalist economy itself.
>
> The most fruitful way to understand the relationship between schooling and economic life in the U.S. is to grasp the essential structural similarity between their respective social relations. The *correspondence* between these social relations is pervasive, and accounts for the ability of the educational system to *reproduce* the social relations of production by reproducing an amenable labor force. The *experience* of schooling, and not merely the *content* of formal learning, is central to this process, and the process is efficacious because the structures of the schooling and work experiences are conformable (1975, 3–4; emphasis in original).

This concept of correspondence is also central to our analysis of the way that the social relations of BCA contribute to the reproduction of the prevailing social relations of production. Experiences with BCA reinforce experiences in the workplace; BCA does not provide divergent experiences of participation and control that could raise disruptive expectations about what might be possible in the realm of production or even give rise to conscious awareness that things might be different. In one way, the link between the social relations of BCA and those of production is closer than that between the social relations of education and of production that I have cited as analogous. In the case of education, the relationship is sequential, with many years of schooling preparing people for many more years of working. For governmental evaluating and choosing among alternative spending and regulatory proposals, however, the correspondence is simultaneous: People experience both the social relations of BCA and the social relations of production throughout their adult lives.

In the theory and practice of BCA, there are a number of important correspondences to capitalist social relations of production. Analysis, evaluation, and decision-making are carried out almost exclusively by experts and politicians; the majority of citizens relate to the process only passively, paying their taxes and living with the consequences of the projects and policies adopted; the structured inequality of these social roles, like those in the workplace, is nonparticipatory and antidemocratic. In the case of public policy determination, notions of "leaving it to the experts" because they "know best" or have "the proper training" echo similar ideas about "leaving it to management." In his analysis of "The Quality of Life and the Limits of Cost-Benefit Analysis," BCA proponent A. J. Culyer notes that the "role of specialists and experts at all levels of the decision-making machinery of supposedly democratic governments . . . is steadily increasing," that people perceive "a trend toward an elite technocracy," and that "society is seen as divided into 'them' and 'us,' the governors and the governed, the decision 'makers' and the decision 'takers' " (1977, 142).

In many cases the tendency in this direction, which follows naturally from the lack of any allotted role for public participation in the process of BCA, is reinforced by practices that operate to put off, discourage, and render ineffective the efforts of those who seek to play a role in the process. The nature of the language used, the form of reports, and the conduct of hearings often contribute to obfuscation of the issues under review, reinforcement of the power of experts and decision-makers, and diminished accountability to the public. Michael Baram cites "the cost-benefit approaches of the Nuclear Regulatory Commission and the National Bureau of Standards [as] examples of complex regulatory decision-records that are virtually incomprehensible and unreviewable except by highly persistent and technically sophisticated individuals" (1980, 490).

It would be an overstatement to claim that BCA never involves citizen participation. But the participation that takes place is generally what Ira Katznelson and Mark Kesselman term "inauthentic" rather than "authentic" participation: "The key issue is thus not whether people participate . . . but what the *terms* of the participation are." In the case of inauthentic participation, "individuals are given the feeling of participating in decision making but are not accorded the power to actually control the decision-making process" (1979, 15). A case study of local government use of BCA in England, for example, concluded that participation was used "not to broaden the base of democracy, but to 'cool out' potential opposition by cooptation" (Bennington and Skelton 1975, 417). Clearly, participation of this sort does not alter the social relations of BCA in a way that threatens capitalist reproduction.[1]

While I have emphasized the way that the social relations of BCA have contributed to the reproduction of the social relations of capitalist production, it is important to recognize that there is also an important causal link operating in the reverse direction. A central reason that there is so little demand for participation in evaluating and deciding on public expenditure and regulatory matters is that people's experiences in the workplace, the most important single source of adult experience in shaping and perpetuating consciousness, do not provide familiarity with participation and control. Carole Pateman (1970) has made this argument persuasively, in some detail and with a great deal of documentation, for the broader case of political participation in general; her *Participation and Democratic Theory* finds the major cause of the low level of political participation in western democracies to be the organization of work that offers workers little opportunity for participation or control. In the terminology I have been using, she demonstrates the existence of a strong correspondence between the social relations of production and the social relations of political life in general. The correspondence between the two spheres mutually reinforces the nonparticipatory nature of each.

Indeed, the lack of participation in decision-making, the unequal outcomes that result from alienated processes, and the stagnation of individual development are all mutually reinforcing. The process is circular and cumulative, and it is stable within the realm of production and also the realm of BCA. The correspondence between these two realms—in addition to their joint correspondence with the social relations in education and in other spheres of social life—adds an even stronger degree of stabilization to each element.

Paolo Freire has written that "to alienate men from their own decision-making is to change them into objects" (1972, 73). That has been one result of the depoliticization of the process of evaluation and determination of public expenditures and regulations by entrusting it almost entirely to experts and politically chosen executives. This is not only greatly destructive of human and social welfare in itself, but it also contributes to the continuation of an exploitative social system. Objects can be manipulated much more easily than subjects; objects do not struggle to change society or to make their own history. To the extent, therefore, that the social relations of benefit-cost analysis successfully contribute to people's alienation from their work and from political life, the theory of BCA and its implementation in practice contribute to the interests of the capitalist class by reinforcing the institutional arrangements of capitalist society.[2]

PREFERENCES AND INTERESTS: FALSE LEGITIMATION

The promotion of capitalist interests will be better served to the extent that BCA is able to contribute to the general acceptance of favored alternatives, as well as to their adoption. One important means by which BCA is able to do this involves the nature of the two basic value judgments of welfare economics that it incorporates. These are, to quote from our discussion in Chapter 2, that "social welfare depends on the individual welfare of the members of society, and only on these individuals' welfares" and that "an individual is regarded as better off if and only if that individual believes that he or she is."

Because these value judgments seem reasonable and appealing, their adoption by BCA tends to lend legitimacy to its conclusions. I.M.D. Little's observation concerning welfare economics in general applies with particular force to the theoretical foundations of BCA: "Much of the importance of the theory lies in the fact that it has been used to give an apparently respectable scientific basis to political arguments" (1957, 258).

The implications and effects of BCA's being based on individual preferences are broader and deeper than an increased legitimacy for the particular selections that it makes. Just as the principal use and effect of theoretical welfare economics has been to provide justification for an economic system based on private property and unregulated markets, the theoretical basis of the BCA paradigm indicates that individual choices can be the primary factor in determining outcomes even in those cases where there is market failure. And if "consumer sovereignty" is the key factor in shaping both private and public sector outcomes, then what possible basis can ordinary members of the society—who in their roles as consumers are, in the final analysis, "sovereign" in capitalist society—have for dissatisfaction with the system? In short, the welfare theory underlying BCA helps to legitimate not only the results of specific applications of BCA, not only the use of BCA as a means of undertaking comparative evaluation of proposed governmental actions, but ultimately the basic institutional arrangements of the capitalist system itself.

This argument is straightforward, and I will not belabor it further. Rather, I will develop the argument that the legitimacy conferred in this way is a false legitimacy. My contention here is that even if BCA were (contrary to what was argued in Chapter 7) fairly and equitably to evaluate alternatives in terms of the entire range of individual preferences, it would still be seriously misleading as an indicator of what actions would contribute the most to the welfare of individuals. This is because people's expressed *preferences* are likely not to reflect their *interests* accurately.

My argument in support of this contention involves a number of parts, which I shall take up in turn: that preferences and interests are logically distinct concepts; that there are good reasons to believe that preferences do in fact frequently diverge from interests; and that preferences are neither exogenous nor immutable but are endogenous to the overall economic system, to the prevailing distribution of income and wealth, and to choices of public expenditures and regulations.

To minimize the possibility of misunderstanding, it may be helpful to emphasize at the outset that my argument here is limited to establishing the propositions that people's preferences are not accurate indicators of their interests and that this divergence undermines the validity of the conclusion that results of BCA will accurately indicate the comparative contributions to social welfare of alternative proposals for expenditures or regulatory policies. The standard response to such claims (which will almost certainly have occurred to the reader by this time, so deeply ingrained in most of our consciousnesses is this component of liberal ideology) is to denounce the apparent desire to substitute someone else's judgment of what is best for people for that of the people themselves. A moment's reflection, however, should make it clear that these criticisms of the BCA paradigm do not in themselves imply anything about the nature of possible alternatives. In particular, they do not imply a paternalistic solution whereby the values or preferences of some elite group are substituted for those of the people themselves. If that were the only remedy, there would indeed be a strong argument that the cure would be worse than the ailment. But that is not the only possible remedy. In Part IV of this book I shall suggest an alternative that explicitly recognizes the existence of a gap between preferences and interests and that seeks to involve people in a self-conscious process of reducing this gap.

In order to stress that the lack of coincidence between preferences and interests affects everyone, including the author and readers of this book, the first person plural will be used in the following pages. The following two sentences are logically equivalent: "We do not have preferences that accurately reflect our interests" and "People do not have preferences that accurately reflect their interests." The latter, however, makes it too easy to think that the argument applies only to other people, less knowledgeable and sophisticated than ourselves.

The Conceptual Distinction between Preferences and Interests

The first step in establishing that preferences are an unreliable indicator of welfare is to argue that the two concepts are not equivalent—that it is logically possible for *preferences*, on the one hand, and *welfare*, or *interests* (I shall use the terms interchangeably), on the other hand, to diverge.[3]

In the "revealed preference" approach that has dominated theoretical welfare economics in recent decades, the possibility of such divergence is simply assumed away. Indeed, welfare (often called "utility") is defined in terms of preferences. In the authoritative account of Graaff, for example, we read that "a person's welfare map is defined to be identical with his preference map.... To say that his welfare would be higher in A than in B is thus no more than to say that he would choose A rather than B, if he were allowed to make the choice" (1967, 5). Similarly, in the words of one BCA text: "We ask whether a person is better off in ... situation A or situation B. If he expresses a preference for B, or if through his market choices he reveals that he likes B better, then we say that he is better off in B than in A. This 'criterion of individual choice' means merely that the individual's preferences are the standard by which we judge his well-being" (Stokey and Zeckhauser 1978, 263). If greater welfare is defined to be identical with preference, and preference with market choice, then it follows immediately that our market choices result in our getting the maximum welfare available (any available alternative not chosen must, by this definition, have offered me less welfare than the alternative I actually chose).

The equation of preference and interest plays an important ideological role because the words have distinct meanings in ordinary language. Thus, when Stokey and Zeckhauser, in the same paragraph quoted from just above, repeat the common assertion that the individual "is the best judge of his own welfare," they seem to be offering a proposition with empirical content. However, the rest of their own paragraph reveals it to be based on a tautology. Our preferences can only be meaningfully ranked in terms of how well they correspond to our welfare (e.g., be "best") if preferences and welfare are distinct things.

The nature of the distinction between preferences and interests as these terms are commonly understood, and as they will be used in this study, can perhaps be expressed most simply by saying that preferences are what we *want*, whereas interests are what we *need*; that preferences are *subjective*, whereas interests are *objective*; that preferences reflect what we would like to have, whereas interests reflect what would increase our well-being. To talk about my welfare is to talk about my being better or worse off, whereas to talk about my preferences is to talk about my beliefs.

Isaac Balbus (1971) has provided an illuminating analysis of these issues from the viewpoint of a political theorist, using the terms "subjective interest" and "objective interest" rather than the terminology adopted here. He observes that an exclusive focus on subjective interest "is to deny the reality of objective interests and the possibility that an individual may be unaware of, or mistaken about, his interests, i.e., that he may be unaware of, or may misjudge the effect that something has on him." He contends that the "unexamined premise that every individual is the best judge of his own interest . . . is either true by definition (if by 'interest' we mean 'subjective interest') or, probably, false (if by 'interest' we mean 'objective interest')." And he argues at length for the proposition that "Marxian theory, because it recognizes both types of interest and is, above all, concerned with their interrelationship, is both behaviorally and normatively superior to [liberal] Pluralist analysis, which consistently refuses to recognize any but subjective interests" (1971, 153, 154, 155).

Although our preferences will often reflect an accurate consciousness of our interests, Balbus points out two ways in which they may diverge: If we fail to recognize that something affects our welfare, we can be said to have a "lack of consciousness"; if we attribute an impact on our welfare to the wrong thing, we can be said to have "false consciousness" (1971, 153-54). Once these categories are pointed out, it would seem difficult to contend that neither is an empirical possibility. Nevertheless, the BCA paradigm, like mainstream welfare economics in general, continues simply to ignore them.

One significant indication that most people are aware of a divergence of preferences and interests is that we prefer some preference structures over others and regard them as superior. In particular, we regard some sets of preferences as better than those we have now and would regard ourselves as better off if we were to attain the preferred preference structure. To take one everyday example, in recent years literally millions of Americans have engaged in efforts to alter their preferences (not just their behavior) concerning the consumption of food and drink. Many have sought to change their preferences toward foods such as whole grains, fresh vegetables, and low-fat dairy products as opposed to foods that are highly processed, heavily salted, and/or have a high fat content; others have sought to develop sophisticated tastes and an enhanced ability to appreciate gourmet meals.

One of the founding fathers of the Chicago School of economists, writing before the rise of the modern welfare economics theory that underlies BCA, expressed the importance of individuals' searching for new preferences as follows: "We cannot accept want-satisfaction as a final criterion of value because we do not in fact regard our wants as final. Life itself is fundamentally an exploration in the field of value itself and not a mere matter of producing given values" (Knight 1935, 42-43). Legal scholar Laurence Tribe has argued the same general point:

> The whole point of personal or social choice in many situations is not to implement a given system of values in light of perceived facts, but rather to define, and sometimes deliberately to reshape, the values—and hence the identity—of the individual or community that is engaged in the process of choosing. The decision-maker, in short, often chooses not merely how to achieve his ends, but what they are and who he is to become (1973, 36).

The clear implication of this argument is that a method of evaluating proposed governmental actions that takes into account only the effects as measured by citizens' existing preferences is using criteria that diverge from those that the citizens themselves regard as superior—and that are likely to diverge from the future preferences of these same citizens.[4]

Because arguments along the lines being pursued here are so readily misinterpreted, it seems important to emphasize once again that I am not arguing for the proposition that we are not the best judges of our own welfare (in fact, I believe that we are). The argument is, rather, that our preferences do not exactly and precisely reflect our interests, and that in many cases there is a substantial divergence between the preferences that we hold and/or express and the choices that would be most in our own interests. Consequently, a set of institutions, or an approach to comparative evaluation of alternative proposed public policies, that results in outcomes that correspond to our preferences does not necessarily deserve endorsement on the basis of promoting our welfare or serving our interests. If preferences and interests do not always and automatically coincide, it is then possible that an alternative set of institutions, or an alternative approach to evaluating proposed public policies, could do a better job of promoting our interests and increasing our welfare.

Preferences and Interests: Reasons for Divergence

There are several ways in which a divergence of our expressed preferences from our interests can result from incomplete and inaccurate information. Our preferences (like our interests) are not given at birth but are shaped by the experiences of our lives. On the basis of information obtained from our experiences, we form ideas about what sorts of things are available for us to choose among (what our "choice sets" are) and how the various alternatives perceived as being in our choice sets would contribute to our welfare.

With respect to the alternatives that are perceived as available, we obtain limited and imperfect information not only because our own direct experience provides an incomplete basis for making accurate and informed assessments, but also because in our daily lives we receive a great deal of information intended to influence our preferences. This information comes to us through socializing institutions such as family, church, and school; from the media; and from other people who constantly express and reinforce prevailing cultural and social values. Given this incomplete and often inaccurate information, it is reasonable to expect that our preferences will not develop in the direction most conducive to our welfare—and that at any given time, our preferences among the alternatives perceived as available will provide inaccurate estimates of the contributions that these alternatives would make to our welfare. To be somewhat more concrete, most Americans do not have enough information, based on personal experience or on any other source, to express preferences accurately reflecting our interests with respect to potential effects of public policy measures involving, for example, major transportation system restructuring; urban renewal, community development, or other major changes in the built environment; changing land use and land-appearance resulting from water resources development; substantially altered health and educational programs; and/or significant changes in environmental regulations.

Perhaps more important than incomplete information concerning those alternatives that are perceived as available, however, is the limitation on what alternatives are so perceived. That is, many highly welfare-conducive alternatives are not perceived as being in the choice set at all. Thus, even if our preferences did accurately reflect our interests with respect to our perceived choice sets, those choice sets themselves may inappropriately exclude desirable alternatives. In other words, the perceived *constraints* on the choice set may be a more important source of preference-interest divergence than failure to choose optimally among alternatives perceived as available.

In examining the concept of the "availability" of alternatives, it is important to note that although individuals expressing their preferences in the marketplace are *alternative-takers*, people analyzing, deciding, and acting collectively can be *alternative-makers*. Thus, the preferences expressed with respect to the more narrow set of options perceived as individually available may offer a very misleading basis for evaluating the changes in individual welfare to be obtained from alternative choices among the expanded, collectively available choice set. The range of feasible options facing public policy makers and BCA analysts is much broader than that facing individuals.

Barrington Moore, Jr.'s distinction between "realistic" and "utopian" preferences relates directly to this argument. Moore (1967) argues that the two sets of preferences coexist but that only the former generally get expressed because people's social experience influences their subjective probabilities for alternative social states. His formulation suggests the existence of widely shared and broadly similar individual preferences for a considerably altered social order that are normally unexpressed because of the lack of mutual awareness of these preferences and of channels for their expression. Only the "realistic" preferences are utilized in BCA, thereby biasing the evaluation process against alternatives perceived by individuals as unlikely—but that may be unlikely *only because* individuals generally perceive them to be so.

A full examination of why we perceive as realistic only a limited subset of the technically feasible and socially attainable set of alternatives is beyond our present scope. But it is important to note that our perceptions and beliefs emerge from our socialization experience and social activity; that an overwhelming amount and variety of experience in U.S. capitalist society tell us that things could not be very much different or better; and that the set of alternatives perceived as available is not random but systematically reflects the reproduction needs of the capitalist system and the limited opportunities for meeting human needs within that system. Thus, while many of the divergences between interests and preferences can be said to result from a lack of full and accurate information, this is a symptom of deeper causes, and the remedy does not lie simply in efforts to provide people with fuller and more accurate information.[5] Nevertheless, attempts to provide better information may be an important part of the effort to deal with the underlying problem itself—that is, the nature of the capitalist system and the power of the capitalist class.

An additional major reason for concluding that the preferences we express in the marketplace may diverge significantly from our interests is the existence of *dual preference structures*. When we are buying or selling commodities, we tend to think of ourselves as self-interested maximizers, and we may act in a way not far removed from that suggested by the traditional assumptions characterizing *Homo economicus*. When we act in our political capacity, however, we may have quite a different set of preferences; our behavior and our choices when we think as citizens about the kinds of public policies that we would like to see adopted may be governed by more public-spirited preferences, reflecting our images of a good society rather than our narrow personal interest. For example, I may place great value, as a citizen, on having a reliable, nonpolluting, and energy-efficient public transportation system in my city and may vote for a candidate who promises to tax gasoline in order to pay for it. And yet, individually, I may often use my car—casting my dollar votes at the gas station rather than the token booth—when I find it even marginally more convenient. Likewise, I may sign petitions and urge my elected representatives to keep fast-food outlets out of my neighborhood—believing they will destroy housing and increase noise and congestion—even though I frequently eat in them when they are built.

An ancient expression of this theme is found in "Plato's distinction between man as a private individual and man as a citizen" (Margolis 1982, 44). More recently, economist Stephen Marglin has contended that "The preferences that govern one's unilateral market actions no longer govern his actions when the frame of reference is shifted from the market to the political arena. The Economic Man and the Citizen are for all intents and purposes two different individuals. . . . Market and political preference maps are inconsistent" (1963, 98).

Although recognition of the coexistence of two such sets of preferences, which are in many cases mutually inconsistent, "has long vexed the theory of public finance,"[6] the issue is ignored by the BCA paradigm. It would seem arbitrary to say that one or the other preference structure reflects our "true" preferences; both are ours, however inconsistent they may be, and which one we invoke depends on the circumstances in which we find ourselves. When the issues under consideration concern selection among alternative proposed governmental actions, a method of evaluation that systematically ignores the possibility of "citizen preferences" can hardly be confidently expected to produce accurate valuations of our interests.

In sum, there are a number of compelling reasons to believe that our expressed preferences do not accurately reflect our interests. And if expressed preferences diverge from interests, then we cannot be confident that the summary quantitative estimates of net benefits produced by BCA will produce a ranking of alternatives that accurately reflects the relative contributions they would make to promoting our interests or to increasing social welfare. The logical basis for the normative claims made on behalf of the methodology of BCA is seriously undermined. This is a strong conclusion. But it is only part of the case against the BCA paradigm that follows from recognizing and taking seriously the preference-interest divergence.

The Endogenousness of Preferences

Even though preferences diverge from interests, it could be the case that preferences were stable or changed only in response to influences that were independent of the alternatives being evaluated. In that case, it might be possible to make a form of *ceteribus paribus* argument in favor of using the market-based WTP criterion—the argument being that in spite of the preference-interest divergence, preferences at least provide a basis for the quantification of benefits and costs that is "objective" in the sense of being independent of the projects being evaluated. However, the premise of any such argument is false. Preferences are not independent of the alternatives being evaluated. Present preferences have been influenced by past public expenditures and regulations, and future governmental decisions can be expected to bring about further changes in our preferences.

My argument that the preferences on which BCA is based are *endogenous* to public expenditures and regulations is closely related to the more general argument—powerfully made by Herbert Gintis (1972b, 1972c, 1974)—that the preferences that theoretical welfare economics takes as the basis for justifying the competitive market and other institutions of the capitalist system are endogenous to that system.[7] If individual development is shaped by people's economic activity, then personalities and preferences are dependent on the relative availability of such economic variables as public and private goods and services, and the nature of work activities as shaped by the social relations of production. Individuals will develop preferences for alternatives that are relatively more available—both because we regularly have experience with these ("associative patterning") and because we consciously plan our own individual development in response to judgments as to future relative availabilities ("cybernetic patterning"). The availabilities of goods and services shape preferences, rather than a given set of preferences determining the relative availabilities. Isaac Balbus underlines the importance of this when he emphasizes "the social fact . . . that an individual's subjective interests are not merely *given* or *randomly* generated, but rather are systematically determined by the way in which his life-chances are objectively affected by objective conditions" (1971, 153).

For example, it seems reasonable to believe that people develop preferences in areas where they have the power to make choices. This general point can be illustrated with the case of workplace safety. Workers who lack any control over their workplace are not likely to have refined preferences concerning alternative possible changes in working conditions that could affect the chances of illness or injury; if they fear that efforts to bring about safer working conditions may jeopardize their jobs, they may actually express preferences against improved safety. Where workers are empowered so that they have some genuine influence on the nature of their working conditions, however, they have an incentive to make the observations, gather the information, and explore the implications of the various consequences of possible alternatives—steps that are an essential part of the process of producing informed preferences.

Because economic institutions tend to give rise to preference structures that justify and reproduce the institutions, these preferences cannot provide an independent or objective bias for evaluation. Gintis concludes that "the development of preferences is governed by the complex of institutions that constitute society itself, among which economic institutions figure prominently. To take these preferences as given in justifying one such set of economic institutions is simply fatuous" (1974, 429).[8]

As it is with economic activity in general, so it is with activities of the state in particular: The consequences of public spending and regulations influence the very preferences that the BCA paradigm relies on for evaluation. Governmental activities in such particular functional areas as safety and health, education, transportation, environmental protection, and housing and community development play a major role in determining the structure of availabilities in those areas and hence people's expressed preferences for additional proposed public expenditures. Because of their endogenousness, it is illegitimate to use these preferences as a basis for making welfare recommendations.

The shaping of preferences also operates at the level of individual programs. Jesse Burkhead describes how a library administrator might use a budget appropriation to operate a community's library program in a way that increases the community's preferences for library services. Burkhead uses the example to "illustrate a number of the characteristics of the operation of the public sector," among which are that an administrator

> can create the demand that additional resources be devoted to the program that is under his supervision . . . [and that] the community does not have a set of values that determine the amount of resources which will be used for the operation of libraries or any other governmental function. These values are operationally determined and are always in the process of being determined. The community decides that it wants a library. The librarian then shapes the community's demand for libraries by the way in which he administers. The kind and size of library will be determined by the librarian's program and by the response of the community to that program (1956, 46-47).

Similarly, the experience of working in, for example, a quiet work environment is likely to influence an individual's willingness to tolerate a noisy one; our ideas about both what is feasible and what is tolerable depend on our experiences. The creation of no-smoking areas on airplanes and restaurants has altered the willingness of nonsmokers to tolerate smokers nearby; what used to be accepted as a matter of course is now perceived as actively annoying.

When preferences are shaped by public expenditures and regulations, then additional public choices made on the basis of these preferences would by definition be what we prefer—but there is no basis for concluding that such expenditures are necessarily those most conducive to our welfare. An alternative pattern of public expenditures and regulations, giving rise to a different set of preferences, might not only be preferred on the basis of this alternative set of preferences but also, and more important, be superior in terms of individual welfares. Endogenous preferences cannot provide an objective basis for welfare comparisons. Their use in justifying the choice of any particular pattern of public expenditures is, indeed, "simply fatuous."[9]

Distribution, Willingness to Pay, and Legitimacy

One particularly significant way that expressed preferences depend on the nature of existing social arrangements—that is, one important aspect of their endogenousness—concerns the distribution of income and wealth. People with low incomes have the same interest in safe cars, pure drinking water, quiet neighborhoods, and accident-free workplaces as those whose incomes are greater, but their limited ability to pay for these things means that these interests are often not reflected in their expressed preferences.

The basic problem with using the willingness to pay (WTP) criterion in a situation characterized by highly unequal income levels can be clarified by introducing a conceptual distinction that is generally assumed away within the BCA paradigm. The literature of welfare economics distinguishes between an individual's compensating variation (CV) and his or her equivalent variation (EV). Consider a hypothetical example where individuals are clearly better off after adoption of regulation X (i.e., in situation A) than before (i.e., in situation B). The CV measures the benefit to an individual of having regulation X as the maximum amount that he or she, assumed to be in situation B, would be willing to pay in order to have the regulation adopted (that is, to be in situation A instead). The EV, on the other hand, measures the benefit as the minimum amount that the individual, assumed now to be in situation A (i.e., already benefitting from the regulation's existence), would accept in return for agreeing to have the regulation abandoned (i.e., for having to return to situation B). The essential difference between these two concepts is that the effect of the CV is to keep the person at the same level of perceived well-being as before the proposed change, while the effect of the EV is to keep him or her at the same level of perceived well-being as after the proposed change.[10]

There is no persuasive reason to regard either of these measures of WTP as better than the other, and the procedures incorporated into the BCA paradigm are based on the assumption that they will give results that are very similar, an assumption that seems to be reasonable for most cases. But when either the CV or the EV is large in relation to a person's income (wealth), the assumption generally fails, and there may be a large gap between these two different measures of an individual's WTP.[11] This condition is not a merely hypothetical possibility: It may be expected to hold in a number of the kinds of expenditure and regulatory proposals to which BCA is routinely applied. Consider the following examples:

- How much would you pay to prevent the flooding of the land where you and family have lived for generations? Now, what is the minimum amount you would accept in return for agreeing to its being flooded?
- Your workplace is very unsafe. How much would you pay to substantially reduce the chance that you will be seriously injured or suffer exposure that would lead to a serious disease? Now, assume that this greater level of safety has been achieved (without significant cost to you). What is the minimum amount you would accept in return for agreeing to have your workplace degraded to the original very unsafe condition?
- How much would you pay for access to a type of surgery that will triple your chances of being alive five years from today? Now, assuming that you have been selected to receive this surgery, what is the minimum you would agree to accept in return for going without it?
- There is a very polluted river near your neighborhood. How much would you pay to have it be clean enough for safe swimming? Now, there is a clean river near your neighborhood; what is the smallest sum you would accept as compensation for agreeing to have it become thoroughly polluted?

In each of these cases, one would expect the second sum (the EV), to be much greater than the first (the CV) because CV is limited by your ability to pay—and the divergence between the two will be especially large for those with low income and wealth. In cases like these, the legitimacy of using market-based information to estimate WTP, and hence the benefits and costs of the alternatives being evaluated, is undermined. Within the framework provided by theoretical welfare economics itself there is no good reason to choose one of these two divergent valuations over the other. The same criticism can also be expressed from a different perspective: People's preferences as measured by WTP cannot be regarded as fixed and exogenous in such cases; they are endogenous in that they depend on the existing distribution of income and wealth as well as on the existing set of regulations and spending programs.

Legal scholar Duncan Kennedy has characterized the divergence between what welfare economists call EV and CV as the "offer-asking problem"—the difference between what an individual will offer to prevent something taking place and what that same individual would ask to give up an assumed right to prevent it from taking place. In his critique of how other legal scholars adopting the "liberal law and economics" approach have used BCA to analyze the proper allocation of legal entitlements, he demonstrates that there is no neutral way to resolve this problem purely on the basis of efficiency considerations; he argues that recognizing this "would deprive the efficiency calculus of some of its bogus air of objectivity" (1981, 389, 401-21).

The Effect of Analysis and Evaluation on Preferences

If we were directly involved in the process of evaluating and choosing among alternative proposed public expenditures, it is reasonable to expect that we would recognize that our initial incomplete information about the available alternatives provided an unsatisfactory basis for good decision-making. We would undertake to inform ourselves about the consequences and to explore and modify our own preferences. As a result of these efforts, including our discussions with one another, we could be expected to emerge from the process of analysis and evaluation with an altered set of preferences, one closer to our interests. The BCA paradigm rules out this important process; it is unable to make constructive use of the fact that, during a process of analysis and evaluation, people's preferences can change in a way that reduces the preference-interest divergence.[12]

The approach of the BCA paradigm in this regard may be illuminated by extending a metaphor originally developed by Paulo Freire—that of a "banking" concept of education (1972, ch. 2). According to this conception, students are passive receptacles for pre-established subject matter that is "deposited" in them during schooling; there is no active student involvement in dialogue or problem solving in the course of the educational process. The role that the BCA paradigm allots to individual citizens in the process of analysis and evaluation of proposed public expenditures and regulations is analogous: Citizens are passive entities from whom analysts make "withdrawals" of pre-established preferences. The conception of people as objects, uninvolved in processes central to their own well-being and development, is strikingly similar—and similarly inhuman. When participation is absent or "inauthentic," political scientists Ira Katznelson and Mark Kesselman observe, individuals "are prevented from arriving at an accurate perception of their interests" (1979, 15).

Since the BCA paradigm is based on the premise that people's expressed preferences accurately mirror their interests, there is no reason from within the paradigm for taking preference change into consideration—and thus no need for people to actively participate in the process of analysis and evaluation. This observation furnishes a clear link between the criticisms of BCA that are offered in this chapter's two major sections—the consequences of the nonparticipatory nature of its social relations and the false legitimacy based on its unjustified equation of preferences and interests. And, again, both aspects of BCA serve to reinforce the equivalent aspects of capitalist society as a whole—the structure of its economic units, and the false legitimacy that the ideology of consumer sovereignty confers on the market system.

NOTES

1. In Chapter 10 I shall have more to say about the nature and significance of the multiple forms that "participation" may take. It may be useful to note at this point, however, that my criticism of the nonparticipatory nature of BCA is not based on any belief that people should participate in every application of BCA that will affect their lives. What is required for the representation of any group's interests in the process of BCA is that at least some of them participate in the process in a meaningful way; and what is required to counter the negative impact on an individual's consciousness and personality from the present social relations of BCA is that he or she participate meaningfully in making at least some of the collective decisions that affect his or her life.

2. The discussion in this section has proceeded on the implicit premise that almost everyone is excluded from participation in BCA. In fact, this is an oversimplification, adopted in order to highlight my central point. The segmented workforce of contemporary U.S. capitalism is one in which some workers have more control over their own working lives than do others. Accordingly, as Bowles and Gintis (1976, esp. ch. 4) have shown, education is not only unequal in quality and amount but also provides students who are from different social backgrounds or who are being prepared for

different sorts of jobs with experiences of correspondingly different sorts of social relations in the education process. Similarly, different segments of the workforce might be expected to participate differently in the process of BCA, and the degrees of participation might be expected to correspond to the degree of participation or autonomy that different groups of workers are allowed in the workplace. Although these hypotheses seem plausible, I have made no systematic attempt to document and confirm them; such an investigation could constitute an interesting research project.

3. Amartya Sen has provided a penetrating critical discussion of the nature of these and related concepts as they are used (and misused) in mainstream economics (1982, Introduction and pt. I, esp. 8-9). The reader will note that I am offering only a minimal characterization of the concept of "interest" (or "welfare") and not a definition. This is because the nature of interests, the extent to which they are determined by one's humanness, by one's social and cultural environment, and/or by one's own unique individuality, and the relationship between our interests and our consciousness of them, are complex issues that need not be resolved here. It may, however, be useful to note that interests (like preferences, as shall be argued below) are historical phenomena—that is, that they are affected by changing social, political, and environmental factors, including public sector resource allocation decisions.

4. This formulation of the issue suggests a possible response from proponents of the BCA paradigm: Since people are aware of their desire for personal change, by acting in accordance with their preferences (including their preferences among alternative preference structures) they will make choices in the market that incorporate this important aspect of individual welfare—and thus there is no need to consider it independently. Indeed, it is logically possible that this might be the case, but conditions necessary to bring about this result are widely at variance with reality, as Gintis (1974) has demonstrated in a rigorous examination of this question.

5. The failure of liberal BCA practitioners to understand this point is highlighted by the title of James Bonnen's (1970) paper "The Absence of Knowledge of Distributional Impacts: An Obstacle to Effective Public Program Analysis and Decisions." This suggests that the educational, water resource development, and agricultural programs he reviews disproportionately benefit the rich because of an accidental absence of knowledge rather than it being the case that the lack of consideration of such data is part and parcel of a larger exercise of political power by the beneficiaries.

6. The issues around dual preference structures and their relationship to economic theory are discussed, with references, by Sagoff (1981) and Margolis (1982). The phrase quoted in the text is from Sagoff (1981, 1286).

7. In this body of work, Gintis is self-consciously developing one of Karl Marx's central insights: that "men, developing their material production

and their material intercourse, alter along with this their real existence, their thinking, and the products of their thinking. Life is not determined by consciousness, but consciousness by life" (Marx 1977 [1846], 164).

8. In the course of her critique of the treatment of democracy in modern political theory, Carole Pateman also strongly emphasizes the extent to which individuals are shaped by institutions and the consequent requirement that an adequate social scientific theory consider individuals and institutions jointly rather than evaluate a set of institutions (and alternatives to it) on the basis of abilities and attributes developed in response to that very set of institutions (1970, esp. 22-29, 42-43, 59).

9. The endogenousness of preferences to the process of choosing and carrying out state activities is not in itself a bad thing, nor is it specific to capitalist society. In any society, patterns of individual development and of preference structures—the very nature of the human beings living in the society—will be shaped by the society's collective resource allocations as well as by the nature of economic and social life in general. What is capable of variation is the *nature* of the relationship between individuals and social resource allocations and therefore whether these allocations are a help or a hindrance to people in achieving personal development and well-being.

10. Most of the BCA texts reviewed in Chapter 2 either ignore the distinction between CV and EV altogether or give it only passing mention. The only thorough treatment is provided by Mishan (1982a, chs. 35, 58, 59).

11. Willig (1976) provides a rigorous technical demonstration of the proposition that, given generally accepted and apparently reasonable assumptions, EV and CV will have very similar values in situations where WTP, however measured, is small in relation to the income of those affected. Only in the final stages of revision of this manuscript, however, did I discover that this generally accepted belief may well be incorrect. Jack Knetsch and J. A. Sinden conducted a series of experiments involving actual cash payments by subjects to acquire, or to subjects to give up, entitlements worth at most a few dollars. Their reported results, as well as their survey of the results of numerous earlier studies involving responses to hypothetical options, provide strong evidence that even when the amounts at issue are very small in relation to income, "the value of entitlements may be substantially greater when measured in terms of compensation required than it is when measured in terms of willingness to pay" [1984, 507].

12. This process will be discussed in more detail in Chapter 10 as one of the major aspects of the alternative mode of analysis and evaluation examined there. As this discussion will emphasize, there need be nothing paternalistic about a process of dialogue and mutual learning that would enable us to develop an improved understanding of our own interests.

9 CONTRADICTIONS, SOCIAL CHANGE, AND THE FUTURE OF BCA

In concentrating on the central themes of class interest, the rise of rationality, the narrow BCA objective function, and the nonparticipatory nature of BCA's social relations, the radical analysis presented so far is, while correct in its essentials, somewhat one-sided. To begin with, one qualification is in order. Public policy-making concerning government expenditures and regulations, like all public policy-making, takes place within an arena of conflict and struggle. Many forces play a role in shaping the ultimate outcomes. Thus, the capitalist class has been only partially successful in using BCA to promote its interests. With respect to the promotion of capitalist interests vis-à-vis those of noncapitalist classes, the actions of the state reflect the nature and level of class struggle and not simply the will of the dominant class for more thorough and effective domination. When the dominance of the capitalist class has been relatively great, as it has generally been in the twentieth-century United States, the state has to a considerable extent acted to promote capitalist interests. Nonetheless, capitalist domination has been far from complete, and popular forces have won significant victories in the state arena. For example, the expansion of social spending in the 1960s and 1970s, while guided and shaped to some extent by capitalist efforts, nevertheless reflected major gains won by working people and their allies (Bowles and Gintis 1982, 68-78; Campen and MacEwan 1982, 5-6).

With respect to promoting the common interests of the capitalist class as a whole vis-à-vis the particular interests of class fractions, the success of BCA—like that of the capitalist state more generally—has again been less than complete. Opposition has come from segments of the capitalist class who stand to lose in particular instances from procedures that emphasize systematic, formally rational analyses of "the public interest." These segments have included, on various occasions, the developers of water resources, the beneficiaries of public works pork barrel projects, the recipients of agricultural subsidies, and the corporations that generate particular forms of pollution. They have been joined in their opposition by legislators and bureaucrats whose own power and influence is tied up with the continuation of particular expenditure and regulatory policies.

All of this qualifies rather than invalidates the central thrust of our earlier arguments. It remains true that BCA has *tended*, with some success, to limit and constrain the impact of special interests in determining actual expenditure patterns. However, there is another, more fundamental, reason why applications of BCA do not always result in the advancement of capitalist class interests. The central argument of this chapter will be that the success of BCA is *self-limited*: that the nature of the BCA paradigm is such that it tends to undermine its own success. In other words, the development of BCA contains inherent *contradictions*. The successful use of BCA to deal with one set of problems that emerged in the process of capitalist development (the need to guide and control an increased economic role for the state) has helped to create a new problem—the possibility that continued use of BCA will contribute to undermining the capital accumulation process and calling into question the reproduction of capitalist institutions.

The arguments developed in this chapter reflect a distinctive feature of the radical political economic perspective—its focus on the contradictions inherent in social reality and on the constantly changing nature of things. My goal is to provide a *dialectical* analysis that captures as much as possible of the complex, contradictory, and changing nature of the theory and practice of BCA in its evolving historical setting.[1] While some of the arguments here may seem to directly contradict arguments presented earlier in Part III, that is not the case. Statements that at first appear inconsistent with each other are attempts to describe different aspects of the same totality, or apply to different points in time.

In understanding the two-sided approach to BCA from the perspective of radical political economics, an analogy to analysis of the welfare state is suggestive, even though imperfect. Radicals criticize the form that the welfare state has taken and emphasize its inherent limitations in improving the conditions of life within capitalist society; accordingly, they envision and work toward the realization of a transformed society that would support an expanded and humanized set of programs able to truly respond to people's needs; yet they also recognize the real gains the welfare state embodies and struggle to defend those gains against conservative attacks (Harrington 1973, 332-34; Gough 1979). Similarly, radical criticism of the nature and role of BCA is accompanied by efforts both to prevent its misuse and to transform and extend its use.

In what follows, I will first identify some of the contradictory elements inherent in the BCA paradigm itself and explore the ways in which its very success leads to the development of forces that undermine its continued successful operation. I will then examine how a major change in political and economic conditions—the emergence and deepening of the economic crisis of the 1970s and 1980s—has rendered BCA an unsuitable means for advancing the altered mission that capitalists have assigned to the state. Finally, I will investigate the extent to which BCA has a progressive potential that is capable of contributing to the struggles of noncapitalist groups to bring about a more democratic, rational, and humane society.

THE CONTRADICTIONS OF BCA

A central feature of the BCA paradigm is that as a formal, impersonal technique for evaluating proposed alternatives, BCA is explicitly outside of the political realm. Its success in promoting the interests of the capitalist class has depended precisely on its operating in an ostensibly rational, impartial, and objective manner. Like the effectiveness of the capitalist state in general, the effectiveness of BCA depends on its *relative autonomy*.[2]

However, this very autonomy of BCA—this independence from direct capitalist control—also creates the possibility that its use will sometimes produce results counter to capitalist interests. This may happen either as a result of the impartial application of the logic of BCA itself, or as a result of conscious efforts by noncapitalist groups to seize on the opportunities arising from the contradictions of BCA and to use it in support of their own interests. Some of the contradictions of BCA emerge only over time—that is, while initial applications may be successful in promoting capitalist interests, its continued use leads to its becoming increasingly ineffective, or even counterproductive, from the capitalist point of view.

Perhaps the most dramatic instance of this general phenomenon is the way in which BCA has become increasingly politicized in recent years, in direct contrast to its original intent. The basic precondition for the politicization of BCA is, of course, the increasing role of the government in the economy; the rise and impact of BCA needs always to be understood in this context, and its politicization is only one aspect of a general politicization of economic affairs in contemporary capitalism (Luria and MacEwan 1976).

At first the use of experts and formal quantitative techniques for arriving at a summary measure of benefits and costs was relatively successful in reducing the effective involvement of noncapitalist groups. The "rise of rationality in government" served to supplement the invisible and automatic operation of the market with an almost equally invisible and automatic process of analysis and choice, based on essentially market criteria. BCA's very success, however, eventually brought it into the spotlight. Once in the spotlight, BCA's emphasis on open, explicit procedures and assumptions revealed it to be a technique that could also be utilized by precisely the kinds of groups that the rise of rationality in government was intended to effectively exclude from the shaping of public policy.

The logic of BCA provides no grounds for withholding from interested parties the reports produced by particular applications of BCA. Over time—especially as citizens have become less trusting of experts and government officials—noncapitalist groups have increasingly grown aware that many of the issues of valuation are inherently political rather than merely technical. Some groups have acquired the knowledge and skills to intervene so that the results of orthodox, pro-capitalist BCA studies seldom reach decision-makers unchallenged. As a result of broad-based public pressure for open governmental procedures, the transmittal of BCA results to decision-makers is generally preceded or accompanied by public hearings at which the assumptions and methods of the analyses can be challenged.

It has become much clearer to the affected parties that however much BCA may make use of market-based criteria, the decisions are actually made by identifiable decision-makers. As the "invisible hand" of the market is replaced by the "visible hand" of governmental decision-making, the potential for politicization grows. And as continued use of BCA gives rise to growing familiarity with and understanding of the pro-capitalist thrust of its methodology, BCA's potential for leading to more rather than less politicization is realized. All sides in controversial issues now attempt to use BCA in support of their positions. Considerable publicity is given to the results of BCA. Analysts increasingly identify for the interested public, as well as for decision-makers, the nature and potential implications of the choices to be made. The consequence is that decision-makers are no longer able very effectively to invoke BCA as a means of disguising the political content of their decisions.

Despite BCA's narrowly specified objective function, moreover, the words "benefit-cost analysis" suggest something more general to most people. As the process of reviewing BCA studies becomes a more politicized one, it becomes increasingly difficult for decision-makers to justify reliance on formal quantitative studies that omit from consideration many benefits and costs that ordinary language or common sense suggest should be included. Theorists and practitioners may continue to debate how and to what extent distributional considerations should be formally integrated into the summary measure of net benefits. But in a politicized environment the ability of BCA to clearly identify gainers and losers from particular proposals will receive great attention, thereby making it more difficult for decision-makers to favor the adoption of measures with regressive distributional consequences. Robert Haveman has pointed out that BCA "has greatly facilitated the successful use of public hearings and adversary proceedings, by focussing the attention of all participants on those questions of who wins and who loses, and by how much" (letter to the author, July 1985). Furthermore, the logic of BCA that calls for taking into account the full range of benefits and costs, whether or not they result in financial flows in the marketplace, readily lends itself to legitimating concern with the kinds of "noneconomic" consequences that are not included directly in the narrow objective function of BCA. Thus, all of the rhetoric about concern for the "public interest" and for "social welfare" can backfire for capitalists when representatives of a broad range of noncapitalist groups become involved in the process and insist on taking these terms literally.

The above contradictions undermine BCA's ability to successfully carry out its selection function. Additional contradictions undermine the contributions that use of BCA is able to make to the reinforcement of the market system and the social relations of capitalist production. For instance, while the falsity of the legitimation provided by BCA may for a considerable period of time not be widely noticed or understood, it is nevertheless vulnerable to exposure. When, and to the extent that, people eventually perceive the divergence between preferences and interests and come to understand the lack of validity of the BCA objective function, the consequences may not only include a loss of credibility and persuasiveness for the results of particular applications of BCA but also contribute to an erosion of belief in and support for the market system itself.

In another way, too, the operation of BCA can contribute to the delegitimizing of capitalist institutions. The BCA paradigm incorporates the propositions that it is reasonable to bring organized human intelligence to bear on the task of guiding the allocation of society's scarce resources and that total (or "social") benefits and costs ought to be taken into account rather than just those consequences ("private" benefits and costs) that are internalized in the marketplace because those who buy and sell are directly affected. These ideas are, at their core, subversive of support for the fundamentally unguided and socially inefficient system of determining outcomes in a highly interdependent economy on the basis of self-interested, profit-seeking behavior in private markets. Mainstream proponents of BCA may argue that it is merely an approach to public policy-making that provides a useful complement to the market in those relatively rare cases characterized by the existence of "market failure," and these arguments may be for a time successful. But the very nature of BCA contains the potential for exposing the basic irrationality of capitalism's fundamental reliance on blind market forces.

Another potential for undermining capitalist reproduction is created by the nonparticipatory social relations of BCA. There is an everpresent danger that exclusion from decision-making may lead not to passivity but rather to anger, frustration, altered consciousness of the unequal distribution of political power, and, ultimately, rebellion. Eric Ashby has noted how the use of elaborate quantitative methodology "may drive the public into disillusion and resentment" and has described how expert presentations at hearings may lead not to respectful acceptance but instead "smother the public with highly sophisticated evidence that mystifies and ultimately enrages them" (1980, 1178). Lack of participation in shaping public expenditures may correspond to lack of participation in shaping the nature of work, but it is inconsistent with a widely shared ideological presumption that people ought to be involved in making decisions that influence their lives, particularly when these decisions are in the political realm with its underlying norm of democratic equality. As the process of BCA becomes increasingly politicized, there is a growing tendency for people to see the democratic political norm rather than the hierarchical, nonparticipatory norm of the capitalist workplace as relevant—and therefore to experience the frustration that comes from unfulfilled expectations.[3]

One additional contradiction inherent in the use of BCA to promote capitalist class interests stems from its being implemented by technical experts and governmental officials. While state managers (bureaucrats and technocrats) operate in an environment characterized by strong structural and instrumental pressures in favor of pro-capitalist behavior, they do nevertheless have interests of their own that can be expected to diverge from those of the capitalist class. Observers of the capitalist state writing from positions ranging from conservative (e.g., Niskanen 1971) to radical (e.g., Block 1977) have emphasized the significance of the collective self-interest of those who occupy positions in the state apparatus. Capitalists, however, must enhance the role and position of state managers in order to gain the contributions to accumulation and reproduction that BCA is capable of providing, at least in the short run. The contradiction is a genuine one, in that recognizing its existence does not allow capitalists to avoid taking the steps that further its development and intensification.

ECONOMIC CRISIS, CONSERVATIVE ASCENDANCE, AND BCA IN THE 1980s

We saw in Chapter 2 that while the basic idea underlying BCA as a means for evaluating proposed public expenditures was published in the 1840s, and it began to be used on a significant scale following the Flood Control Act of 1936, the theoretical developments that led to what I call the BCA paradigm only took place in connection with the expanding number of applications of BCA in the period after World War II. In Chapter 7 I argued that the growth and development of BCA during the postwar period can be understood as a response to the changing nature of the capital accumulation process. An expanding economic role for the state was accompanied by the development of BCA as one means to help guide and direct the growth of public expenditures (and, somewhat later, regulations) in ways that would further the achievement of capitalist needs for accumulation and reproduction.

As the process of capitalist development proceeds, however, the circumstances within which economic activity takes place continually change, and the problems that capitalists must confront in order to continue the capital accumulation process and bring about the reproduction of the basic institutional arrangements of capitalism change as well. This suggests the possibility that BCA, although well adapted for successfully carrying out its selection and reinforcement functions during one historical period, may not be an effective means for promoting capitalist interests in a later period that is characterized by very different economic, political, and social circumstances. This in turn suggests the further possibility that attempts to use BCA in these altered circumstances may be not only unsuccessful in promoting capitalist goals but actually counterproductive.

The central contention of the present section is that these possibilities have been realized in the 1980s. The way that BCA developed in response to the needs of an earlier period characterized by relative prosperity, expanding government, and the political ascendancy of a liberal coalition has resulted in its being an unsuitable means for advancing capitalist objectives in a period of relative stagnation, government cutbacks, and conservative political ascendancy. The initial attempts of the Reagan administration to use BCA in support of its efforts to reduce government regulation and social spending played an important role in developing a widespread perception of BCA as a conservative tool. As the administration soon discovered, however, this is not the case. BCA has not been very helpful to them in advancing their goals, and in some cases it has even backfired. They have curtailed its use. (This recent experience is consistent with my argument in Part II that BCA is, essentially, a liberal methodology.

If that argument is valid, it should not be surprising to find that a conservative administration in a conservative era has had difficulty utilizing BCA for its own purposes.)

Throughout its history, the process of capitalist development has been punctuated by serious crises.[4] Periods of economic expansion cannot be sustained indefinitely because capitalist expansion itself gives rise to forces that undermine its continuation. The resulting crisis periods, however, are not merely times of slow growth, high unemployment, financial instability, and political turmoil; they also provide the opportunity for establishing the conditions that can make possible another period of profitable capital accumulation. The United States underwent major economic crises in the 1890s and again in the 1930s; in each case, resolution of the crisis involved the establishment of a new set of institutional arrangements, including major expansions of the economic role of the state.

The transformed set of institutional arrangements that was put into place during and after the Great Depression and World War II included three basic foundations for the long period of relative prosperity that began in the late 1940s: a set of international economic arrangements based on U.S. hegemony; an understanding between organized labor and big business in which the former's right to share in the fruits of prosperity through collective bargaining and political lobbying was obtained in response for its cooperation in production and its respect for capitalist arrangements; and a new role for the government in maintaining the conditions for profitable capital accumulation, especially through greatly increased levels of spending and a commitment to use macroeconomic policy to sustain a high level of aggregate demand. Beginning from the particular historical conditions that existed in the aftermath of more than fifteen years of depression and war, this institutional framework was able to support the most rapid period of sustained economic growth in U.S. history. During this period, with its growing governmental outlays, the use of BCA became significant, spreading from application in the water resources area to the whole range of physical investment projects during the 1950s, then to human resources and social spending programs during the 1960s, and finally to the area of social regulation in the 1970s.

As the expansion continued, however, its success gave rise to developments that undermined its ability to continue. Each of the three major institutional foundations of the long expansion was transformed into a source of problems. Other nations successfully challenged U.S. international dominance. Labor-capital cooperation in promoting growth gave way to conflict over the distribution of a relatively stagnant level of economic output. And the government's maintenance of high levels of demand produced unprecedented inflation rather than real economic growth. By the early 1970s, prosperity had been transformed into a full-blown economic crisis. The inability of the previously dominant liberal political coalition to deal with the economic crisis resulted in the ascendancy of conservative ideologies and conservative politicians, together with increasing acceptance of conservative economic theories and policy recommendations. The national elections in November 1980, resulting in the presidency of Ronald Reagan and a Republican majority in the Senate, demonstrated the extent of the conservative ascendancy by the end of the decade.

While there were, and are, a number of varieties of contemporary U.S. conservatism, with differing views on both economic theory and economic policy, there is broad agreement among conservatives on several matters. Among these are the goals of reducing the government's economic role — by shrinking government domestic spending, lowering taxes, and cutting back regulation of private businesses — and of tilting the distributional impact of public policies toward those corporations and households that already have a disproportionate share of income, wealth, and power. Creating the incentives for capitalists and for workers that will allow markets to work effectively requires, in the conservative view, keeping taxes on investors low, minimizing bureaucratic oversight of working conditions or pollution-generating activity, and eliminating government-provided benefits that could provide an alternative to labor income for working people.

The extent to which such a conservative program may contribute to successful resolution of the current economic crisis is an interesting and important question, but well beyond the scope of our present inquiry.[5] The issue to be addressed here is whether the use of BCA can contribute to the realization of the program. That leading members of the Reagan administration thought that it could is clearly indicated by the promulgation of Executive Order 12291 within a month of the president's inauguration. Events since that time, however, have provided a strong basis for skepticism. BCA was developed to help capitalists guide the expansion of government during a long upswing of the capitalist economy. The resulting nature of the BCA paradigm is such that it is ill-suited to serve the conservative goal of simultaneously shrinking government and restructuring its distributional impacts.

This is not to deny that conservatives have been quite successful in their efforts to implement their program. My argument here is the more limited one that BCA has not, on balance, contributed to the conservative successes. The reduction of the federal tax burden in ways particularly favorable to high-income households, the massive expansion of military spending in ways highly profitable to the large corporations who are leading military contractors, the domestic spending cutbacks that have hurt moderate- and low-income households, and the substantial reductions in occupational health and safety regulation at the expense of working people—all have been brought about primarily by the exercise of political power. Where the conservative agenda has been less successfully implemented, as in the area of environmental regulation, this has been the result of resistance by politically powerful forces. In such areas, I would argue, BCA has been used to greater effect by those who have opposed the conservative onslaught than by those who have engineered it. The resistant political groupings have been able to use BCA results in appealing to open-minded, uncommitted legislators, bureaucrats, and citizens.

One starting point for understanding this phenomenon is recognizing that conservatives never intended to use BCA to help *guide* them in their reduction and reorientation of the government's economic role. Their agenda, as outlined above, was established in advance. Almost any boost in military spending was ipso facto good, as was virtually any cut in domestic social spending or any reduction in government regulatory activity. Whereas liberal use of BCA during the long period of postwar expansion had been based on the recognition of "market failure" and the attempt to calculate the outcome that markets would have produced in the absence of such failure, the newly ascendant conservative ideology simply assumed away the existence of market failure altogether. Almost anything done by the government was thus seen as producing a less desirable result than what the free-market system would produce if left on its own. Conservatives saw no need for detailed analysis of particular cases; the proper course of action was, in their view, predetermined by their fundamental faith in well-functioning markets. Whereas liberals in power had tried to use BCA to help them identify those situations where government intervention (spending or regulation) was likely to be most beneficial to broad capitalist interests, the position of the ascendant conservatives could be accurately represented by extending the scope of Milton Friedman's alleged aphorism that "I never met a tax cut I didn't like" to include cuts in domestic spending and social regulation as well. For conservatives, the question was not what they wished to cut—since they already knew that they wished to cut everything—but what they could succeed in cutting.

In accordance with this basic position, conservatives viewed BCA simply as a means to provide justification, a veneer of apparently objective scientific backing, for policy proposals that they had selected in advance. In a manner very similar to the way that the U.S. Army Corps of Engineers had formerly manipulated the assumptions underlying its analyses of proposed water projects to guarantee that a favorable benefit-cost ratio would emerge, the Reagan administration now undertook to carry out BCAs whose manipulated assumptions would guarantee support for lower levels of social regulation and domestic spending. Their effort was similarly unsuccessful. Of course, the Corps of Engineers built a lot of dams and canals, and the Reagan administration has made many cuts in spending and regulatory programs. But it seems highly unlikely that there were many cases where a rigged BCA enabled either the Corps or the Reaganauts to do what they wouldn't have been able to do in the absence of BCA altogether. One reason for this conclusion is the sheer transparency of the effort in both cases. Misuse and abuse were so unsubtle and pervasive that no impartial or undecided observer could give much credibility to the results of these studies.

But BCA was not merely ineffective in helping Reagan administration conservatives implement their predetermined agenda. It may actually have been counterproductive.[6] Their attempts to use BCA unleashed a process of analysis, evaluation, and review that they could not control—a process that tended to work against the selection of their favored alternatives. There are three major reasons for this conclusion, each based on an inherent feature of the BCA paradigm.

First, a properly conducted BCA must include an explicit statement of the assumptions that underlie its procedures and valuations. Even though these may be effectively invisible to those people who look only at the report's bottom line, they can be identified by other analysts. In situations where there is significant opposition to the alternative that conservatives are attempting to promote through use of BCA (and it is only in situations with such opposition that adoption of their favored alternative is problematical), the opposition is able to subject individual analyses to detailed scrutiny by experts and to publicize their findings of inappropriate assumptions and methods. In short, the formal and explicit nature of BCA makes it hard for its abuse in support of preselected alternatives to escape detection.

The second reason for concluding that conservative use of BCA in the 1980s has tended to be counterproductive applies, as does the third, to cases where conservatives make good-faith attempts to carry out BCA, in the belief that a fair and honest evaluation will support their position. One of the central propositions incorporated into the BCA paradigm is the explicit goal and criterion of selecting alternatives that favor the general, or public, interest. While this is an effective orientation for promoting the general interests of the capitalist class as a whole against the particular interests of various class fragments, the principal thrust of the conservative program for the early 1980s is quite different. It seeks instead to redistribute the benefits and burdens of government programs in favor of capitalists generally, at the expense of the large majority of the population. However, the assumption underlying all discussion of distribution in the BCA literature is that the goal of public policy is, and should be, to improve the position of those who are currently *dis*advantaged or *less* well off. We saw in Chapter 2 that even those who argue against formal incorporation of distributional consequences into the summary quantitative measure of net benefits for each alternative that constitutes an analysis's "bottom line" agree on the value of explicitly identifying and displaying each alternative's distributional impact, as a means of providing information that decision-makers and other interested parties may wish to take into consideration. BCA thus provides a means of identifying the regressive distributional impacts of the proposals favored by conservatives. Increased public availability of such information almost certainly decreases rather than increases the chances of these proposals' being adopted.

A third possible reason for BCA's use being counterproductive for conservatives is that its rationale is based on explicit recognition of the potential appropriateness of governmental actions in cases characterized by market failure; BCA provides an analytical framework for investigating the existence of market failures and their consequences. Because most of the government spending and regulatory programs targeted by conservatives have in fact arisen in response to market failures, their continued existence is likely to be vindicated by a carefully and honestly conducted application of BCA. Thus, the BCA paradigm provides a vehicle for focusing attention in a direction that must be ignored in order for the conservative agenda to gain support.

It must be emphasized that none of these three reasons for the counterproductiveness of BCA for conservatives during the current historical period is based on an automatic mechanism. Each depends on the existence of a significant opposition to the proposals under consideration, an opposition with the resources and the sophistication to intervene in the process of reviewing and publicizing the results of those BCAs sponsored by conservatives and, perhaps, to themselves sponsor competing BCAs. Given the stakes involved, and the increasing politicization of governmental decision-making in recent years, this condition is one that is generally satisfied.

THE PROGRESSIVE POTENTIAL OF BCA

The idea that BCA may have the potential to contribute to progressive social change is implicit in the preceding discussion of its counterproductiveness for conservative capitalists. I would argue that BCA does indeed contain such potential—not only for helping to bring about policies that are more in the interests of the majority of the population, but also for contributing to the efforts of those who are engaged in the longer-run struggle to bring about a democratic socialist society.

The claim here is that BCA, whose development was promoted and shaped by capitalist efforts in pursuit of their class interests in accumulation and reproduction, and whose past use has actually advanced those interests, may now play a role in bringing about fundamental change in the very institutional arrangements that it has previously helped to reproduce. This claim cannot be fully understood or evaluated apart from the more general conceptual framework provided by radical political economics. Radicals understand capitalist development as a contradictory process that generates within itself forces that tend to undermine its own success and ultimately its survival. They view capitalism itself as playing a historically progressive role in breaking down restrictive social relationships, unleashing unprecedented productive powers, and establishing the necessary material preconditions for the development of socialism.

The progressive potential of BCA lies in two of its basic features. The first is its nature as a means of systematically using organized human rationality to identify and evaluate the consequences of proposed collective decisions. The second is its orientation toward valuing all benefits and costs, whether or not they enter into the financial calculations of individuals or firms—that is, its concern with "social" rather than merely with "private" benefits and costs. The mainstream BCA paradigm resulted from the particular ways in which these basic features were developed; being highly critical of the resulting theory and practice of BCA does not necessarily involve rejecting these two underlying features. For example, critical analysis of the narrow and distorted form of rationality that characterized what I termed "the rise of rationality in government" in no way implies a rejection of rationality itself. On the contrary, at the very core of the progressive, or socialist, agenda lies the goal of developing a society where application of humane and democratic rationality replaces the undemocratic and irrational bases of social decision-making in contemporary capitalism.

BCA has the potential to contribute toward the realization of this goal precisely because it does raise the possibility that people should, consciously and systematically, evaluate proposed expenditure programs or regulatory policies in terms of their effects on the welfare of all of those who would be affected. Given this general orientation, it is entirely natural—as well as politically and popularly appealing— to suggest that those who will be affected should be involved in the process of evaluation and review, and that the terms *benefit* and *cost* be interpreted in a broader sense than the one incorporated into the BCA paradigm. The underlying orientation of BCA suggests bringing decision-making about economic matters out of the corporate boardroom and the marketplace and into the public, political realm. This "socialization" of economic decision-making contains a distinct progressive potential.

I am contending only that BCA contains this *potential*, not that there is any guarantee that the potential will be realized. Like other aspects of the "socialization" of economic life (e.g., the growth of the public sector and the increasing size of productive enterprises), BCA has a negative potential for contributing to the further development of an authoritarian, undemocratic state apparatus as well as a positive one for contributing to the development of a set of humane and democratic governmental institutions and practices. The future character of BCA will be shaped by the level and form of political struggles in the state arena during the years ahead. Its progressive potential cannot be realized unless progressive forces, aware of the way that BCA has been used to promote capitalist interests, engage in serious efforts to make BCA live up to the claims that are made for it. Only by insisting that BCA be applied in ways that come as close as possible to really identifying those alternatives that will make the greatest contribution to human well-being (that is, to the "public interest" or to "social welfare," as these terms are understood in everyday language), can progressives contribute to transforming the nature of BCA.

I remarked at the beginning of this chapter that an illuminating analogy can be made between analysis of BCA from the perspective of radical political economics and a similarly based analysis of the welfare state within modern capitalism. The strength of this analogy is suggested in the way that radical analyses of these two subjects lead to similar implications for political action, as is indicated by the following excerpt from the "Political Postscript" to Ian Gough's *The Political Economy of the Welfare State*—which I have altered only by substituting "BCA" for "the welfare state" in the places indicated:

> Once the contradictory nature of [BCA] and its contradictory impact on capitalism is appreciated, then the political strategy of all who work in it, use it, or are concerned with it can be refined. The positive aspects of [BCA] need defending and extending, its negative aspects need exposing and attacking. It is at this stage that the concept of "human needs" becomes relevant in clarifying what is positive and what is negative. In this way, a struggle may be mounted to realize in practice the ideology of [BCA] propounded in many orthodox textbooks: a system for subjecting economic forces to conscious social control and for meeting human needs. It will not develop in this direction without continuous and informed struggle (1979, 153).

What might BCA be like if its progressive potential were able to be realized without the constraints imposed by the capitalist framework within which it has developed historically? What vision of a transformed mode of BCA could inspire and guide current efforts to make it operate in a more humane and democratic manner? We turn now to consideration of such questions.

NOTES

1. Although it is frequently misused and misunderstood, the term *dialectical* remains indispensable in characterizing Marxist approaches to understanding social reality. For a readable and informative introduction to the concept, see Heilbroner (1980, ch. 2). A concise but much more demanding survey is provided by Roy Bhaskar (1983).
2. In advanced capitalist society, the state has a considerable amount of independence from direct control by capitalists. This relative autonomy contributes to its effective operation in two major ways. First, autonomy is essential to the task of serving the interests of capitalists as a class; Ralph Miliband (1973, 85) has argued that the very notion of promoting the common interests of the class implies that the state must be separated from the control of particular capitalists. Second, autonomy allows the state to play its role in interclass struggle; in order to promote the legitimacy of the capitalist system, the state cannot be perceived by working people as simply an instrument for capitalist class domination but must be seen as potentially responsive to their needs—and the best way to have it perceived that way is to have it be that way in fact. The autonomy of the state and its real, even though limited, responsiveness to popular pressures add both resiliency and legitimacy to the system.
3. Samuel Bowles and Herbert Gintis discuss the nature and consequences of the problematical coexistence of "the social relations of capitalist production [and] the social relations of liberal democracy" (1982, 52) in the contemporary United States.
4. There is a large and growing body of radical political economic writing about capitalist economic crises in general, and about the origins and nature of the economic crisis of the 1970s and 1980s in particular. For a more detailed presentation of my own analysis, together with bibliographic guidance to this literature, see Campen (1981, 36-43) and Campen and MacEwan (1982, 2-7).
5. For analyses of alternative capitalist strategies in response to the current economic crisis, and of their prospects for success, see Campen (1981, 43-50); Campen and MacEwan (1982, 7-20); and Bowles, Gordon, and Weisskopf (1983, pt. 2).
6. Examples and illustrations of many of the points made in the rest of this section have already been presented—in the final section of Chapter 4 ("Exposing Misuse and Abuse of BCA") and in the second section of Chapter 5 ("The Pro-Liberal Impact of BCA"). These are not repeated here. Instead, the argument is developed in general terms, and the reader is encouraged to reread those two sections in light of the propositions advanced in this chapter.

IV TRANSFORMING BCA AND TRANSFORMING SOCIETY

10 TOWARD A PARTICIPATORY ALTERNATIVE

We saw in Part II that the defenders of BCA rest their case ultimately on the argument that its critics are unable to offer a superior alternative—an argument that tends to be persuasive, given the mainstream economics paradigm and the acceptance of the institutional arrangements of modern U.S. capitalism by BCA's critics and defenders alike. The goal of this concluding chapter is to respond to that argument by identifying an alternative mode of BCA that is superior to that represented by the prevailing BCA paradigm.

I will begin by describing three principal elements of a participatory mode of analyzing proposed expenditures and regulatory policies that provide sharp contrasts to the corresponding features of the mainstream BCA paradigm: a more inclusive objective function, a process of dialogue and mutual learning about both options and preferences, and an egalitarian set of social relationships. Taken together, these elements characterize an alternative form of BCA designed to become a means for promoting human liberation rather than for perpetuating class domination. That is, all three elements of the participatory alternative described here contribute to the goal of having BCA serve the people rather than serve the powerful.

Just as the most fundamental criticisms of the BCA paradigm concern its roles within the current capitalist system, any alternative form of evaluating proposed public expenditures or regulatory decisions must also be considered within a broader institutional setting. Thus, I turn next to examining the socialist social setting for the practice of a transformed mode of BCA. This will involve first outlining a vision of a set of democratic, participatory, egalitarian economic institutions that could constitute a democratic socialist society's underlying framework for a participatory mode of analyzing resource allocation problems, and then considering the possible relationships between alternative ways of undertaking BCA in the present and the movement struggling to bring about such a society.

The single most important feature of the alternative mode of BCA is its *participatory* nature, which characterizes and ties together all three of its principal elements. Because participation is both so important and so problematical (e.g., we all know from personal experience that it is costly as well as beneficial), the chapter's third major section will examine the issues involved in establishing an optimal level and structure of participation.

While the following examination of an alternative for BCA illustrates a number of its arguments with references to some of the many attempts to implement participatory and egalitarian approaches to resource allocation, it does not attempt to provide a survey of that broad body of potentially relevant experience. Among the relevant experiences that might be investigated in such a survey are those of progressive local governments such as Madison, Wisconsin, in the 1970s and Burlington, Vermont, and Santa Monica, California, in the 1980s; community organizing activities in the tradition established by Saul Alinsky; the many facets of the "citizen participation" movement; the extensive and varied experience with workers' self-management of productive enterprises both in the United States and overseas; the alternative institutions that flourished in the 1970s; initiatives by the social democratic governments of Western Europe; and the practices of countries, such as China and Cuba, that have undergone socialist revolutions.[1] Examining this large and diverse range of experience to illuminate questions about the desirability and feasibility of a participatory alternative mode of BCA for the United States—and for insights and ideas about how such an alternative might be structured and implemented most effectively—represents a formidable undertaking. If the present volume helps to encourage others to pursue this task, it will have achieved at least one of its objectives.[2]

ELEMENTS OF A PARTICIPATORY ALTERNATIVE

This section discusses three major features of a mode of analyzing and evaluating proposed uses of public resources that stand in strong contrast to the corresponding characteristics of the prevailing mode of BCA. This alternative mode is characterized as *participatory* because that is its single most important characteristic, the aspect that ties all three elements together; other suitable one-word characterizations would be *egalitarian* and *democratic*.

The word *elements* signifies that this is not a complete description of an alternative process of BCA. In particular, no attention is paid here to the details of analytical techniques or organizational structures. Although such details are essential to practitioners of any mode of BCA, they are less useful in understanding and evaluating it than are the basic outlines of the social and political relationships it embodies: What goals are considered worthy of being included in the objective function? What view of the content and formation of preferences forms the basis for the analysis? In whose interest is the analysis carried out? Who takes part in the process, and how do the various participants relate to one another? These are the sorts of questions with which this section is concerned.

For example, many of BCA's current analytical techniques—involving complicated equations, rigorous statistical estimation, and sophisticated mathematical manipulation—would continue to play a role; the problems lie not in the techniques themselves but in the way that they are used. Paul Baran and Paul Sweezy have expressed this point very well, and the example they use to illustrate it is particularly relevant to an alternative mode of BCA:

> There is everything to be said for the adoption of all the advanced, mathematical and non-mathematical, techniques of observation and analysis developed by bourgeois economics.... Much of what has been established in bourgeois economics—but constitutes under capitalism a manifestation of naive, ahistorical rationalism and turns inevitably into apologetics for the status quo—can be effectively used under socialist planning. To take one example among many: the theory of consumer's behavior conveys under capitalism the false, ideological notion that the "autonomous" consumer is the sovereign ruler of the economy, while in fact it is the capitalist system itself

that determines the nature of his wants, tastes, standards, spending habits, and so forth. The very same theory of consumer's behavior, however, can be employed (and developed) under socialism as a powerful means for ascertaining needs and wants of consumers within an entirely different social setting (1968, 307-08).

Not only are the details of an alternative mode less important than its general nature, but they are also more difficult to predict with any confidence. The precise shape of a participatory alternative for evaluating and choosing among proposed uses of public resources will emerge from the ideas and experiences of those who struggle to bring it into being—and will vary with the nature of the people and the alternatives involved in particular decision contexts. Underlying this considerable unpredictability and variation, however, the elements identified in this section together provide a broad foundation for a radically transformed mode of BCA that is both welfare-conducive and historically progressive.

A More Inclusive Objective Function

We saw in Part III that the prevailing BCA paradigm focuses on a narrow subset of the welfare-relevant consequences of proposed public expenditures and regulations—with the contributions that changed levels of goods and services make to the economic welfare of individuals, as defined by their existing preferences. The objective function could and should be made to be more inclusive in at least three major ways.

First, within the realm of satisfying existing individual preferences, the evaluation process would include several sets of consequences that are excluded from consideration by the prevailing BCA paradigm. Among these important *"noneconomic" consequences* are changes in people's productive activities (in addition to changes in their consumption); effects on the social relations that individuals enter into with each other; ecological consequences (based on a consciousness of and appreciation for the natural world as something more than a potential contributor to human economic welfare); aesthetic consequences; and ethical and moral consequences. All of these consequences are valued by people, and all of them contribute in significant ways to human welfare. A fully adequate mode of evaluating alternative ways of using public resources would take all of them into account (Pearl and Pearl 1971; Goulet 1971).

Second, in addition to the satisfaction of existing preferences, the evaluation process ought to be concerned with the effects of public decisions on *personal development*. Analysis of the desirability of alternative proposals should take into account the sorts of people that they will tend to make us become, their effect on what we are and can do, as well as on what we have or consume (Albert and Hahnel 1981, 305). The fetishism of commodities embodied in the prevailing BCA paradigm serves to obscure what may well be the most important determinant of human welfare—personal development.

Third, a historically progressive mode of public evaluation and choice must give attention to the *political aspects* of the alternatives under consideration. To what extent will the expenditure or regulation contribute to bringing about a better society by aiding the development of a strong progressive movement or by better enabling that movement to transform society? To what degree will it contribute to the achievement of such politically important goals as equality and solidarity? How will it influence power relationships in society? These are the sorts of central political questions that should be addressed within the framework provided by a more inclusive objective function for BCA.

Dialogue and Learning

Proponents of neoclassical welfare economics sometimes acknowledge that expressed preferences are not a perfect indicator of interests, but they argue that these are the best available indicator, far better than the imposed preferences of some dictator or elite.[3] There is, however, an alternative that is superior to accepting people's existing preferences, while it remains respectful of citizens' sovereignty over the public decisions that will affect their lives. This alternative explicitly recognizes the problem of preference-interest divergence and self-consciously confronts it. It does so in a way that transforms, rather than simply rejects, the willingness to pay criterion.

The essence of this element of the alternative is *dialogue and learning*. If our existing preferences do not accurately reflect our interests, then we ought to be able to recognize this and take steps to attain a better understanding of what our interests are. These steps involve a process of investigation, analysis, and exploration of a particular decision problem that makes use of people with expert knowledge and includes face-to-face discussions with others affected by the consequences of the contemplated decision. This better understanding—that is, our altered and more accurate preferences—can then be used as the basis for a choice more conducive to our welfare than the choice that would have resulted from the application of the BCA paradigm.

The notion that people do not accurately understand their own interests applies to all people. The argument here is not that some enlightened people understand the interests of other people better than they do themselves (even though this may sometimes in fact be the case), but that in many of the areas of potential public expenditure and regulation, we have not had enough personal experience or devoted enough attention to the area to have an accurate sense of our own interests. The problem is a universal one that applies to economists, planners, and benefit-cost analysts as much as to anyone else.

We recognize this problem whenever we seek to educate ourselves before making important personal expenditures decisions, rather than simply making top-of-the-head judgments based on our existing preferences. Similarly, in the case of proposed public expenditures that could have significant consequences for our lives, we could benefit from "the opportunity to make an extended analysis of the precise nature of [our] own self interest"—to use the words of the proposal for a project aimed at giving people a chance to do just that (Carr et al. 1971a, 10-11). Such an opportunity is one that most people would be likely to welcome—provided they have a good basis for believing they are in control of information flows and of the process of investigating and changing their preferences, and that their modified preferences will play an important role in determining choices among the available alternatives.

Even in cases where a process of dialogue and learning is initiated by those who believe that they have, in some respects, a better understanding of people's interests than the people do themselves (perhaps because they have previously engaged in processes of dialogue and learning in the area, or have other relevant experience), the process can and should be respectful of people's own understanding of their preferences. Paolo Freire's (1972) discussion of education for liberation repeatedly emphasizes the necessity of always dealing with people's own views of the world and advocates a process of dialogue between teacher and student (in the present case, that would translate to analyst and citizen) beginning and learning from these views, in order to bring about a more accurate perception of the world. For example, Freire notes that "One cannot expect positive results from an educational or political action program which fails to respect the particular view of the world held by the people.... It is not our role to speak to the people about our own view of the world, nor to attempt to impose that view on them, but rather to dialogue with the people about their view and ours" (1972, 84-85).

In short, the process advocated here does not involve one group of people imposing "correct" preferences on others, but rather a self-conscious process of exploration, analysis, and dialogue—of self- and mutual education—whereby we ourselves can bring about a closer correspondence of our objective and subjective interests, of our needs and wants, of our interests and awareness. The process can provide an opportunity to discover needs that we were previously unaware of, to bring repressed needs to the level of conscious awareness.[4] The main result of such a process will be a conscious change in our preferences, in ways that will make them better indicators of our interests—and thus will make public expenditure and regulatory decisions based on the revised preferences more welfare-conducive.

An important aspect of the process is dialogue among those who would be affected by the alternatives under consideration. Not only is such a collective process itself an activity that can contribute to individual welfare, but also a process of mutual education and exchange of ideas can lead to more effective learning than could be achieved by individuals attempting to investigate and analyze their interests in isolation from each other.[5]

There is an important additional benefit of such a collective process: Individual preferences can be brought into closer agreement with those of other individuals, as a result of dialogue concerning the reasons for the initial disagreement. Even though individuals will certainly not always come to agree, the fact of dialogue at least provides an opportunity to eliminate a portion of those differences based on inaccurate understanding. Indeed, when people engaged in dialogue do not have antagonistic interests, better understanding of interests ought to lead to closer agreement of preferences. This possibility stands in strong contrast to the complete absence within the framework provided by the BCA paradigm of any possibility of people learning from each other and coming to closer agreement. Within that paradigm citizens are restricted to a passive role; as a result, any differences among individuals' preferences are frozen and perpetuated.[6]

One final advantage of the use of dialogue and learning also deserves emphasis. By involving people directly in a process of identifying interests and needs, there is a much greater chance that decisions will be based on those needs rather than on the simple application of market criteria within the public sphere. Such a procedure thus offers one promising mechanism for moving toward realization of what has been termed a system of "needs-based allocation" as opposed to the current system of primarily "market-based allocation" (Bowles, Gordon, and Weisskopf 1983, 269).

Altered Social Relations: Egalitarian and Participatory

The unequal, nonparticipatory and alienated social relations of the prevailing BCA paradigm are characterized by their correspondence to the social relations of production in the capitalist economy and their compatibility with the strongly antidemocratic ideology that has accompanied the "rise of rationality in government." The social relations embodied in an alternative mode of BCA would be very different: Relationships among citizens as well as those between citizens and professionals (experts, analysts, decision-makers) would be dramatically transformed. Three interdependent dimensions of these altered social relations are particularly significant: increased participation, transformed roles for the relations between citizens and professionals, and shifts in the locus of power and accountability.

First, the people who would most directly be affected by the consequences of proposed public expenditures and regulations would be actively involved in the process of analyzing, evaluating, and choosing among them. This participation would take many forms, ranging from meetings in small face-to-face groups for extensive discussion and dialogue with neighbors, fellow citizens, or co-workers to the use of advanced communications and data processing technology that could involve very large numbers of people simultaneously.

The extensive involvement of those affected could be expected to lead to public policy choices more in line with their interests, but this is only one of several welfare-relevant consequences. Most important, the process of participation is itself a welfare-relevant activity, and it can also contribute to the individual development of those who are involved. Bowles and Gintis have emphasized that "The central prerequisite for personal development . . . lies in the capacity to control the conditions of one's life. Thus a society can foster personal development roughly to the extent that it allows and requires personal interaction along the lines of equal, unified, participatory, and democratic cooperation and struggle" (1976, 265-66). At the same time, by contributing to personal development and to ties among people, the process of participation can contribute to the sort of individual politicization and popular-based political movement essential to building and maintaining a democratic socialist society in general—and to exerting effective popular control over the professionals involved in the BCA process in particular.

Second, increased participation of citizens in the process of evaluation and choice should be accompanied by major changes in the role of the professionals involved. Analysts and other experts could work hard at clarifying and explaining their concepts and techniques for citizens, rather than engaging in obfuscation in order to confuse and intimidate citizens and thereby enhance their own power. Experts would work to convey skills to citizens rather than to keep them to themselves; one of the roles mandated for professionals should be "to develop and transfer skills which allow people to do their own analysis and decision-making" (Carr et al. 1971b, 7). The role of experts would increasingly be to structure and facilitate a process whereby the citizens themselves could carry out and control the analysis and evaluation necessary in making good decisions. One important product of a participatory planning and evaluation process would be a continually enlarged capacity to plan (Alperovitz and Faux 1984, 278).

Even if all of these things were to be done, however, there would still be a need for some people to have special skills and knowledge and to play a more central role in the analysis and evaluation process. A participatory mode of BCA would not eliminate experts, but it would transform their relations with the rest of the population (Albert and Hahnel 1981, 271-72, 278). This process of transformation would involve experts learning from citizens as well as vice versa. As Freire has envisioned in the area of education: "Education must begin with the solution of the teacher-student contradiction, by reconciling the poles of the contradiction so that both are simultaneously teachers *and* students" (1972, 59). For example, the citizens who will live with the consequences of a proposed expenditure or regulation know much more about the nature of their individual and community life than any outside expert ever could. The goal must be to have a collaborative, mutual-learning process between professionals and citizens where differences in knowledge and skills are seen as the result of differences of specialization, and each acknowledges the areas in which they can learn from the other. Specialized expertise need not be incompatible with democratic equality.

The third major dimension of the altered social relations of BCA concerns the issues of power and accountability. Ultimately, BCA could be confidently expected to serve the people if and only if the people have control over the processes and the personnel involved. The skills, knowledge, and techniques used by experts are much less important than their accountability to those who can hire and fire them. Although there is an inherent tendency for power to go with expertise, we saw in Chapter 7 that those who carry out the BCA process in this country do not themselves control the process but are accountable to representatives of the capitalist class. In a participatory alternative mode of BCA, the experts and others who carry out the work would instead be popularly accountable. Just as the capitalist class has evolved means of controlling experts, so can means of exercising popular control and democratic accountability be devised and implemented in a participatory socialist society.

As before, the basic issue is that of power—not the existence of a corps of experts but how it is chosen, to whom it is accountable, whose interests it serves. Popular control of expertise would be facilitated by pervasive social equality. If analysts or decision-makers have greater status, wealth, or power in other spheres of society, this is likely to carry over into the realm of BCA. But if those who fulfill expert roles in the BCA process have the same general lifestyle as other citizens, and a similar amount of wealth and status in the society at large, citizens and experts will tend to relate as equals in the process of analyzing and evaluating proposed public expenditures and regulations. The two aspects of altered social relations discussed earlier—a high level of citizen involvement in the BCA process and a transformation of the roles of expert and citizen—would also contribute to the likelihood of effective popular control over analysts and other experts.

A SOCIALIST SOCIAL SETTING

Just as the prevailing mode of BCA needs to be understood in its corporate capitalist setting, a genuinely alternative mode of BCA could not exist apart from an alternative social system. Branko Horvat has emphasized the general point that "No radical change or improvement of any important social institution—that is, of a *subsystem*—is possible if the social *system* remains unchanged" (1982, xviii). Much closer to the specific concern of this book, Stephen Marglin has written that "If planning is to be democratic in process and end product, the *entire structure* of the capitalist economy must be overhauled to become significantly more participatory" (1980, 23-24; emphasis added). Thus, the previous section's discussion of the key elements of a participatory alternative for BCA necessarily appears utopian and unrealistic when considered in isolation; if nothing else were to change, no such alternative could be implemented.

In the long run, to fully realize the alternative mode of BCA requires a *democratic socialist society*. But it does not therefore follow that nothing can be done until "after the revolution." What I call a socialist social setting can also be provided by a *progressive movement* within capitalist society, to the extent that such a movement gains control over resources as a result of attaining power within governmental units, or other political or economic institutions. Such control creates space for the potential implementation of a participatory alternative approach to decision-making concerning resource allocation. Before discussing each of these two types of "socialist social settings," however, two preliminary comments may be helpful.

First, the tasks of envisioning a possible socialist future and of building a movement that can struggle toward such a future are complementary. Without a plausible and inspiring socialist vision, it is unlikely that a mass socialist movement could be built or that the movement would direct its efforts in appropriate directions. On the other hand, it is inconceivable that a democratic socialist society could be realized except through the struggles of a broad-based socialist movement, and it seems highly implausible that a democratic society could result unless the movement that successfully struggled for it was itself democratic in nature.[7]

Second, nothing in what follows should be interpreted as suggesting that the creation of a democratic socialist society would bring about a solution to all social problems. Democratic socialism would provide a favorable arena within which people could struggle, individually and collectively, with a wide range of problems and opportunities—favorable because of the lack of concentrated private economic power and because of the pervasive emphasis on equality. Socialists claim no more than that the replacement of capitalism by socialism is a necessary precondition for the creation of a democratic and humane society.

Socialist Visions, Socialist Institutions, and Economic Democracy

The traditional characterization of a socialist economic system focused on two central institutional principles: public ownership and control of productive wealth, and comprehensive economic planning. These stand in sharp contrast to the corresponding institutional principles of capitalism: private ownership and control of productive wealth, and the determination of economic outcomes by the market mechanism. In the traditional view, socialism was seen as substituting social ownership and control for the highly concentrated private ownership of the means of production that inevitably occurs under capitalism, and as substituting the conscious application of organized human intelligence for the blind, uncoordinated operation of market forces in addressing important problems of resource allocation and distribution.

Some of the important potential consequences of such arrangements are immediately apparent. The material basis of the primary class division under capitalism—that between those who own the means of production and those who own only their own labor power and have to sell that labor power to survive—would be abolished, along with the economic basis for capitalist class domination of the state. The distribution of economic well-being and political power could be substantially equalized. Productive and other economic decisions could be made on the basis of people's needs rather than in accordance with the market-determined dictates of private profit maximization, thus creating the possibility of an end to the periodic crises, high unemployment, persistent inflation, uneven regional development, and other irrationalities that characterize capitalist development.

While this is a very attractive vision, the actual experience of countries that have had socialist revolutions has in many ways diverged greatly from the sorts of potential results just mentioned. In particular, most socialists recognize that the Soviet Union is now characterized by some of the very features that socialism was intended to eliminate, including pervasive economic and political inequality. A relatively small elite makes important decisions, while the majority of people participate in the economy only as workers and consumers.

Socialists have come to realize that implementation of the two traditional socialist principles need not lead automatically to the kind of economy and society that they desire; they now recognize that these two principles by themselves are also compatible with another sort of society, one where political and economic life is dominated by an authoritarian state controlled by party officials and bureaucrats. Although there has been considerable debate among socialists about how such states are best understood and described— we shall follow Erik Olin Wright in using the term *statism* as a shorthand for "statist mode of production" (1983, 81–112)[8]—there has been general agreement that statism represents a serious danger that socialists must struggle to avoid bringing about.

Socialists have devoted much work to investigating the question of under what circumstances a socialist society could bring about a desirable alternative to the continued development of contemporary U.S. capitalism. The central conclusion that has emerged from this work is that *economic democracy* must be regarded not only as a goal or result of socialism but also as a third principle of socialist economic organization, at least as important as social ownership and public planning. Preventing the emergence of statism requires political and economic institutions that are both based on and contribute to the reproduction of an active, politicized, and informed population. Popular control over leaders, experts, managers, and bureaucrats depends on an expansion of democracy into all areas of social life. The creation of a democratic socialist society does not result from the transfer of economic power from private corporations and wealthy individuals to the state or to any small elite claiming to represent the population as a whole: Power must be effectively democratized, so that the ability to shape social, economic, and political outcomes is spread throughout the population in a highly equal way.

A number of recent contributions have begun to undertake the essential task of examining in more detail what the realization of political and economic democracy might involve in terms of institutional arrangements and day-to-day life (Albert and Hahnel 1981, chs. 7-8; Albert and Hahnel 1983; Cohen and Rogers 1983, ch. 6; Gintis 1983; Green 1983; Sirianni 1981). I wish to discuss briefly the implications of economic democracy in two areas with particular importance for BCA—productive activity and economic planning.

A participatory alternative for BCA could be successful only if it corresponded to a radically transformed organization of people's work experiences. (Recall Chapter 8's discussion of the *correspondence* between the hierarchical social relations of capitalist production and the structured inequality and nonparticipatory character of the prevailing mode of BCA.) Michael Albert and Robin Hahnel argue that "only by moving toward an equity of job complexes as our real goal [so that "everyone's ... overall workdays are comparable"] will work's qualitative effects on personality, consciousness, and skill in each work place begin to 'produce workers' who have comparable capacities to participate in work place decision-making" (1983, 131); extending their argument to make workplace equity a prerequisite for implementation of egalitarian decision-making processes outside the workplace is straightforward. Philip Green has similarly emphasized the necessity of "a division of labor so constituted as to maximize every person's capacities and opportunities for participation in equal self-governance"; he contends that only such a "democratic division of labor" could make possible a truly democratic, egalitarian society (1983, 446). Maintaining an essentially unchanged social division of labor, where a relatively small elite is charged with "conception" and the majority devote their entire working lives to "execution," will doom to failure any attempt to transform social relations in an egalitarian direction. Green also argues that individuals' responsibilities in the workplace should be organized in a way that provides "regularized and normal opportunities for participating in the civic activities and decision-making processes of one's own choice and capacities" (1983, 461). In short, unless the principle of economic democracy is incorporated into the structure of productive activity itself, it will be futile to hope for democratization of political decision-making in general, or for the success of a participatory, egalitarian mode of BCA in particular.

Advocates of economic democracy and democratic socialism emphasize too that the conscious economic planning that would play a central role in resource allocation must be democratic and participatory in nature. This will entail a substantial amount of decentralization in the planning process. Decentralized, participatory, democratic planning is an alternative to *both* central planning *and* reliance on markets. An understanding of economic democracy thus makes it possible to understand the falsity of a dilemma frequently posed by mainstream economists who claim that there are really only two basic modes of resource allocation available to an advanced industrial economy—either centralized, bureaucratic planning or a decentralized market mechanism—and that critics of one must necessarily be in favor of the other.[9] Economic democracy would involve both significant decentralization of political-economic decision-making authority and a complex, multilayered system of cooperative interaction in order to achieve coordination among units at various levels.[10]

A set of socialist institutions pervaded by such economic democracy would bring about unprecedented opportunities for the development of social life in general and of BCA in particular. Socialism could mean the end of the sort of basic institutions that operate to determine social outcomes in a manner that is invisible, outside of direct conscious control or direction by those most directly affected. For the first time it might be possible for social outcomes to be chosen—democratically, consciously, openly, actively—by those members of society who will be affected by them. Thus, in a socialist society, the economic sphere—more particularly, the forces and social relations of production—need no longer be predominant; it need no longer be the case that the arrows of causation run almost exclusively from the productive sectors to other spheres of social life. In a future socialist United States, people might be able collectively and consciously to choose the nature of economic, political, cultural, social, and other institutions simultaneously. The production and distribution of material goods and services could become simply one of many aspects of social organization and activity that contribute to people's welfare.[11] The prospects for this would be enhanced by the substantial reduction in the hours of socially necessary labor time that could be made possible by development of technology, elimination of waste and irrationality, and reduced emphasis on material goods.

Furthermore, because the role of the market and of private investment would be greatly reduced by the rise of social ownership and democratic planning, the scope of the public sector in the economy would greatly increase. Almost all investment decisions would become public investment decisions. And as the process described in the preceding paragraph proceeds, the separateness and distinctness of the "economic" sphere would become blurred and disappear. In short, there is a sense in which the public sector would grow to include essentially the whole economy and the economy would become inseparably bound up with all of social life.

Thus, in a socialist society of the kind envisioned here, BCA would no longer be a distinct activity confined to a relatively narrow and well-defined domain. It would be one important aspect of society's process of analysis, evaluation, and choice, all aspects of which would be characterized by the three features discussed in the preceding section.

Progressive Programs, the Socialist Movement, and Economic Democracy

In the last several years, economic democracy has emerged as a central theme not only of those who have attempted to articulate a positive vision of what a socialist United States might be like, but also of those who have attempted to develop strategies and programs for building a broad progressive movement. A number of recent sets of programmatic suggestions have placed special emphasis on broad-based, participatory, democratic control of economic life.[12] It is thus possible for those who are struggling to transform the practice of BCA to understand their work as constituting one particular aspect of a much broader set of struggles being undertaken by people who share similar analyses of what is wrong with contemporary capitalist society, and similar visions of how things might be different and better. Those working to transform BCA can turn to this broader movement not only for insights and improved understanding, but also for political support.

To the extent that this movement, in the course of its struggles, achieves successes that give it control over the allocation of resources by particular governmental bodies or other institutions (for example, a local city council, a state government planning agency, a worker-controlled enterprise, a school, or a recreational facility), it may attempt to make use of a participatory mode of BCA to guide and inform its decision-making. In this way, there may be socialist social settings for the practical implementation of an alternative form of BCA on a limited scale long before a socialist transformation of the whole country is a realistic possibility.

At the same time, efforts to envision and to implement a participatory alternative for the theory and practice of BCA can contribute to the broader effort to envision and to struggle for the realization of a democratic socialist society. For example, while the sets of programmatic suggestions noted above emphasize the principles of participatory, decentralized, democratic planning of investment decisions in particular, and of resource allocation more generally, they stop short of providing specific descriptions of how the analysis and decision-making involved in such planning might be organized and carried out. The thinking and experiences of those engaged in efforts to transform BCA could make important contributions to this necessary task. And our earlier examination of three principal elements of a participatory mode of BCA represents an attempt to contribute to filling in one important part of the emerging general outline of the program and the vision being developed by the broader progressive movement.

BENEFITS AND COSTS OF PARTICIPATION

We have seen that participation not only is a central defining feature of our alternative mode of BCA but also is a pervasive feature of democratic socialism more generally. The term *participation*, like the term *natural*, seems to carry a generally positive connotation, but it also has been used and misused in many ways. Throughout this chapter, I use *participation* to refer to involvement in the process of evaluation and decision-making by people who have the power to influence the outcome of the decision-making process. Participation in this sense is both a means of empowering those who are affected by decisions and a mechanism for exercising that empowerment. It is important to recognize that in recent years much of what has been called "participation" has not satisfied this criterion. Instead, various "participatory" techniques have been implemented by powerful groups in order to control, manipulate, or pacify those who are affected by decisions.[13]

Even genuine participation involves a potential pitfall: Many of the most important benefits of high levels of participation accrue to the society in general, while many of its most important costs are borne by individuals. As a result, the levels of participation normally chosen by individuals on the basis of their own interests will tend to be less than the socially optimal level. An important task, then, is to identify, and to suggest measures for achieving, a level of participation that is both great enough to be effective in realizing the potential social benefits and limited enough to be acceptable to the large majority of the population.

The Social Benefits and Individual Costs of Participation

Widespread participation in the process of evaluation and decision-making about proposed public expenditures and regulations, to review briefly, has several important social benefits. First, because participation involves a process of education and dialogue, it is able to establish more accurate information about the actual benefits and costs of the alternatives being evaluated—and this better information should lead to better decisions. Second, widespread participation provides a means of controlling the elites (leaders, experts, managers)— who may otherwise tend to perform their tasks in ways that benefit themselves and their families, that consolidate their own authority and control, and that ultimately are incompatible with an egalitarian and democratic society. Those who participate are much more likely to have their interests reflected in the final decisions than those who are excluded. A third major benefit from widespread participation in the process of BCA goes beyond the nature of the resulting decisions, to the nature of society itself and of the personalities of those who live within it. Active and effective participation in one area of social life is likely to increase people's interest in, and abilities for, additional future participation, and to reinforce participation elsewhere, including participation in the area of work. To say the same thing the other way around, the active workers' self-management in the productive sphere that is central to a democratic socialist society will be facilitated and reinforced by participation in areas such as BCA.

All of these benefits are "social" not in the sense that they accrue to some abstract entity called "society" but in the sense that they are automatically shared by everyone in the society (unlike "private benefits," which can be withheld from people who do not purchase them).[14] From the point of view of any single individual, the extent to which the social benefits of widespread participation are realized is not measurably affected by his or her own participation; in a society of substantial size, these benefits are created overwhelmingly by the participation of others. To the extent that the individual undertakes a self-interested rational calculation, taking as given the level of participation by others, he or she will recognize that personal enjoyment of these social benefits is virtually unaffected by whether or not he or she participates. A rational, self-interested individual will therefore choose whether or not to participate on the basis of his or her private costs and benefits. The resulting bias is clear: Because social benefits are not taken into account, such individual decision-making will tend to bring about a less than optimal amount of participation in social decision-making.[15]

This problem is a significant one, because participation in social decision-making can involve substantial costs for those who participate. The process may be unpleasant and frustrating (I shall return to this point below), but even if the process itself is enjoyable, it tends to be very costly in terms of one precious commodity—time. The opportunity cost of the time required for effective participation in the management of social institutions will be familiar to many readers of this book from their own experience, and the potentially great amount of time spent in participating in the management of a participatory democratic society has been frequently commented on. In an often quoted quip, Oscar Wilde complained that "The trouble with socialism is that it would take too many evenings," a sentiment echoed in the weary complaint of Chinese peasants in the village described in William Hinton's *Fanshen* (1966): "Under the Kuomintang, too many taxes; under the Communists, too many meetings."[16] There is humor in such statements, but they are addressed to a very serious problem—that of envisioning a system of social self-management where participation is widespread enough to provide its crucial social benefits but still limited enough to ensure that it can and will be provided voluntarily.

Toward Optimal Participation

The preceding discussion strongly suggests that the proper goal for those involved in the design and implementation of a participatory mode of BCA is an *optimal* level of participation, rather than a *maximum* one. A central element in determining such an optimal level involves finding the point at which the social benefits to be obtained from additional participation begin to be outweighed by the opportunity costs of the time that additional participation requires. This is only one part of the overall problem, however, for we have seen that there are good reasons to expect that individual decisions will result in a level of participation considerably below the level determined to be optimal. It is therefore necessary to consider how the actual level of participation might be raised to this optimal level. Although neither of these tasks can be undertaken in detail here—indeed, they are themselves tasks in social benefit-cost analysis that should be undertaken in a democratic, participatory way by those who will be affected!—some relevant considerations can be presented and discussed.

In order to realize the important social benefits identified above, two conditions must be satisfied. There must be a substantial amount of participation in the making of every important decision, and every person must engage in a significant amount of participatory activity. These conditions are imprecise, but they have three clear implications. First, they do not entail that every person participate in every decision that affects him or her. Second, they require a level of participation much greater than the present level. And third, there is no need for society to choose *either* participation *or* representation; a substantial amount of representation could exist in a participatory system that met these conditions (Gintis 1983).

Now, how could an optimal level of participation be achieved? Governments provide most public goods by levying taxes—compulsory payments—on their citizens. This has proven increasingly problematical in recent years, as pressure for lower taxes has grown, but at least the usefulness of the tax revenues themselves is not affected by how grudgingly they are paid. When the requirement is for participation rather than money, however, compulsion does not provide as satisfactory a solution. Some minimum requirements for such things as participating on committees, attending meetings, and serving on decision-making bodies can—and probably should—be established and maintained, but neither individual nor society is likely to benefit from participation that is undertaken grudgingly.

A distinction analogous to that between labor power and labor is illuminating here: Just as employers who buy a worker's time (labor power) still have the problem of getting the worker actually to work productively (provide labor), getting an individual to fulfill a participation commitment specified in terms of memberships, meetings, and the like does not guarantee actual participation that is either willing or productive. While employers in capitalist society have solved the problem of extracting labor from the labor power that they have purchased through a range of techniques that reduce worker discretion and autonomy (Braverman 1974), these techniques are completely antithetical to any attempt to bring about genuine participation. It is difficult to conceive of any successful system of genuine participation that is not based on voluntary decisions by individuals to play an active role in taking part in making the collective decisions that in large measure determine the circumstance of their lives.

There are several approaches to encouraging effective participation in the process of evaluating and deciding among proposed public expenditures and regulations. One is to alter people's perceptions of their circumstances and their assessments of benefits and costs. For instance, educational campaigns could increase awareness of the social benefits of participation and increase socialist (as opposed to individualist) consciousness—so that people will give significant positive weight in their individual decision-making to behaving in ways that will contribute to the realization of these social benefits.

A second approach involves structuring the process of participation itself so that it is an enjoyable and satisfying activity for those who take part, rather than being unpleasant and frustrating. To some extent this can be promoted through the use of resources to provide physically comfortable meeting spaces, refreshments, travel and lodging, and technical support. On another level, it involves taking conscious steps to make the human interactions that participants enter into be positive rather than negative experiences; to provide procedures that facilitate effective involvement by all participants, rather than domination by those individuals who are more articulate, better educated, louder, or more self-confident; and to provide participation skills to those who initially lack them.

A third approach is to create a broad, varied, and flexible structure of opportunities for participation. This could involve, for example, making it possible for people to participate selectively, on matters of particular concern to them, without necessarily having also to become involved in other matters in which they are not especially interested. It could also involve exercising social control over the design and development of new technology so that it can facilitate broad participation in democratic decision-making.

Taken together, these approaches provide promising beginning points for the demanding project of shaping sets of institutional arrangements and procedures capable of eliciting and sustaining an optimal amount of participation. In addition, Chapter 8's points concerning the endogenous nature of preferences—their being shaped by opportunities and experiences, rather than being given and immutable—become relevant here. When people become genuinely empowered, when they see that their participation can and does have a real effect, then increased preferences for participation will both accompany and contribute to a rise in the levels of participation itself.

WHAT IS TO BE DONE? A CONCLUDING NOTE

In closing, I return again to the distinction between the public policy perspective of mainstream economics and the perspective of radical political economics. The former adopts an essentially prescriptive approach toward BCA and is oriented toward providing information and analysis that will be useful to policy-makers. The latter seeks to develop a broad critical understanding of BCA in its historical, institutional, ideological, and political–economic contexts and then to communicate this understanding in ways that will contribute toward the growth of broad-based movements that are struggling for fundamental change. The critiques of BCA presented in Parts II and III of this book are fundamentally different. The radical political economics perspective is able to provide an understanding of the nature, development, and impact of BCA that is simply unattainable within the framework of mainstream economics.

It is thus very interesting to note the similarity of the practical guidelines concerning involvement with BCA that emerged at the end of Part II's liberal analysis and those that were suggested at the conclusion of the radical analysis offered in Part III. In spite of the very different conceptual frameworks and political motivations that underlie these two approaches, and the very different constituencies whose actions they aim to inform, their implied agendas with respect to BCA have much in common. Both would emphasize careful oversight and scrutiny of the work done by analysts to ensure that BCA is conducted in as open and honest a manner as possible. Both would emphasize broad participation in the process of reviewing the analyses that are prepared. Both would seek to use BCA not only defensively (to expose abuse and misuse of the technique in the analyses sponsored by conservatives in their campaign to cut social expenditure and regulatory programs), but also offensively (to buttress positive, constructive campaigns to maintain and expand socially beneficial expenditures and regulations). In short, there may be little if any discernible difference between the day-to-day activities and arguments of liberals and of radicals who both are involved with preparing or reviewing benefit–cost analyses in any particular area.

There is an important difference, however, in the way that they view these short-run struggles to extend and transform the use of BCA as a means of genuinely identifying and promoting those proposals that will make the greatest contribution to human welfare. For those with a public policy perspective, this goal is seen as ambitious but nevertheless possibly attainable within our present society. For those with a radical political economic perspective, however, efforts toward this goal are undertaken with the understanding that there are real constraints on the extent to which they can be successful within the institutional framework of contemporary capitalism. In other words, radical political economists understand that the progressive potential contained within BCA could be fully realized only in a transformed society. They believe that insofar as the resistance that frustrates efforts to realize this potential within capitalism comes to be more broadly understood as reflecting the constraints imposed by existing political and economic arrangements, the need to struggle for a democratic socialist society will become more broadly recognized, and the movement dedicated to carrying out this struggle will grow.

In short, I have tried to suggest that a radical political economic analysis of BCA, combined with a vision of a democratic socialist society, has useful guidance to offer those involved in trying to influence the formulation of public policy. There are approaches to working with BCA in the present that are consistent both with Part III's critical analysis of the relationships between BCA, economic structure, and political power, and with the desire to bring about progressive social change. Involvement with benefit–cost analyses, like involvement in many other areas of public policy making, provides opportunities both to contribute to the adoption of outcomes more in the interest of the great majority of people and to help build a broad-based movement for progressive social change.

NOTES

1. There is a substantial literature about each of these areas of experience. The following works provide good points of entry into several of these bodies of literature: Carnoy and Shearer (1980); Langton (1978); Peterson (1984); Case and Taylor (1979); Nelkin (1977); Pfeffer (1972); and Horvat, Markovic, and Supek (1975). Additional guidance to materials published by the early 1970s is available in my annotated bibliography of items relevant to thinking about the possibilities of socialist alternatives for America (Campen 1974).
2. My own contribution toward this task reports on the impressive efforts of the community of Isla Vista, California, to become self-managing (Campen 1986). These efforts involved attempts to implement each of the three principal elements of a participatory alternative approach to evaluating collective resource allocation problems that are discussed here.
3. See Robert M. Solow (1970, 104–05) for a typical example of such an argument.
4. For an insightful survey of the issues involved in eliciting people's preferences through such a process, see Fischhoff, Slovic, and Lichtenstein (1980).
5. The processes of dialogue and self- and mutual learning about interests are discussed and advocated in a number of places. See, for example, Freire (1972, 82–85, 184–85); Friedmann (1973, xvi–xix, ch. 7); and Kuenzlen (1972, 98, 104). The Ecologue project, carried out in Cambridgeport (a neighborhood in Cambridge, Massachusetts) during 1971–72 under the guidance of a team of planners from MIT, tried self-consciously to implement many of these ideas; the *Research Plan, Manual of Methods*, and

Final Report prepared by the project leaders are insightful and informative in connection with the issues raised here (Carr et al. 1971a, esp. 10-12; 1971b, esp. 6; and 1972, esp. 1, 4-5); Gary Hack (1976, ch. 13) provides a careful exposition and analysis of the project's history.

6. This point is developed by Thayer (1973, 11-12) and by Albert and Hahnel (1983, 255, 262-63). In a related context, David Collingridge has argued that

> Making a social choice is not finding some reasonable compromise between the fixed values of the individuals concerned. On the contrary, disagreement is resolved by some of the people involved in the decision changing their views about what their interests are, realizing that their original opinions about what the group should choose were mistaken. Each person tries to convince those in opposition to him that the option which really serves their individual interests is the one which he thinks serves his own. Thus *debate* and not *compromise* is the key to the making of social decisions (1982, ix).

7. These points are widely recognized among socialist scholars. For example, on the former point, William Tabb has contended that as an integral part of movement building, "we will have to develop concepts of collective decision-making and a participatory version of American economic democracy" (1984, 377). On the latter point, Joshua Cohen and Joel Rogers have sought to "underscore the importance of achieving compatibility between the objects of political struggle and the organization of that struggle" (1983, 173), while Erik Wright has emphasized that, for precisely this reason, "projects for socialist transformation should be militantly democratic" (1983, 124).

8. Another important analysis of what he terms "etatism" and describes as "a blend of traditional socialism and authoritarian state" is provided by Yugoslavian political economist Branko Horvat (1982, ch. 2; quote is from p. 22).

9. For a classic statement of this position, see Assar Lindbeck's widely hailed critique of *The Political Economy of the New Left* (1971, pt. 2, esp. 32-33).

10. The most ambitious attempts to spell out in detail how such a system of democratic, decentralized planning might be organized of which I am aware are those of Horvat (1982, pt. 3) and of Albert and Hahnel (1981, pt. 3).

11. The resulting contrast with contemporary capitalist society would be dramatic. One can do a pretty good job of explaining most major features of contemporary U.S. society by tracing the effects of the normal functioning of capitalism's basic economic institutions. Most important social outcomes are not the direct result of conscious choices but are determined by the invisible institutional aggregation of the actions taken by individuals confronted with a narrowly delimited set of alternatives. Personality struc-

tures and cultural values (individualism, competition, acquisitive striving) correspond to the needs of the capitalist economy. The educational system, the political apparatus, technological development, the nature of community, the spatial distribution of population, and the relations between males and females, whites and nonwhites, children, adults, and the aged, Americans and others, and people and nature are all significantly shaped by the normal functioning of the basic economic institutions of capitalism. In a socialist society, this need not be so.

12. These include books by Bowles, Gordon, and Weisskopf (1983); Carnoy and Shearer (1980); Carnoy, Shearer, and Rumberger (1983); and Alperovitz and Faux (1984). In this book, I use the term *socialist* to characterize the social setting that is essential for the full realization of a participatory alternative mode of BCA—just as I have used the term *capitalist* to characterize the social setting for the theory and practice of the prevailing BCA paradigm—because it is the most direct and straightforward way of indicating what I mean. I regard the analyses and proposals presented in the books just cited to be essentially socialist, even though the authors of these discussions of economic alternatives for the United States apparently decided to free their ideas of the negative associations that many Americans bring to anything labeled with that term.

13. Pateman has written of "pseudo participation," involving, for example, "techniques used to persuade employees to accept decisions that have *already* been made by the management" (1970, 68-69). Katznelson and Kesselman have discussed "inauthentic participation," where "individuals are given the feeling of participating in decision making but are not accorded the power to actually control the decision-making process" (1979, 15). Nelkin concluded that the "European Experiments in Public Participation" noted in the subtitle of her influential book "surely represent more an effort to convince the public of the acceptability of government decisions than any real transfer of power" (1977, 99). And Alford and Friedland's review of the "bureaucratic participation without power" that was fostered by federal government's War on Poverty beginning in the middle 1960s concludes that it "institutionalized participation as a form of social control" (1975, 455-64, 472-74; quotes from 455, 472). Other important contributions to the literature on nongenuine participation include Arnstein (1969), Aleshire (1970), and Cott (1978).

14. "Social benefits" are thus one instance of what economists call *public goods*. For a good textbook survey of the economic theory of public goods, see Musgrave and Musgrave (1984, chs. 3-4).

15. This conclusion would have to be qualified to the extent (which I believe is small) that there are social *costs* of participation, which individuals would also tend to ignore.

16. This important point was given perhaps its most extreme statement in Michael Walzer's (1968) antiutopian response to Karl Marx's famous depiction, in *The German Ideology*, of communist society as making it "possible for me to do one thing today and another tomorrow, to hunt in the morning, fish in the afternoon, rear cattle in the evening, criticize after dinner, just as I have a mind, without ever becoming hunter, fisherman, cowherd, or critic" (1977 [1846], 169). Walzer offers a caricature of participatory socialism as a society where the socialist citizen of the future has no time at all to hunt, fish, rear cattle, or criticize because he is so busy all day long attending meetings about each of these matters (1968, 243–44).

REFERENCES

Ackerman, Bruce A., Susan Rose-Ackerman, James W. Sawyer, Jr., and Dale W. Henderson. 1974. *The Uncertain Search for Environmental Quality.* New York: Free Press.
Albert, Michael, and Robin Hahnel. 1981. *Socialism Today and Tomorrow.* Boston: South End Press.
_____. 1983. "Participatory Planning" and "Rejoinder." In *Socialist Visions*, edited by Stephen R. Shalom, pp. 247-74 and 287-93. Boston: South End Press.
Aleshire, Robert A. 1970. "Planning and Citizen Participation: Costs, Benefits, and Approaches." *Urban Affairs Quarterly* 5, no. 4 (June): 369-93.
Alford, Robert R., and Roger Friedland. 1975. "Political Participation and Public Policy." In *Annual Review of Sociology*, vol. 1, edited by Alex Inkeles, James Coleman, and Neil Smelser, pp. 429-79. Palo Alto, Calif.: Annual Reviews.
Alperovitz, Gar, and Jeff Faux. 1984. *Rebuilding America.* New York: Pantheon.
Alpert, Irvine, and Ann Markusen. 1980. "Think Tanks and Capitalist Policy." In *Power Structure Research*, edited by G. William Domhoff, pp. 173-98. Beverly Hills, Calif.: Sage.
American Public Health Association. 1982. "Resolution 8103: Use of Cost-Benefit Analysis in Public Health Regulation." *American Journal of Public Health* 72, no. 2 (February): 196-97.
American Textile Manufacturers Institute v. Donovan. 1981. 101 S. Ct. 2478, 69 L. Ed. 2d 185.
Arnstein, Sherry R. 1969. "A Ladder of Citizen Participation." *Journal of the American Institute of Planners* 35, no. 4 (July): 216-24.

Ashby, Eric. 1980. "What Price the Furbish Lousewort?" *Environmental Science and Technology* 14, no. 10 (October): 1176-81.
Ashford, Nicholas A. 1979. "Testimony" and "The Usefulness of Cost-Benefit Analysis in Decisions Concerning Health, Safety, and the Environment." In *Use of Cost-Benefit Analysis by Regulatory Agencies*, pp. 64-89. See U.S. Congress, House (1979).
_____. 1981. "Alternatives to Cost-Benefit Analysis in Regulatory Decisions." *Annals of the New York Academy of Sciences* 363 (April 30): 129-37.
Ashford, Nicholas A., Christopher T. Hill, William Mendez, Jr., Roger K. Chisholm, Richard Frenkel, George R. Heaton, Jr., and W. Curtiss Priest. 1980. *Benefits of Environmental, Health, and Safety Regulations.* Prepared for the Senate Committee on Governmental Affairs, 96th Cong., 2d sess. Committee Print. Washington, D.C.: U.S. Government Printing Office.
Babson, Steve. 1979. "A Pound of Flesh." *Technology Review* 82, no. 2 (November): 12-13.
Balbus, Isaac D. 1971. "The Concept of Interest in Pluralist and Marxist Analysis." *Politics and Society* 1, no. 2 (February): 151-77.
Ball, Michael. 1979. "Cost-Benefit Analysis: A Critique." In *Issues in Political Economy: A Critical Approach*, edited by Francis Green and Petter Nore, pp. 63-88. London: Macmillan.
Baram, Michael S. 1980. "Cost-Benefit Analysis: An Inadequate Basis for Health, Safety, and Environmental Regulatory Decision-Making." *Ecology Law Quarterly* 8, no. 3: 473-531.
_____. 1981. "The Use of Cost-Benefit Analysis in Regulatory Decision-Making Is Proving Harmful to Public Health." *Annals of the New York Academy of Sciences* 363 (April 30): 123-28.
Baran, Paul A., and Paul M. Sweezy. 1968. "Economics of Two Worlds." In *Marx and Modern Economics*, edited by David Horowitz, pp. 291-311. New York: Monthly Review.
Bennington, John, and Paul Skelton. 1975. "Public Participation in Decision-Making by Governments." In *Benefit-Cost and Policy Analysis, 1974: An Aldine Annual on Forecasting, Decision-Making, and Evaluation*, edited by Richard Zeckhauser, Arnold C. Harberger, Robert H. Haveman, Laurence E. Lynn, Jr., William A. Niskanen, and Alan Williams, pp. 417-55. Chicago: Aldine.
Bhaskar, Roy. 1983. "Dialectics." In *A Dictionary of Marxist Thought*, edited by Tom Bottomore, pp. 122-29. Cambridge: Harvard University Press.
Block, Fred. 1977. "The Ruling Class Does Not Rule: Notes on the Marxist Theory of the State." *Socialist Revolution* 7, no. 3 (May/June): 6-28.
Boden, Leslie I. 1979. "Cost-Benefit Analysis: Caveat Emptor." *American Journal of Public Health* 69, no. 12 (December): 1210-11.
Bonnen, James T. 1970. "The Absence of Knowledge of Distributional Impacts: An Obstacle to Effective Public Program Analysis and Decisions." In

Public Expenditure and Policy Analysis, edited by Robert H. Haveman and Julius Margolis, pp. 246–70. Chicago: Markham.
Booth, Douglas E. 1978. "Collective Action, Marx's Class Theory, and the Union Movement." *Journal of Economic Issues* 12, no. 1 (March): 163–85.
Botner, Stanley B. 1970. "Four Years of PPBS: An Appraisal." *Public Administration Review* 30, no. 4 (July/August): 423–31.
_____. 1972. "PPB under Nixon." *Public Administration Review* 32, no. 3 (May/June): 254–55.
Bowles, Samuel. 1974. "Economists as Servants of Power: The Poverty of Policy." *American Economic Review* 64, no. 3 (May): 129–32.
Bowles, Samuel, and Herbert Gintis. 1976. *Schooling in Capitalist America: Educational Reform and the Contradictions of Economic Life.* New York: Basic.
_____. 1982. "The Crisis of Liberal Democratic Capitalism: The Case of the United States." *Politics and Society* 11, no. 1: 51–93.
Bowles, Samuel, Herbert Gintis, and Peter Meyer. 1975. "The Long Shadow of Work: Education, the Family, and the Reproduction of the Social Division of Labor." *Insurgent Sociologist* 5, no. 4 (Summer): 3–22.
Bowles, Samuel, David M. Gordon, and Thomas E. Weisskopf. 1983. *Beyond the Wasteland: A Democratic Alternative to Economic Decline.* Garden City, N.Y.: Anchor.
Braverman, Harry. 1974. *Labor and Monopoly Capital: The Degradation of Work in the Twentieth Century.* New York: Monthly Review.
Buchanan, James M. 1960. *Fiscal Theory and Political Economy.* Chapel Hill, N.C.: University of North Carolina Press.
Burkhead, Jesse. 1956. *Government Budgeting.* New York: Wiley.
Business Week. 1979. "Cost-Benefit Trips Up the Corps." February 19.
Campen, James T. [Jim]. 1974. *Materials Relevant to Constructive Thinking about Socialist Alternatives for America: A Bibliography.* Resource Materials in Radical Political Economics, vol. 1. New York: Union for Radical Political Economics.
_____. 1981. "Economic Crisis and Conservative Economic Policies: U.S. Capitalism in the 1980s." *Radical America* 15, no. 1-2 (Spring): 33–54.
_____. 1986. "The Struggle for Self-Management in Isla Vista." Unpublished paper, University of Massachusetts at Boston.
Campen, James T., and Arthur MacEwan. 1982. "Crisis, Contradictions, and Conservative Controversies in Contemporary U.S. Capitalism." *Review of Radical Political Economics* 14, no. 3 (Fall): 1–22.
Carnoy, Martin. 1984. *The State and Political Theory.* Princeton, N.J.: Princeton University Press.
Carnoy, Martin, and Derek Shearer. 1980. *Economic Democracy: The Challenge of the 1980s.* White Plains, N.Y.: Sharpe.

Carnoy, Martin, Derek Shearer, and Russell Rumberger. 1983. *A New Social Contract: The Economy and Government after Reagan.* New York: Harper & Row.
Carr, Stephen, Philip Herr, William Cavellini, and Philip Dowds. 1971a. "Ecologue: A Methodology for Community Development." Unpublished, Department of Urban Studies and Planning, MIT.
———. 1971b. "Ecologue: A Manual of Methods for Resident Planning." Unpublished, Department of Urban Studies and Planning, MIT.
———. 1972. "Ecologue/Cambridgeport Project: Final Report," Unpublished, Department of Urban Studies and Planning, MIT.
Case, John, and Rosemary C.R. Taylor. 1979. *Co-ops, Communes, and Collectives: Experiments in Social Change in the 1960s and 1970s.* New York: Pantheon.
Chase, Samuel B., Jr., ed. 1968. *Problems in Public Expenditure Analysis.* Washington, D.C.: Brookings Institution.
Cohen, Joshua, and Joel Rogers. 1983. *On Democracy: Toward a Transformation of American Society.* New York: Penguin.
Collingridge, David. 1982. *Critical Decision Making: A New Theory of Social Choice.* New York: St. Martin's.
Committee for Economic Development. 1966. *Budgeting for National Objectives: Executive and Congressional Roles in Program Planning and Performance.* New York: Committee for Economic Development.
Connerton, Marguerite, and Mark MacCarthy. 1982. "Cost-Benefit Analysis and Regulation: Expressway to Reform or Blind Alley?" National Policy Papers, no. 4. Washington, D.C.: National Policy Exchange.
Cott, Katharine. 1978. "Local Action, Not Citizen Participation." In *Marxism and the Metropolis: New Perspectives on the Urban Political Economy*, edited by William K. Tabb and Larry Sawers, pp. 297–311. New York: Oxford University Press.
Crandall, Robert W. 1981. "The Use of Cost-Benefit Analysis in Regulatory Decision-Making." *Annals of the New York Academy of Sciences* 363 (April 30): 99–107.
Culyer, A.J. 1977. "The Quality of Life and the Limits of Cost-Benefit Analysis." In *Public Economics and the Quality of Life*, edited by Lowdon Wingo and Alan Evans, pp. 141–53. Baltimore: Johns Hopkins University Press.
Dasgupta, Ajit K., and D.W. Pearce. 1972. *Benefit-Cost Analysis: Theory and Practice.* New York: Barnes and Noble.
Dasgupta, Partha, Stephen A. Marglin, and Amartya Sen. 1972. *Guidelines for Project Evaluation.* New York: United Nations Industrial Development Organization.
Domhoff, G. William. 1968. "*The Power Elite* and Its Critics." In *C. Wright Mills and the Power Elite*, edited by G. William Domhoff and Hoyt B. Ballard, pp. 251–78. Boston: Beacon.

———. 1971. *The Higher Circles: The Governing Class in America.* New York: Vintage.

———. 1974. "State and Ruling Class in Corporate America." *International Socialist Review* 35, no. 8 (September): 4-11.

———. 1979. *The Powers That Be: Processes of Ruling-Class Domination in America.* New York: Vintage.

———, ed. 1980. *Power Structure Research.* Beverly Hills, Calif.: Sage.

———. 1983. *Who Rules America Now? A View for the '80s.* Englewood Cliffs, N.J.: Prentice-Hall.

Dorfman, Robert. 1978. "Forty Years of Cost-Benefit Analysis." In *Econometric Contributions to Public Policy*, edited by Richard Stone and William Peterson, pp. 268-84. London: Macmillan.

———, ed. 1965. *Measuring Benefits of Government Investments.* Washington, D.C.: Brookings Institution.

Dupuit, J. 1968 [1844]. "On the Measurement of the Utility of Public Works." In *Transport*, edited by Denys Munby, pp. 19-57. Baltimore: Penguin.

Eakins, David W. 1966. "The Development of Corporate Liberal Policy Research in the U.S., 1885-1965." Ph.D. dissertation, University of Wisconsin.

———. 1972. "The Origins of Corporate Liberal Policy Research, 1916-1922: The Political-Economic Expert and the Decline of Public Debate." In *Building the Organizational Society*, edited by Jerry Israel, pp. 163-79. New York: Free Press.

Eckstein, Otto. 1958. *Water Resource Development.* Cambridge: Harvard University Press.

———. 1961. "A Survey of the Theory of Public Expenditure Criteria." In *Public Finances: Needs, Sources, and Utilization*, edited by James M. Buchanan, pp. 439-504. Princeton, N.J.: Princeton University Press.

Edel, Matthew. 1979. "A Note on Collective Action, Marxism, and the Prisoner's Dilemma." *Journal of Economic Issues* 13, no. 3 (September): 751-61.

Edwards, Richard C. 1979. *Contested Terrain: The Transformation of the Workplace in the Twentieth Century.* New York: Basic Books.

Fischhoff, Baruch. 1977. "Cost-Benefit Analysis and the Art of Motorcycle Maintainance." *Policy Sciences* 8, no. 2 (June): 177-202.

———. 1981. "Cost-Benefit Analysis: An Uncertain Guide to Public Policy." *Annals of the New York Academy of Sciences* 363 (April 30): 173-88.

Fischhoff, Baruch, Sarah Lichtenstein, Paul Slovic, Steven L. Derby, and Ralph L. Keeney. 1981. *Acceptable Risk.* New York: Cambridge University Press.

Fischhoff, Baruch, Paul Slovic, and Sarah Lichtenstein. 1980. "Knowing What You Want: Measuring Labile Values." In *Cognitive Processes in Choice and Decision Behavior*, edited by T.S. Wallsten, pp. 117-41. Hillsdale, N.J.: Erlbaum.

Foley, Duncan K. 1978. "State Expenditure from a Marxist Perspective." *Journal of Public Economics* 9, no. 2 (April): 221-38.
Franklin, Raymond S. 1977. *American Capitalism: Two Visions*. New York: Random House.
Freeman, A. Myrick, III. 1977. "Project Design and Evaluation with Multiple Objectives." In *Public Expenditure and Policy Analysis*, 2d ed., edited by Robert H. Haveman and Julius Margolis, pp. 239-56. Chicago: Rand McNally.
———. 1979. *The Benefits of Environmental Improvement: Theory and Practice*. Baltimore: Johns Hopkins University Press.
Freire, Paulo. 1972. *Pedagogy of the Oppressed*. New York: Herder and Herder.
Friedmann, John. 1973. *Retracking America: A Theory of Transactive Planning*. Garden City, N.Y.: Anchor.
Gintis, Herbert. 1969. "Alienation and Power: Towards a Radical Welfare Economics." Ph.D. dissertation, Harvard University.
———. 1970. "On Commodity Fetishism and Irrational Production." Discussion Paper no. 121. Cambridge: Harvard Institute of Economic Research.
———. 1972a. "Towards a Political Economy of Education: A Radical Critique of Ivan Illich's *Deschooling Society*." *Harvard Educational Review* 42, no. 1 (February): 70-96.
———. 1972b. "Consumer Behavior and the Concept of Sovereignty: Explanations of Social Decay." *American Economic Review* 62, no. 3 (May): 267-78.
———. 1972c. "A Radical Analysis of Welfare Economics and Individual Development." *Quarterly Journal of Economics* 86, no. 4 (November): 572-99.
———. 1974. "Welfare Criteria with Endogeous Preferences: The Economics of Education." *International Economic Review* 15, no. 2 (June): 415-30.
———. 1975. "John Stuart Mill and the Foundations of Welfare Theory." Unpublished paper. University of Massachusetts at Amherst.
———. 1983. "A Socialist Democracy for the United States: Representation and Participation." In *Socialist Visions*, edited by Steve Rosskamm Shalom, pp. 11-34. Boston: South End Press.
Gordon, David M. 1977. "General Perspectives: Radical, Liberal, Conservative." In *Problems in Political Economy: An Urban Perspective*, 2d ed., edited by David M. Gordon, pp. 1-14. Lexington, Mass.: Heath.
Gordon, David M., Richard Edwards, and Michael Reich. 1982. *Segmented Work, Divided Workers: The Historical Transformation of Labor in the United States*. New York: Cambridge University Press.
Gough, Ian. 1979. *The Political Economy of the Welfare State*. London: Macmillan.
Goulet, Denis. 1971. *The Cruel Choice: A New Concept in the Theory of Development*. New York: Atheneum.
Graaff, J. de V. 1967. *Theoretical Welfare Economics*. New York: Cambridge University Press.

———. 1975. "Cost-Benefit Analysis: A Critical View." *South African Journal of Economics* 43, no. 2 (June): 233-44.

Graham, John D., and James W. Vaupel. 1983. "The Value of a Life: What Difference Does It Make?" In *What Role for Government? Lessons from Policy Research*, edited by Richard J. Zeckhauser and Derek Leebaert, pp. 176-86. Durham, N.C.: Duke University Press.

Gramlich, Edward M. 1981. *Benefit-Cost Analysis of Government Programs.* Englewood Cliffs, N.J.: Prentice-Hall.

Green, Mark, and Norman Waitzman. 1979. *Business War on the Law.* Washington, D.C.: Public Citizen. Reprinted in U.S. Congress, House (1979: 141-316).

Green, Philip. 1983. "Considerations on the Democratic Division of Labor." *Politics and Society* 12, no. 4: 445-85.

Greider, William. 1982. *The Education of David Stockman and Other Americans.* New York: Dutton.

Grubb, W. Norton, Dale Whittington, and Michael Humphries. 1984. "The Ambiguities of Cost-Benefit Analysis: An Evaluation of Regulatory Impact Analyses under Executive Order 12291." In *Environmental Policy under Reagan's Executive Order: The Role of Benefit-Cost Analysis*, edited by V. Kerry Smith, pp. 121-64. Chapel Hill, N.C.: University of North Carolina Press.

Haber, Samuel. 1964. *Efficiency and Uplift: Scientific Management in the Progressive Era, 1890-1920.* Chicago: University of Chicago Press.

Hack, Gary. 1976. "Environmental Programming: Creating Responsive Settings." Ph.D. dissertation, MIT.

Halvorsen, Robert, and Michael G. Ruby. 1981. *Benefit-Cost Analysis of Air Pollution Control.* Lexington, Mass.: Heath, Lexington Books.

Hammond, Richard J. 1960. *Benefit-Cost Analysis and Water-Pollution Control.* Stanford, Calif.: Food Research Institute, Stanford University.

———. 1966. "Convention and Limitation in Benefit-Cost Analysis." *Natural Resources Journal* 6, no. 2 (April): 195-222.

Hanke, Steve H. 1981. "On the Feasibility of Benefit-Cost Analysis." *Public Policy* 29, no. 2 (Spring): 147-57.

Hanke, Steve H., and Richard A. Walker. 1974. "Benefit-Cost Analysis Reconsidered: An Evaluation of the Mid-State Project." *Water Resources Research* 10, no. 5: 898-908. Reprinted in and cited from Haveman and Margolis (1983, 324-49).

Harberger, Arnold C. 1971. "Three Basic Postulates for Applied Welfare Economics: An Interpretive Essay." *Journal of Economic Literature* 9, no. 3 (September): 785-97.

———. 1978. "On the Use of Distributional Weights in Social Cost-Benefit Analysis." *Journal of Political Economy* 86, no. 2, pt. 2 (April): S87-S120.

——— . 1983. "Basic Needs versus Distributional Weights in Social Cost–Benefit Analysis." In *Public Expenditure and Policy Analysis*, 3d ed., edited by Robert H. Haveman and Julius Margolis, pp. 105–26. Boston: Houghton Mifflin.

Harberger, Arnold C., Robert Haveman, Julius Margolis, William A. Niskanen, Ralph Turvey, and Richard Zeckhauser, eds. 1972. *Benefit–Cost Analysis 1971: An Aldine Annual*. Chicago: Aldine.

Harrington, Michael. 1973. *Socialism*. New York: Bantam.

Haupt, Georges. 1982. "Marx and Marxism." In *Marxism in Marx's Day*, vol. 1 of *The History of Marxism*, edited by Eric J. Hobsbawm, pp. 265–89. Brighton, England: Harvester.

Haveman, Robert H. 1972. *The Economic Performance of Public Investments: An Ex Post Evaluation of Water Resources Investments*. Baltimore: Johns Hopkins Press.

——— . 1973. "Efficiency and Equity in Natural Resource and Environmental Policy." *American Journal of Agricultural Economics* 55, no. 5 (December): 868–78.

Haveman, Robert H., Arnold C. Harberger, Laurence E. Lynn, Jr., William A. Niskanen, Ralph Turvey, and Richard Zeckhauser, eds. 1974. *Benefit–Cost Analysis 1973: An Andile Annual on Forecasting, Decision-Making, and Evaluation*. Chicago: Aldine.

Haveman, Robert H., and Julius Margolis, eds. 1970. *Public Expenditure and Policy Analysis*. Chicago: Markham. Selections from U.S. Congress, Joint Economic Committee (1969).

——— . 1977. *Public Expenditure and Policy Analysis*. 2d ed. Chicago: Rand McNally.

——— . 1983. *Public Expenditure and Policy Analysis*. 3d ed. Boston: Houghton Mifflin.

Hays, Samuel P. 1964. "The Politics of Reform in Municipal Government in the Progressive Era." *Pacific Northwest Quarterly* 55, no. 3 (October): 157–69.

——— . 1972. "The New Organizational Society." In *Building the Organizational Society*, edited by Jerry Israel, pp. 1–13. New York: Free Press.

Heilbroner, Robert L. 1980. *Marxism: For and Against*. New York: Norton.

Hinrichs, Harley H., and Graeme M. Taylor, eds. 1969. *Program Budgeting and Benefit–Cost Analysis: Cases, Texts, and Readings*. Pacific Palisades, Calif.: Goodyear.

Hinton, William. 1966. *Fanshen: A Documentary of Revolution in a Chinese Village*. New York: Vintage.

Hitch, Charles J., and Roland N. McKean. 1960. *The Economics of Defense in the Nuclear Age*. Cambridge: Harvard University Press.

Horvat, Branko. 1982. *The Political Economy of Socialism: A Marxist Social Theory*. Armonk, N.Y.: Sharpe.

Horvat, Branko, Mihailo Markovic, and Rudi Supek, eds. 1975. *Self-Governing Socialism: A Reader.* 2 vols. White Plains, N.Y.: International Arts and Sciences Press.

Hymer, Stephen, and Frank Roosevelt. 1972. "Comment." In "Symposium: Economics of the New Left." *Quarterly Journal of Economics* 86, no. 4 (November): 644-57.

Jessop, Bob. 1982. *The Capitalist State: Marxist Theories and Methods.* New York: New York University Press.

Junger, Peter D. 1976. "A Recipe for Bad Water: Welfare Economics and Nuisance Law Mixed Well." *Case Western Reserve Law Review* 27, no. 1 (Fall): 3-335.

———. 1979. "The Inapplicability of Cost-Benefit Analysis to Environmental Policies." *Ekistics* 46, no. 276 (May/June): 184-94.

Just, Richard E., Darrell L. Hueth, and Andrew Schmitz. 1982. *Applied Welfare Economics and Public Policy.* Englewood Cliffs, N.J.: Prentice-Hall.

Karpf, Beth. 1982. "*American Textile Manufacturers Institute v. Donovan.*" *Ecology Law Quarterly* 10, no. 1: 87-96.

Katznelson, Ira, and Mark Kesselman. 1979. *The Politics of Power: A Critical Introduction to American Government.* 2d ed. New York: Harcourt Brace Jovanovich.

Kelman, Steven. 1981. "Cost-Benefit Analysis: An Ethical Critique." *Regulation* 5, no. 1 (January/February): 33-40.

Kennedy, Duncan. 1981. "Cost-Benefit Analysis of Entitlement Programs: A Critique." *Stanford Law Review* 33, no. 1 (February): 387-445.

Knetsch, Jack L., and J.A. Sinden. 1984. "Willingness to Pay and Compensation Demanded: Experimental Evidence of an Unexpected Disparity in Measures of Value." *Quarterly Journal of Economics* 94, no. 3 (August): 507-21.

Knight, Frank H. 1935. *The Ethics of Competition.* New York: Harper.

Kolko, Gabriel. 1967. *The Triumph of Conservatism: A Reinterpretation of American History, 1900-1916.* Chicago: Quadrangle.

Krutilla, John V. 1981. "Reflections of an Applied Welfare Economist." *Journal of Environmental Economics and Management* 8, no. 1 (March): 1-10.

Krutilla, John V., and Otto Eckstein. 1958. *Multiple Purpose River Development.* Baltimore: Johns Hopkins Press.

Kuenzlen, Martin. 1972. *Playing Urban Games: The Systems Approach to Planning.* New York: Braziller.

Kuhn, Thomas S. 1962. *The Structure of Scientific Revolutions.* Chicago: University of Chicago Press.

———. 1970. *The Structure of Scientific Revolutions.* 2d ed. Chicago: University of Chicago Press.

Langton, Stuart, ed. 1978. *Citizen Participation in America.* Lexington, Mass.: Lexington.

Layard, Richard, ed. 1972. *Cost-Benefit Analysis.* Baltimore: Penguin.
Levi, Arrigo. 1973. *Journey among the Economists.* La Salle, Ill.: Library Press.
Levin, Henry M. 1983. *Cost-Effectiveness: A Primer.* Beverly Hills, Calif.: Sage.
Lindbeck, Assar. 1971. *The Political Economy of the New Left: An Outsider's View.* New York: Harper & Row.
Lindblom, Charles E. 1982. "The Market as Prison." *Journal of Politics* 44, no. 2 (May): 324-36.
Linnerooth, Joanne. 1979. "The Value of Human Life: A Review of the Models." *Economic Inquiry* 17, no. 1 (January): 52-74.
Lipsey, R.G., and Kelvin Lancaster. 1956-57. "The General Theory of the Second Best." *Review of Economic Studies* 24, no. 63: 11-32.
Little, I.M.D. 1957. *A Critique of Welfare Economics.* 2d ed. New York: Oxford University Press.
Little, Ian M.D., and James A. Mirrlees. 1968. *Social Cost Benefit Analysis.* Vol. 2 of *Manual for Industrial Project Analysis in Developing Countries.* Paris: Organization for Economic Cooperation and Development.
Luke, Jacquelyn. 1977. "Environmental Impact Assessment for Water Resource Projects: The Army Corps of Engineers." *George Washington Law Review* 45, no. 5 (August): 1095-1122.
Luria, Daniel, and Arthur MacEwan. 1976. "International Crisis and the Politicization of Economic Activity." *American Economic Review* 66, no. 3 (May): 34-39.
Lyden, Fremont J., and Ernest G. Miller, eds. 1968. *Planning, Programming, Budgeting: A Systems Approach to Management.* Chicago: Markham.
———. 1972. *Planning, Programming, Budgeting: A Systems Approach to Management.* 2d ed. Chicago: Markham.
Maass, Arthur, Maynard M. Hufschmidt, Robert Dorfman, Harold A. Thomas, Jr., Stephen A. Marglin, and Gordon M. Fair. 1962. *Design of Water Resource Systems: New Techniques for Relating Economic Objectives, Engineering Analysis, and Government Planning.* Cambridge: Harvard University Press.
Mansbridge, Jane J. 1973. "Time, Emotion, and Inequality: Three Problems of Participatory Groups." *Journal of Applied Behavioral Science* 9, no. 2/3 (March/June): 351-68.
———. 1983. *Beyond Adversary Democracy.* Chicago: University of Chicago Press.
Mansfield, Edwin. 1982. *Microeconomics: Theory and Applications.* 4th ed. New York: Norton.
Marglin, Stephen A. 1962. "Objectives of Water Resource Development: A General Statement." In *Design of Water Resource Systems*, pp. 17-87. See Maass et al. 1962.
———. 1963. "The Social Rate of Discount and the Optimal Rate of Investment." *Quarterly Journal of Economics* 77, no. 1 (February): 95-111.

———. 1967. *Public Investment Criteria: Benefit-Cost Analysis for Planned Economic Growth.* Cambridge: MIT Press.

———. 1980. "Resolutions for the 1980s." *Harvard Magazine* 82, no. 3 (January/February): 23-24.

Margolis, Howard. 1982. *Selfishness, Altruism, and Rationality: A Theory of Social Choice.* Chicago: University of Chicago Press.

Marx, Karl. 1977 [1846]. *The German Ideology.* Selections reprinted in *Karl Marx: Selected Works,* edited by David McLellan, pp. 159-91. New York: Oxford Univeristy Press.

Marx, Thomas J. 1983. "The Cost of Living: Life, Liberty, and Cost-Benefit Analysis." *Policy Review,* no. 25 (Summer): 53-58.

McKean, Roland N. 1958. *Efficiency in Government through Systems Analysis.* New York: Wiley.

Means, Thomas C. 1977. "Note: The Concorde Calculus." *George Washington Law Review* 45, no. 5 (August): 1037-65.

Merewitz, Leonard, and Stephen H. Sosnick. 1971. *The Budget's New Clothes: A Critique of Planning-Programming-Budgeting and Benefit-Cost Analysis.* Chicago: Markham.

Miliband, Ralph. 1973. "Poulantzas and the Capitalist State." *New Left Review* no. 82 (November/December): 83-92.

———. 1983. "The State." In *A Dictionary of Marxist Thought,* edited by Tom Bottomore, pp. 464-68. Cambridge: Harvard University Press.

Miller, James C., III, and Bruce Yandle, eds. 1979. *Benefit-Cost Analyses of Social Regulation.* Washington, D.C.: American Enterprise Institute.

Mishan, E.J. 1974. "Flexibility and Consistency in Project Evaluation." *Economica* 41, no. 1 (February): 81-96.

———. 1982a. *Cost-Benefit Analysis.* 3d ed. Boston: Allen and Unwin.

———. 1982b. "The New Controversy about the Rationale of Economic Evaluation." *Journal of Economic Issues* 16, no. 1 (March): 29-47.

Moore, Barrington, Jr. 1967. "The Society Nobody Wants: A Look beyond Marxism and Liberalism." In *The Critical Spirit,* edited by Barrington Moore, Jr. and Kurt Wolff, pp. 401-18. Boston: Beacon.

Musgrave, Richard A., and Peggy B. Musgrave. 1984. *Public Finance in Theory and Practice.* 4th ed. New York: McGraw-Hill.

Nelkin, Dorothy. 1977. *Technological Decisions and Democracy: European Experiments in Public Participation.* Beverly Hills, Calif.: Sage.

Niskanen, William A., Jr. 1971. *Bureaucracy and Representative Government.* Chicago: Aldine.

Niskanen, William A., Arnold C. Harberger, Robert H. Haveman, Ralph Turvey, and Richard Zeckhauser, eds. 1973. *Benefit-Cost and Policy Analysis, 1972: An Aldine Annual on Forecasting, Decision-Making, and Evaluation.* Chicago: Aldine.

Tribe, Laurence H. 1973. "Policy Science: Analysis or Ideology?" In *Benefit-Cost and Policy Analysis, 1972*, pp. 3–47. See Niskanen et al. 1973.
U.S. Bureau of the Budget. 1952. *Budget Circular A-47.* Washington, D.C.: Bureau of the Budget.
U.S. Bureau of the Census. 1975. *Historical Statistics of the United States, Colonial Times to 1970, Bicentennial Edition.* Washington, D.C.: Government Printing Office.
U.S. Congress, Joint Economic Committee. 1969. *The Analysis and Evaluation of Public Expenditures: The PPB System.* 3 vols. A compendium of papers submitted to the Subcommittee on Economy in Government, 91st Cong., 1st sess. Joint Committee Print. Washington, D.C.: U.S. Government Printing Office.
U.S. Congress, House Committee on Interstate and Foreign Commerce. 1976. *Federal Regulation and Regulatory Reform.* Report by the Subcommittee on Oversight and Investigations, 94th Cong., 2d sess. Subcommittee Print. Washington, D.C.: U.S. Government Printing Office.
———. 1979. *Use of Cost-Benefit Analysis by Regulatory Agencies.* Joint Hearings before the Subcommittee on Oversight and Investigations and the Subcommittee on Consumer Protection and Finance, 96th Cong., 1st sess. Serial no. 96-157. Washington, D.C.: U.S. Government Printing Office.
———. 1980. *Cost-Benefit Analysis: Wonder Tool or Mirage?* Report by the Subcommittee on Oversight and Investigations, 96th Cong., 2d sess. Committee Print 96-IFC 62. Washington, D.C.: U.S. Government Printing Office.
U.S. Congress, Senate. 1970. *Planning, Programming, Budgeting: Budget Bureau Guidelines of 1968.* Submitted by the Subcommittee on National Security and International Operations to the Committee on Government Operations. 90th Cong., 2d sess. Washington, D.C.: Government Printing Office.
U.S. Federal Inter-Agency River Basin Committee. 1950. *Proposed Practices for Economic Analysis of River Basin Projects ("Green Book").* Report by the Subcommittee on Benefits and Costs. Washington, D.C.: U.S. Government Printing Office.
U.S. Inter-Agency Committee on Water Resources. 1958. *Proposed Practices for Economic Analysis of River Basin Projects ("Green Book")* (revision of 1950 *"Green Book"*). Report by the Subcommittee on Evaluation Standards. Washington, D.C.: U.S. Government Printing Office.
U.S. President's Water Resources Council. 1962. *Policies, Standards, and Procedures in the Formulation, Evaluation, and Review of Plans for Use and Development of Water and Related Land Resources.* Printed as Senate Document 97, 87th Cong., 2d sess. Washington, D.C.: U.S. Government Printing Office.
U.S. Water Resources Council. 1973. *Principles and Standards for Planning Water and Related Land Resources. Federal Register* 38, no. 174 (September 10): 24, 778–869.

Waitzman, Norman. 1982–83. "Externality, Cost–Benefit Analysis, and Commodity Fetishism." *Economic Forum* 13 (Winter): 121–25.

Walzer, Michael. 1968. "A Day in the Life of a Socialist Citizen." *Dissent* 15, no. 3 (May/June): 243–47.

Weinstein, James. 1968. *The Corporate Ideal in the Liberal State, 1900–1968*. Boston: Beacon.

Weisbrod, Burton A. 1968. "Income Redistribution Effects and Benefit–Cost Analysis." In *Problems in Public Expenditure Analysis*, edited by Samuel B. Chase, Jr., pp. 177–209. Washington, D.C.: Brookings Institution.

Whittington, Dale, and W. Norton Grubb. 1984. "Economic Analysis in Regulatory Decisions: The Implications of Executive Order 12291." *Science, Technology, and Human Values* 9, no. 1 (Winter): 63–71.

Wildavsky, Aaron. 1966. "The Political Economy of Efficiency: Cost–Benefit Analysis, Systems Analysis, and Program Budgeting." *Public Administration Review* 26, no. 4 (December): 292–310.

Williams, Alan. 1972. "Cost–Benefit Analysis: Bastard Science: and/or Insidious Poison in the Body Politick?" *Journal of Public Economics* 1, no. 2 (August): 199–226. Reprinted in and cited from Haveman and Margolis 1983, pp. 535–60.

Williams, William Appleman. 1966. *The Contours of American History*. Chicago: Quadrangle.

Willig, Robert D. 1976. "Consumer's Surplus without Apology." *American Economic Review* 66, no. 4 (September): 589–97.

Wolff, Robert Paul. 1968. *The Poverty of Liberalism*. Boston: Beacon.

Wright, Erik Olin. 1983. "Capitalism's Futures." *Socialist Review* 13, no. 2 (March/April): 77–126.

Zeckhauser, Richard. 1981. "Preferred Policies When There Is Concern for Probability of Adoption." *Journal of Environmental Economics and Management* 8, no. 3 (September): 215–37.

Zeckhauser, Richard, Arnold C. Harberger, Robert H. Haveman, Laurence E. Lynn, Jr., William A. Niskanen, and Alan Williams, eds. 1975. *Benefit–Cost and Policy Analysis, 1974: An Aldine Annual on Forecasting, Decision-Making, and Evaluation*. Chicago: Aldine.

INDEX

Ackerman, Bruce A., 63
Administrative Procedure Act, 63
Albert, Michael, 195, 199, 204, 215
Aleshire, Robert A., 216
Alford, Robert R., 216
Alinsky, Saul, 192
Alperovitz, Gar, 199, 216
Alpert, Irvine, 144
American Journal of Public Health, 68
American Public Health Association, 52
American Textile Manufacturers Institute v. Donovan, 63
Army Corps of Engineers, 16, 53, 86-87, 94, 134, 182
Arnstein, Sherry R., 216
Ashby, Eric, 58-59, 63, 177
Ashford, Nicholas, 63, 67, 68-69, 92, 94, 98

Babson, Steve, 59
Balbus, Isaac, 156-57, 163
Ball, Michael, 12
Baram, Michael, 45, 52, 53, 60, 61, 63, 67-68, 73, 94, 100, 104, 151
Baran, Paul, 193-94
Bennington, John, 152
Bhaskar, Roy, 187
Block, Fred, 177

Boden, Leslie I., 68
Bonnen, James, 169
Booth, Douglas E., 143
Boston Globe, 112
Botner, Stanley, 144
Bowles, Samuel, 111, 124, 138-39, 143, 149-50, 168, 171, 187, 198, 199, 216
Braverman, Harry, 126, 211
Brookings Institution, 129, 131, 132
Buchanan, James, 111-12
Budget and Accounting Act of 1921, 132
Budgeting for National Objectives (Committee for Economic Development), 132
Bureau of Reclamation, 53-54, 86-87, 94
Bureau of the Budget, 17, 18, 86, 129, 130, 131, 132, 133, 134
Burkhead, Jesse, 164
Business Council, 129
Business Week, 87

Campen, James T., 118, 171, 187, 214
capitalism:
    acceptance of, by liberals and conservatives, 8
    alternatives to, 5; *see also* socialism

critique of, by radicals, 8, 9
potential of benefit-cost analysis for undermining, 176–77, 184–86
reinforcement of, by benefit-cost analysis, 136–39, 145–47, 149–54
role of the state in, 112–16; *see also* capitalist class, use of the state by
social relations of production under, 147, 149, 151, 152, 211
capitalist class:
control of experts by, 200
fragments of, with interests different from overall class interest, 113, 117, 122, 133, 136, 172, 183
struggle of, with other classes, 113, 115, 149, 171, 175–76
use of the state by, 112–16, 121–23, 124–25, 128–30, 146, 171
value of benefit-cost analysis to, 117, 121–22, 133–35, 183
Carnegie Foundation, 129
Carnoy, Martin, 114, 118, 214, 216
Carr, Stephen, 196, 199, 215
Carter, Jimmy, 4, 20, 87
Case, John, 214
Chase, Samuel B., Jr., 132
Cohen, Joshua, 204, 215
Collingridge, David, 215
Committee for Economic Development (CED), 126, 129, 131, 132
compensating variation (CV), 165–67
Connerton, Marguerite, 55
conservatives:
difficulties in using benefit-cost analysis to further goals of, 181–84, 213
distinguished from liberals, 6–8, 111, 180, 181–82
see also Reagan administration
"consumer sovereignty," 154, 168
consumers' surplus, 34, 35, 46–47, 74
cost-benefit analysis (alternative wording), 12, 46
Cott, Katharine, 216
Council on Wage and Price Stability (COWPS), 73
Crandall, Robert, 81
Culyer, A. J., 62, 63, 151

Dasgupta, Ajit K., 80
Dasgupta, Partha, 45

decision-making:
benefit-cost analysis as an input for, 25–27, 40–41, 44–45, 62–63, 83–84, 92–93, 94–95
exclusion from, of most people who will be affected by the decisions, 147, 148–49, 150–53, 167–68, 176–77
participatory alternative to present form of, 5, 185–86, 198–212
removal of, from the "political" realm, 122–23, 124–28, 131, 133
role of benefit-cost analysis in facilitating wider participation in, 101, 174–76
Defense Department, 18, 97, 131–32
Design of Water Resource Systems, The (Harvard Water Resources Program), 131
discount rate, 38–40, 47, 60
discounting, 24
distribution effects, 40–42, 96–97, 101–2, 175, 183
difficulty of incorporating into benefit-cost analysis, 33, 41–42, 55–58, 101–2
Domhoff, G. William, 129–30, 132, 143, 144
Dorfman, Robert, 51, 87, 102–3, 132
Dukakis, Michael, 114
Dupuit, Jules, 17

Eakins, David, 126–27, 143, 144
Eckstein, Otto, 17, 25, 145
Ecology Law Quarterly, 61
Economics of Defense in the Nuclear Age (Hitch and McKean), 18
Edel, Matthew, 143
Edwards, Richard C., 149
Engels, Friedrich, 113–14
Enthoven, Alain, 131–32
Environmental Protection Agency, 66–67, 73
equivalent variation (EV), 165–67
Executive Order 12044 (Carter), 20, 73, 100
Executive Order 12291 (Reagan), 3, 20, 55, 61, 66–67, 74, 76, 84, 88, 98, 100, 180
experts, 122, 123, 126, 130, 133, 135, 136, 148, 151, 153, 174, 177, 199–201

Fanshen (Hinton), 209
Faux, Jeff, 199, 216
Fischhoff, Baruch, 13, 53, 58, 62–63, 85, 87, 94, 101, 214
Flood Control Act of 1936, 16, 17, 97, 131, 178
Foley, Duncan K., 143
Ford, Gerald, 4
Ford Foundation, 129, 131
Franklin, Raymond S., 118
Freeman, A. Myrick, 75, 112
Freire, Paolo, 153, 167, 196–97, 200, 214
Friedland, Roger, 216
Friedman, Milton, 182
Friedmann, John, 214

General Accounting Office, 55
Gintis, Herbert, 137–38, 139, 140–41, 143, 149–50, 162, 163, 168, 169, 169–70, 171, 187, 199, 204, 210
Gordon, David M., 118, 149, 187, 198, 216
Gough, Ian, 143, 173, 186
Goulet, Denis, 195
government, growing role of, in economy, 115, 116, 121, 171, 174
Graaff, J. de V., 69, 71, 72, 76, 82, 106, 155–56
Graham, John D., 66, 73, 75
Gramlich, Edward M., 12, 15, 24, 26, 30, 31, 33, 34, 35, 41, 46, 47, 48, 57–58, 76, 80
Green, Mark, 98, 106
Green, Philip, 204
Green Book, 17
Greider, William, 95
Grubb, W. Norton, 45, 54, 66–67, 74, 76, 84, 87, 97, 131

Haber, Samuel, 126, 128, 143
Hack, Gary, 215
Hahnel, Robin, 195, 199, 204, 215
Halvorsen, Robert, 12, 22, 24, 28, 30, 37, 40, 46, 47, 48, 89
Hammond, Richard J., 16, 45
Hanke, Steve H., 53–54, 77, 99
Harberger, Arnold, 27, 40–41, 45
Harrington, Michael, 173
Harvard Water Resources Program, 131
Haupt, Georges, 9

Haveman, Robert, 45, 46, 89, 94, 133, 175
Hays, Samuel P., 125, 127, 128, 143
Heilbroner, Robert L., 187
Hitch, Charles J., 18, 131–32
Hoos, Ida R., 52
"horse and rabbit stew," 102–3
Horvat, Branko, 201, 214, 215
Hueth, Darrell L., 46
human life, attempts to calculate value of, 59, 60, 65–66, 73
Humphries, Michael, 45, 54, 66–67, 74, 76, 84, 87, 131
Hymer, Stephen, 140

Institute for Government Research, 132
intangible effects:
  defined, 33–34
  difficulty of incorporating into BCA, 35–36, 65–69, 102–4, 137–38
  environmental, safety, and health issues as, 59, 60, 61, 63–67, 94, 98, 102–3; *see also* human life, attempts to calculate value of

Jessop, Bob, 113–14, 118
Johnson, Lyndon, 3, 19, 97
Junger, Peter, 52, 64, 76
Just, Richard E., 46

Kaldor-Hicks criterion, 30
  see also potential Pareto improvement criterion
Karpf, Beth, 61
Katznelson, Ira, 151–52, 168, 216
Kaufman, Herbert, 52
Kelman, Steven, 59
Kennedy, Duncan, 12–13, 167
Kennedy administration, 97
Kesselman, Mark, 151–52, 168, 216
Knetsch, Jack, 170
Knight, Frank H., 157–58
Kolko, Gabriel, 125, 143
Krutilla, John V., 17, 77
Kuenzlen, Martin, 214
Kuhn, Thomas, 22, 46

Lancaster, Kelvin, 71, 76
Langton, Stuart, 214
Layard, Richard, 45
Levi, Arrigo, 4–5

Levin, Henry M., 13
liberals:
  as critics of benefit-cost analysis, 3, 51-78, 117, 133-34
  as initial advocates of benefit-cost analysis, 3-4
  corporate, 127, 128
  distinguished from conservatives, 6-8, 111, 181-82
  suitability of benefit-cost analysis for advancing the goals of, 51, 95-99, 181-82, 213
Lichtenstein, Sarah, 214
Lindbeck, Assar, 215
Lindblom, Charles E., 146
Lipsey, R.G., 71, 76
Little, I.M.D., 28, 45, 76, 153
Luke, Jacquelyn, 19
Luria, Daniel, 173
Lyden, Fremont J., 45, 133, 144

Maass, Arthur, 131
MacCarthy, Mark, 55
MacEwan, Arthur, 118, 171, 173, 187
Mansfield, Edwin, 71
Marglin, Stephen A., 45, 54, 142, 161, 201
Margolis, Howard, 161, 169
Margolis, Julius, 45, 46, 89
market failures, 31, 34, 70, 96, 111, 136, 138, 146, 176, 181, 183-84
Markovic, Mihailo, 214
Markusen, Ann, 144
Marx, Karl, 9, 113-14, 143, 170, 217
Marx, Thomas J., 59
Marxist political economics, 9, 113, 157
McKean, Roland N., 17, 118
McNamara, Robert, 18, 97, 131
Means, Thomas C., 54
Merewitz, Leonard, 13, 45, 103
Meyer, Peter, 150
Miliband, Ralph, 187
Mill, John Stuart, 141
Miller, Ernest G., 45, 133, 144
Miller, James C., III, 45
Mirrlees, James A., 45
Mishan, E.J., 12, 25, 26, 41, 46, 48, 72, 102, 170
Moore, Barrington, Jr., 160

movements, popular, for change in society, 5, 192, 199, 201-2, 206-7, 213, 214
  desire of radicals to encourage, 9, 110
Musgrave, Peggy B., 25, 40, 46, 216
Musgrave, Richard A., 25, 40, 46, 216

Nash, C.A., 12, 13, 46, 48, 62, 70, 89
National Civic Federation, 129
Nelkin, Dorothy, 214, 216
net present value (NPV), 38, 39, 40, 43
New York Bureau of Municipal Research, 129
Niskanen, William A., 19, 45, 177
noneconomic considerations. *See* intangibles

Occupational Safety and Health Administration (OSHA), 61, 67
O'Connor, James, 125, 139, 143
Office of Management and Budget, 54, 74, 88, 133, 134
Ollman, Bertell, 114, 118
Olson, Mancur, Jr., 143-44
opportunity costs, 29

Pareto improvement, 29, 30
Pareto superiority, 29-30, 70
Participation and Democratic Theory (Pateman), 152
participatory democracy, 5
Pateman, Carole, 141, 152, 170, 216
Pear, Robert, 52
Pearce, D.W., 12, 13, 25, 40, 42, 45, 46, 47, 48, 62, 70, 80, 89
Pearl, Arthur, 195
Pearl, Stephanie, 195
pecuniary effects (vs. real effects), 32-33
Peskin, Henry, 23, 55, 89
Peterson, James C., 214
Pfeffer, Richard M., 214
planning-programming-budgeting system (PBBS), 3, 18, 20, 132, 144
Political Economy of the Welfare State (Gough), 186

potential compensation criterion. *See* potential Pareto improvement criterion
potential Pareto improvement criterion (PPIC), 30–31, 32, 40, 41–42, 57, 71
preferences, 140–41, 147, 148, 153–54
  difference between, and interests, 154–62, 168, 176, 195–98
  effect of public policies on, 162–66, 170, 212
Prest, A.R., 45, 80
producers' surplus, 34, 74
production, social relations of, 147, 149–51, 152, 204–5, 209
Proposed Practices for Economic Analysis of River Basin Projects, 17
public policy perspective, 9, 10, 25, 105, 109–10, 146, 212–13

radical political economics, 5, 6, 10, 105–6, 110–11, 117, 118, 140, 146, 149, 172, 184–85
  defined, 8–10
  use of, to understand benefit-cost analysis, 116–17, 212–14
  views of, on the state, 112–16, 121
radical political economists, 173, 184–85, 213
radicals. *See* radical political economists
Rand Corporation, 18, 131
"rationality, rise of, in government," 122–28, 132, 135, 174, 185
  relation of benefit-cost analysis to, 123–24, 131–35
Reagan, Ronald, 3, 20, 55, 97, 180
Reagan administration, use of cost-benefit analysis by, 1, 4, 20, 54, 87, 95, 100, 123–24, 178–79, 180–84
regulations:
  application of benefit-cost analysis to, 20, 24–25, 52
  growth of, in 1960s and 1970s, 20, 179
  Reagan administration's hostility to, 3, 20, 54–55, 87, 123–24

Reich, Michael, 149
Resources for the Future, 129, 131
reversals, 71–72
Review of Radical Political Economics, 118
River and Harbor Act of 1902, 16
Roberts, Paul E., 53, 94
Rockefeller Foundation, 129, 131
Roemer, John E., 143
Rogers, Joel, 204, 215
Roosevelt, Frank, 140
Roosevelt, Franklin, 97
Rowen, Henry S., 131–32
Ruby, Michael G., 12, 22, 24, 28, 30, 37, 40, 46, 47, 48, 89
Rumberger, Russell, 216

Sagoff, Mark, 119, 169
Salzman, Harold, 144
Samuelson, Paul, 21
Schick, Allen, 45, 144
Schmitz, Andrew, 46
Schriftgeisser, Karl, 126, 132
Schultze, Charles L., 3, 89
Scitovsky, T. de., 71
Second best, theory of the, 71
Self, Peter, 80
Sen, Amartya, 45, 119, 169
sensitivity analysis, 40, 43
Seskin, Eugene, 23, 55, 89
shadow prices, 35, 39, 74
Shearer, Derek, 214, 216
Sinden, J.A., 170
Sirianni, Carmen, 204
Skelton, Paul, 152
Slovic, Paul, 214
Smith, V. Kerry, 45
social opportunity cost of capital, 39
social rate of time preference (SRTP), 39
socialism, 199, 201–7, 213
Solow, Robert M., 214
Sosnick, Stephen H., 13, 45, 103
Soviet Union, 203
Squire, Lyn, 45
state, role of in capitalist society, 111–16
State-Local Finances Project (George Washington University), 129
Steiner, Peter O., 19, 45

Stockman, David, 95
Stokey, Edith, 12, 24, 26, 29, 44, 46, 47, 97, 110, 156
Sugden, Robert, 12, 22, 26, 29, 30-31, 33, 34, 35, 42, 46, 47, 48, 88
Supek, Rudi, 214
Sweezy, Paul, 193-94

Tabb, William, 215
Taylor, Rosemary C.R., 214
Thayer, Frederick C., 215
Thompson, Mark S., 12, 41, 46, 47
Thurow, Lester, 4-5
Titmuss, Richard M., 137
Tolchin, Martin, 52
Tribe, Lawrence, 64, 158
Turvey, Ralph, 45, 80

van der Tak, Herman G., 45
Vaupel, James W., 66, 73, 75
Viner, Jacob, 15

Waitzman, Norman, 12, 98, 106
Walker, Richard A., 53-54, 99
Walzer, Michael, 217
water resource projects, 16-17, 86-87, 131, 179
    see also Army Corps of Engineers; Bureau of Reclamation; Water Resources Council
Water Resources Council, 17-19, 84
Weidenbaum, Murray, 133
Weinstein, James, 125-26, 128, 143, 144
Weisbrod, Martin A., 76

Weisskopf, Thomas E., 187, 198, 216
welfare economics:
    applied, 81-82
    benefit-cost analysis as an area of applied, 15-16, 24, 27-31, 58, 69, 72, 86, 105, 153, 154
    radical alternative to, 138, 141-42
    shortcomings of, 30, 69-72, 104, 118, 140-42, 157
    theoretical, 69-72, 154, 155, 157, 165
Whittington, Dale, 45, 54, 66-67, 74, 76, 84, 87, 97, 131
Wildavsky, Aaron, 87
Wilde, Oscar, 209
Williams, Alan, 12, 22, 26, 29, 30-31, 33, 34, 35, 42, 46, 47, 48, 80-81, 85, 88, 89
Williams, William Appleman, 128, 143
Willig, Robert D., 170
willingness to pay (WTP) criterion, 28-29, 32, 34, 35-36, 37, 47, 72, 97, 137, 148, 165-67
Wisecarver, Daniel, 27
Wolff, Robert Paul, 142
work, 139-40
    see also capitalism, social relations of production under
working class, 112, 117, 128, 133, 149
Wright, Erik Olin, 203, 215

Yandle, Bruce, 45

Zeckhauser, Richard, 12, 26, 29, 44, 45, 46, 47, 57, 97, 110, 156

ABOUT THE AUTHOR

James T. Campen is Associate Professor and Chairperson of the Department of Economics at the University of Massachusetts/Boston. He received an M.A. in Economics and Political Science from Cambridge University and a Ph.D. in Economics from Harvard. He has taught at Harvard, the University of California/Riverside, and the Cambridge Center for Adult Education; served for many years as an editor of *Dollars & Sense* magazine; and worked with numerous government agencies at both the federal and state level.